The Law of Electronic Commerce
EDI, Fax, and E-mail

THE LAW OF ELECTRONIC COMMERCE

EDI, FAX, AND E-MAIL: TECHNOLOGY, PROOF, AND LIABILITY

BENJAMIN WRIGHT

MEMBER, TEXAS BAR

Little, Brown and Company

Boston Toronto London

Library of Congress Catalog Card No. 91-61353
ISBN 0-316-95632-5

Third Printing

PUBLISHER'S NOTE

This publication is designed to provide accurate and authoritative information in regard to the subject matter covered. It is sold with the understanding that the publisher is not engaged in rendering legal, accounting or other professional services. If legal advice or other expert assistance is required, the services of a competent professional person should be sought.—From a Declaration of Principles jointly adopted by a Committee of the American Bar Association and a Committee of Publishers.

EB

Published simultaneously in Canada
by Little, Brown & Company (Canada) Limited

Printed in the United States of America

To Becky and Mitch

Summary of Contents

Contents

Contents

PART V ELECTRONIC CONTRACT ISSUES 233

Chapter 14 Industry Codes and Model Trading Agreements 235

Chapter 15 The Trading Partner Relationship 247

PART VI NETWORK SERVICE PROVIDERS AND CUSTOMERS 331

Chapter 18 Liability for Deficient Service 333

Chapter 19 Confidentiality and Control of Data 361

Table of Figures

Preface

Hear the courts of Canada:

> The law has endeavored to take cognizance of, and to be receptive to, technological advances in the means of communication. . . . The conduct of business has for many years been enhanced by technological improvements in communication. Those improvements should not be rejected automatically when attempts are made to apply them to matters involving the law. They should be considered and, unless there are compelling reasons for rejection, they should be encouraged, applied and approved.

Beatty v. First Exploration Fund 1987 & Co.
25 B.C.L.R.2d 377 (S.C. 1988)

> Where technological advances have been made which facilitate communications and expedite the transmission of documents we see no reason why they should not be utilized. Indeed, they should be encouraged and approved.

Rolling v. Willann Investments Ltd.
70 O.R.2d 578 (C.A. 1989)

Commerce is experiencing a revolution. For centuries paper has reigned as the supreme and ubiquitous medium for effecting formal legal transactions such as contracts and regulatory filings. Today, electronic messages are dethroning the monarch, with fax, electronic mail, electronic data interchange (EDI), and videotex swiftly installing a new order in business and government.

Real estate buyers are faxing offers to buy land, and sellers are faxing back acceptances. Offers plus acceptances create contracts; buyers and sellers become legally bound. EDI users are issuing electronic (computer-to-computer) purchase orders to buy goods, and their trading partners are responding with EDI purchase order acknowledgments to accept those orders. Again, we have offers and acceptances and therefore contracts.

Contracts and other binding business transactions will raise legal issues. See, for example, the protracted lawsuit *Bazak International Corp. v. Mast Industries,*[1] which turned on the legal effect of five faxed purchase orders for $103,330 worth of textiles. The American Bar Association's Section on Business Law now has a large and very active group working on electronic commercial practices. Its most celebrated product is the Model EDI Trading Partner Agreement published in June 1990. A legal issues committee now works under the American National Standards Institute, Accredited Standards Committee X12, the largest EDI standards-setting body in North America. The EDI Council of Canada and the EDI Council of Australia each have prolific committees examining legal and audit issues.

[1]73 N.Y.2d 113, 538 N.Y.S.2d 503, 535 N.E. 633 (1989).

A REBELLION AGAINST PAPER

The reason for the rebellion against paper is that it is inefficient. Paper costs too much, occupies too much space, and requires too much time and labor to transport and process. The market is decisively embracing paper's replacements.

This phenomenon is global. Fax machines now saturate the business world. In addition, according to the 1989 and 1990 issues of the journal *EDI Forum,* no fewer than 30 countries boast EDI initiatives of one sort or another. These include all of North America, most of Europe, the Soviet Union, and the leading trade nations of the Pacific Rim. Few technical problems inhibit electronic transactions across national borders, especially between the technologically advanced nations.

Business law should not, and largely will not, stand in the way of this revolution. The law's mission is to make commerce as easy as possible, so long as certain public policies are met. Ink and pulp are not vital to those policies. With proper techniques, electronic messages can achieve all the essential legal goals that paper achieves. In fact, they can do it better.

This book's theme is that, if implemented intelligently, electronic communication can confidently be used for legal transactions. It rejects the attitude that technology deserves suspicion.

Old habits and rusty thinking drive lawyers to act inefficiently. Hence, they have been known in 1990 to jet from city to city for the sole purpose of quickly securing original autographs on paper. Such ink worship is expensive and unjustified in the age of the fax machine.

We must nevertheless be thoughtful in our use, control, and recording of electronic messages, just as we were in the use, control, and retention of paper documents.

Recent, well-publicized legal controversies highlight the critical role electronic messages play in modern business and government. In the aftermath of the 1989 oil spill by Exxon Co. U.S.A. in Alaska's Prince William Sound, a federal court ordered Exxon to preserve all records relating to the spill. A hapless computer operator inadvertently erased records of some relevant electronic mail messages. He consequently lost his job, and the incident became a public issue in the government's investigation of the spill.[2]

In the Iran-Contra scandal, an important source of evidence for the criminal prosecution of former National Security Advisor John Poindexter was one of his private electronic mail messages. The message, sent to Colonel Oliver North via an IBM "PROFS" system, indicated Poindexter's approval of North's testimony before Congress. A record of this communication was admitted as evidence in the trial.[3]

Today, electronic data contain oceans of valuable, sensitive information. Corporations, regulatory agencies, and law enforcement authorities now must understand the current policies concerning the recording, purging, and confidentiality of such data. In some cases new policies may need to be articulated.

ABOUT THIS BOOK

This book covers commercial and government, but not consumer, transactions. It builds upon a prior book, *EDI and American Law: A Practical Guide,* which was researched with the generous support of the Electronic Data Interchange As-

[2]*See* Eckerson, E-mail Nets Pose Hidden Legal Issues, Network World, July 31, 1989, at 1, col. 5.

[3]Transcript of Trial, at 1722-1769, United States v. Poindexter (Crim. No. 88-0080-1) (D.D.C. 1990). *See* §§5.4 n.17, 5.5 n.1, 6.4 n.7, 8.5 n.3, 8.6 n.7. *See generally* Johnston, 5,000 Files Erased from Poindexter's Computer, N.Y. Times, Mar. 16, 1990, at A11. col. 4 (natl. ed.).

sociation of Alexandria, Virginia, the subsequent publisher of the volume. The present book carries forward some of the ideas expressed in *EDI and American Law,* but it has a different scope. It looks not just at EDI, but at all electronic messaging technology, probing the core legal doctrines much more deeply, and substantiating its analysis with traditional legal scholarship.

This book is intended to serve both lawyers and laypeople. The purpose is to educate both. Business people should understand commercial law, since it is impractical to expect lawyers to monopolize the development and application of legal analysis in day-to-day commerce. Appendices A and B (suggestions for implementing fax and EDI) should be especially useful to business implementors.

I do not mean to say this book furnishes legal advice, will replace the company lawyer, or will turn laypeople into attorneys. Businesses do need expert counsel. Yet this book can help business managers, accountants, and consultants to recognize issues, follow the advice of their lawyers, intelligently interact with them, and even challenge them to think. The best solutions to legal issues will come from team efforts, where each member has different knowledge but still comprehends what the other has to say.

I have taken pains to define and explain many basic legal concepts. American attorneys may find some of this tedious, but it should help laymen and lawyers from other countries.

In many places this book explores legal theory. That subject may not interest some laypeople, so I have tried to summarize my conclusions in a way that helps them skim and move on.

Many of the names given by manufacturers and sellers to their products and services are claimed as trademarks. In this book, I have used initial caps or all caps for these names when I knew about such claims.

The field of electronic commercial law is vast. With selected exceptions, this volume ignores several important areas that must be addressed in a future work: antitrust, electronic "partnerships," Uniform Commercial Code Article 4A (wholesale electronic funds transfers), international trade and trade finance, conflicts of law, electronic negotiable instruments, information property rights, and the regulation of electronic financial markets.

This book represents "ultra-software." It is neither a computer nor instructions that make a computer work. Instead, it is knowledge that helps and encourages people to exploit computer power. It promotes economic efficiency and worker productivity.

I invite all comments.

Benjamin Wright
Attorney and Counselor
3420 Granada, Suite 400
Dallas, Texas 75205
Telephone: 214-526-5254
CompuServe: 73457,2362
Internet: 73457.2362@compuserve.com

April 1991

The Law of Electronic Commerce
EDI, Fax, and E-mail

PART I

THE TECHNOLOGIES AND THEIR APPLICATIONS

Chapter 1

The Technologies

§1.1 PRIMARY TECHNOLOGIES

This chapter briefly introduces electronic messaging technologies. The categories here are indistinct because the technologies blend. Computers can (within limits) convert messages from one technology to another. For example, a message may start as electronic mail, but an intermediary service provider may reformat it and deliver it to a telex terminal, to a fax machine, or as paper in the postal mail. Some product innovators are creating hybrid electronic mailboxing systems that fold messages from several different technologies—fax, electronic mail, voice messaging, and so forth—into the same system.[1]

§1.1.1 Fax

Fax, sometimes called telecopy, is a form of electronic transmission conforming to facsimile standards set by the International Telegraph and Telephone Consultive Committee (CCITT). Fax technology has been used for many years, but its popularity exploded in the 1980s.

The most popular fax device is a stand-alone machine that plugs into the telephone system. (*See* Figure 1-1.) The machine sends by scanning a paper document and converting its image to a digital signal that is then transmitted through the telephone system. The same machine can receive by interpreting such a signal and printing the image onto a

FIGURE 1-1

Fax

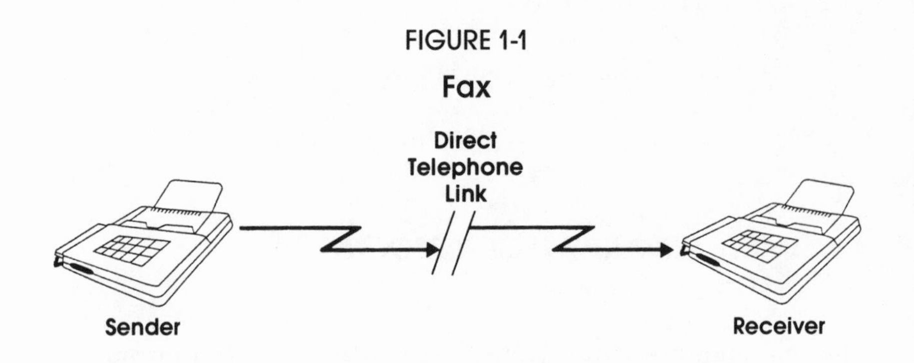

§1.1 [1]*See* Keller, One Bin for Voice Mail, Electronic Mail and Faxes, Wall St. J., Sept. 18, 1990, at B1, col. 2 (s.w. ed.).

new sheet of paper. Older machines print on thermal paper, which archives poorly. The image it captures can fade when exposed to heat or after only a year or two. More advanced machines print on plain paper. Computers can be configured, with special "fax boards," to send or receive faxes.

An incoming fax need not necessarily be immediately printed on paper. A sophisticated fax machine can temporarily store messages until a user instructs it to print. Faxes received by computer can be stored on disk indefinitely. Yet this storage is in fax format. The words that may be on the fax are not stored as alphanumeric characters (such as one sees on a word processing or spreadsheet display), but as human readable images (such as one sees in a computer graphics display).

Alphanumeric characters are much more useful in a computer system. So inventors are racing to find ways to convert fax images into characters. Optical character recognition technology may soon solve the problem. The goal is to permit a remote party to fax data typewritten (or even handwritten) on paper to a computer so it can convert the data from images to characters.

The conversion of alphanumeric data to fax, however, is not a technical problem. A computer can be configured with a "fax board" to permit the conversion of characters from, say, a word processing program to a fax signal.

Some value-added networks (VANs), such as MCI, "store and forward" fax transmissions. A fax sender can deliver a transmission to the VAN, which temporarily stores it. When later convenient, the VAN forwards the fax to the recipient. Or, the fax can wait in an electronic "mailbox" until the recipient requests it. (*See* Figure 1-2.)

Fax is also becoming a tool for accessing information in computer databases. Some systems permit users to request fax printouts from databases containing such information as classified advertisements and newsletter summaries. A user submits the request either by faxing a special form, which

FIGURE 1-2
Fax via VAN

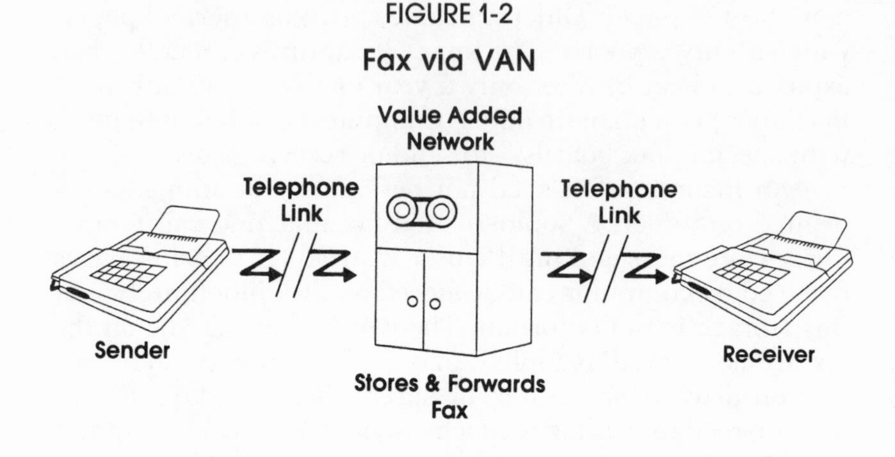

the receiving system can interpret, or by pressing keys on a touch-tone telephone.[2]

§1.1.2 E-mail

Electronic mail (e-mail) is the telecommunication of messages from one computer to another. Usually these are alphanumeric character messages, written in free-form text, intended for human reading. Thus, e-mail is symbolic communication that uses no paper. (In a literal sense, the things that are transferred between the computers are electronic impulses that the receiving computer can interpret as alphanumeric characters.)

Technically, the sending and receiving computers could be linked directly to one another with a cable. Usually, however, they are linked through an intermediary computer system or network, perhaps a local area network or a public VAN such as CompuServe. (*See* Figure 1-3.)

[2]*See, e.g.*, Markoff, Marrying the PC and Fax Machine, N.Y. Times, May 2, 1990, at C8, col. 1 (natl. ed.); Miles, I've Got Your Number, InformationWeek 58 (Apr. 23, 1990).

FIGURE 1-3
E-mail

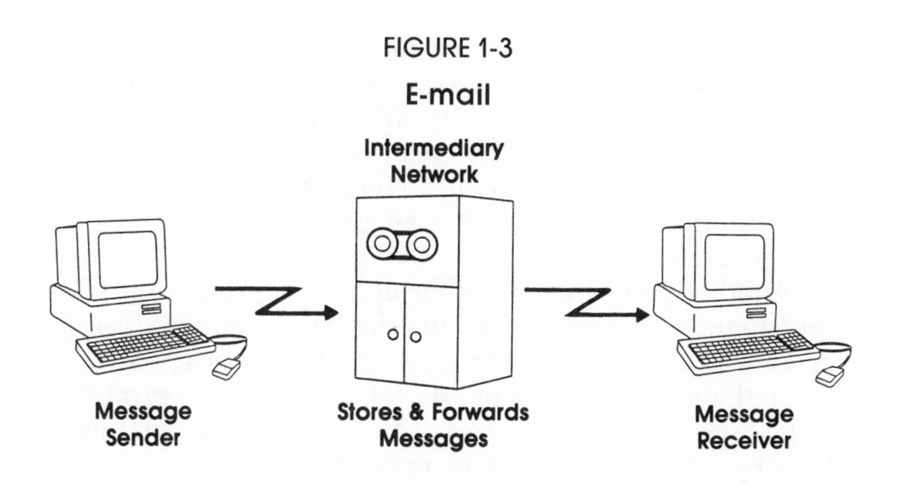

One or more networks may interconnect so that the customer of one can send a message to the customer of another. Public network interconnection (internetworking) challenges the e-mail industry because it requires the development of uniform standards and procedures for accounting for and managing messages.[3] Store and forward is a common feature of e-mail systems.

E-mail can be communicated without a record of the message being made. The users, however, can choose to record the message on computer media, such as a magnetic disk, or to print it out on paper.

§1.1.3 Telegraph and Telex

Telegraph has been used for transacting business for well over a century. A telegram is a message submitted to an independent carrier, called a record carrier. The message starts as an oral or written instruction to an operator em-

[3]*See* Valentine & Heywood, International Electronic-Mail Services: Ready for Takeoff?, Data Comm. 145 (Dec. 1989).

ployed by the carrier. The operator converts the message to transmittable text, and the carrier relays the message through its cable/satellite network to its office nearest the recipient. The carrier then delivers the telegram to the recipient by telephone or messenger, with a confirmation copy sent in the postal mail. A mailgram is a telegram that is, on its final leg, delivered by mail only.

Another record carrier offering, telex, grew from telegraph in the middle of this century. In the conventional sense, a telex is an electronic text message created at one teleprinter terminal and delivered to another. Both terminals print paper transcripts of the message. The receiving terminal usually does not need an operator present.

Each telex terminal has a unique "answerback," an alphanumeric code that the terminal, automatically at certain times and on request at others, transmits to the other terminal. Usually, a terminal's answerback is publicly known. With the old teleprinter terminals, the answerback derived from a rotating metal drum that the record carrier initialized and built into the terminal. The answerback signals, as printed on the transcripts, evidence which terminal originated a message and which received it. It is not impossible to forge an answerback signal, however.[4]

Telex messages contain audit numbers, which the carrier adds automatically. These can aid an inquiry into a telex printout's origin and authenticity.

Traditionally, telex communication was in "real-time," which means the sending and receiving terminals interacted directly and instantaneously (as telephones do). If an operator was at each terminal, communication could be like a printed conversation. In recent years, telex has become much like e-mail. Telex carriers have adopted store and forward techniques (although real-time connections are still possible), and computer terminals have replaced many old tele-

[4]*See* §4.2, describing the shortcomings of telex.

printer terminals. Incoming messages can be stored in an electronic mailbox or on computer disk rather than being printed immediately. Telex is still slow and expensive compared with e-mail, however.

Record carriers keep, for seven years, billing records (identity of sending and receiving machines and time and duration of transmission) for all telex transmissions. Additionally, if a message travels through a store-and-forward facility, rather than via a direct connection, the carrier keeps a record of the message's content for six months.[5]

§1.1.4 EDI

Electronic data interchange (EDI) is a hot topic, a business buzzword—touted in both the business and the popular media as signaling the rise of the information age.[6] EDI is the movement of electronic business messages, such as purchase orders, from computer to computer. Technically, EDI messages are transmitted in much the same way that e-mail messages are transmitted. They can be recorded on computer media or printed out on paper, just as e-mail messages can.

EDI's distinguishing feature is that its messages are structured and coded (generally in alphanumeric characters) in accordance with a standard agreed upon by sender and receiver. (*See* Figure 1-4. The code "850," for example, means "this message is a purchase order.") The standard is a language that adheres to a prescribed syntax. The beauty of structured and coded data is that the receiving computer can automatically transfer it into diverse application programs such as inventory management software. This is unlike data on or in paper, fax, telex or e-mail, which can only be read

[5]Telephone interview with Larry Cohen, Director of Technical Sales Support, TRT Telecommunications Corp. (Nov. 2, 1990).

[6]*See* A. Toffler, Powershift 120-125 (1990).

FIGURE 1-4

EDI Message

ST * 850 * Blue Co. * 111 **
RX @ ** 7742 MKB * . . .

by humans and must be rekeyed in order to reach application programs. Hence, a computer receiving an EDI purchase order can understand that the message is an order. It can, without human intervention, log the order into the recipient's order-fulfillment, product-shipping, and accounting programs so the order can be tracked, shipped, and booked.[7]

Significantly, the elimination of human intervention reduces data entry errors.

The agreed EDI standard can be proprietary or public. The former is designed by an individual company or small group of companies. Many proprietary standards exist, and they continue to proliferate. Proprietary standard users may not even label their work EDI; they may just call it a data exchange.

Large industry committees set public EDI standards. The best known standards are ANSI X12 (developed by American National Standards Institute, Accredited Standards Committee X12) and EDIFACT, or EDI for Administration, Commerce, and Transport (developed under the United Nations). Standards setting is a slow, expensive, bureaucratic process. Public EDI standards are in a constant state of revision. In practice, users often modify public standards to varying degrees to suit their specific needs. Sometimes they concoct their own message designs, borrowing principles from the public standards. An industry group, such as the Auto-

[7]Just because it is technically possible for EDI to be read and acted on automatically does not necessarily mean that is the way industry always implements it. Some EDI receivers lack the software to read and use EDI data. So the receiving computer may just print messages for operators to read.

motive Industry Action Group, may develop guidelines for EDI implementation within its industry.

EDI can travel directly between the sender's and receiver's computers (point-to-point), via (1) the physical delivery of a computer tape containing the data (tape-to-tape exchange) or (2) a link through the telephone or some other telecommunications system. Alternatively, EDI data can move through an intermediary computer network, called perhaps a VAN, a third-party network, or an EDI service provider. General Electric Information Services and BT Tymnet are two well-known EDI VANs. Sometimes a VAN performs store and forward services. It may also track the status of messages, keep message audit records, check messages for conformance with standards, translate (or convert) messages from one standard to another (such as from a proprietary to a public standard), and perform other services. As with e-mail, internetworking has been an important and challenging facet of EDI network service.

EDI today is usually communicated in a "batch" mode, so that responses to messages are not immediate or real-time. Yet the day of "interactive" EDI is coming, where computers link in real-time sessions during which messages and responses go in both directions, like a conversation. Futurists see the day when computers negotiate. One computer will offer to buy 500 widgets, and the second counteroffer with 300. The first will accept the counteroffer to form a contract.

§1.1.5 EFT

An electronic funds transfer (EFT) is a transmittal of value between banks via computer or other electronic message. Some EFT messages are structured and coded to conform with a banking industry standard. Put differently, these EFT messages are a subset of EDI. In this book, EFT refers only to wholesale or large dollar transfers (sometimes called wire transfers) and not consumer transfers.

§1.1.6 Videotex

E-mail and EDI are sent in batches as individual messages from sender to recipient. Videotex makes a mass of information available to remote computer users in a real-time, interactive mode. The most simple form of videotex is the electronic bulletin board, where information resides in a central database for simultaneous access by multiple computer users. (*See* Figure 1-5.) With designated commands, videotex users navigate through the database and initiate purchase and other transactions. Information is often organized in a

FIGURE 1-5
Videotex

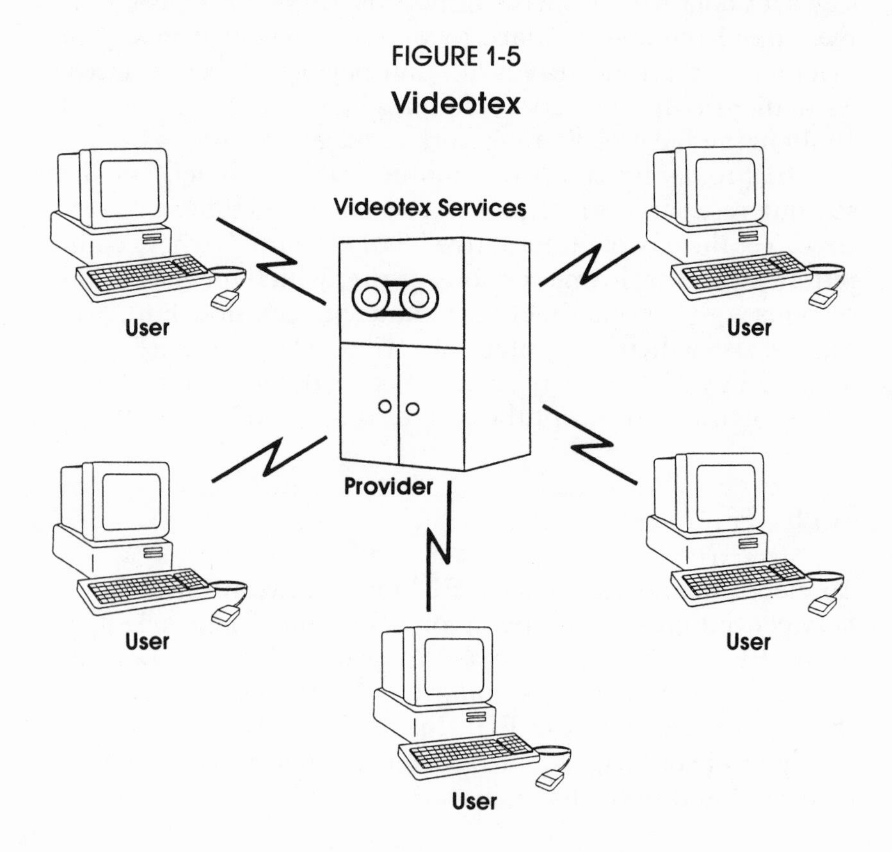

tree structure of pages that users see as they give appropriate commands.[8]

§1.2 TELECOMMUNICATIONS AND DATA COMMUNICATIONS

Any of several types of intermediaries are necessary to link two electronic message users. Frequently, a telecommunications common carrier, such as a local or long distance telephone company, is involved. A conventional fax, for example, can travel from one machine to another through a direct and immediate dial-up or leased line connection provided by the telephone system. The two fax machines operate simultaneously. Similarly, two EDI trading partners can exchange data by linking their computers "point-to-point" through a telecommunications common carrier or a network service provider dedicated to data communications.

VANs are another electronic message bridge. To some extent, the VAN industry grows out of the computer time-sharing and "service bureau" industry. A service bureau is a company with a large computer system and technical staff; it sells data processing services to others lacking computer resources.

VANs can provide much more service than just a communications link. They often store, forward, mailbox, and translate messages. This makes communication easier and more secure because the VAN customer who has, say, 50 trading partners can funnel all communication through one secure and professionally maintained channel.[1] The cus-

[8]Kusekoski, Corporate Videotex: A Strategic Business Information System, MIS Q. 446 (Dec. 1989).

§1.2 [1]Collins-Schnabel, The Role of the Value-Added Network in EDI, EDI Forum 144 (1989).

tomer can unload the many technical burdens of coordinating communication with these partners onto the VAN. Because the VAN can accumulate stored messages in a mailbox, the customer need only connect with the VAN periodically to receive the multiple messages its trading partners may have sent. VANs often rely on other service providers, such as telecommunications common carriers and packet switching and other data communications networks, to link VANs to their customers and to link one VAN to another.

VANs and other data communications networks employ various public and proprietary protocols for controlling, tracking, routing, facilitating, and accounting for messages. Two international standards developed under the CCITT, X.400 and X.500, merit mention. X.400 facilitates the exchange of electronic messages among many different types of computing systems. X.400 protocols establish agreed-upon methods for grouping, addressing, and enveloping messages. Message contents may be in one or more of many formats: free-text e-mail, structured EDI, fax, spreadsheet, and so forth. X.400's distinguishing attributes are that it provides for an audit trail that spans from sender to receiver (despite the crossing of multiple network boundaries) and furnishes automatic message tracking and acknowledgments. X.500 is a companion series of standards for electronic directory services. It permits the construction of electronic message user directories, which can include such information as names and electronic addresses.[2]

§1.3 SECURITY AND CONTROL

A well-managed electronic messaging network features multiple security attributes. Access to the network to send or

[2]*See* Houldsworth, Applying Electronic Messaging, Telecommunications 55 (Aug. 1990).

receive is commonly restricted to those with user identification codes and secret passwords. A network may deter password guessing by giving a user a limited number of opportunities (such as three) to enter it. Some networks require the user to have a unique token, such as a "smart card" (which looks like a credit card but contains a secure computer microprocessor), to gain access. Network management software, which is generally very reliable and incorporates overlapping control features, checks, assigns control numbers to, and keeps track of messages to ensure complete and orderly delivery. Many networks automatically return acknowledgments and message status reports to senders. Some networks have regular reviews by external auditors to confirm security and control.[1]

Admittedly, both public and private networks suffer some control and security risks. Messages can be lost, lines can be tapped, and criminals can break into systems. But the skeptical newcomer should know that the commercial messaging industry is a very sophisticated business that takes security and control seriously.

Many schemes are available to confirm a message's origin to the recipient. None is perfect. One simple method is for an intermediary network to inform the recipient who the sender is, based on the sender's password disclosure to the network. Another is for the sender and recipient to agree on a secret password to be included in the message text.[2]

A more sophisticated method employs a "test key," or algorithmic test code, long used in banking for EFT, letters of credit, and guarantees communicated by telex or fax.[3] The sender adds to the message a test key, that is, a series of characters that represents the product of a mathematical formula previously agreed-upon by sender and receiver.

§1.3 [1]Draper, Technical Solutions, *in* EDI and the Law (I. Walden ed. 1989).

[2]*See* §5.5.

[3]Beware! Fax Attacks!, ABA Banking J. 52 (June 1990).

The formula commonly uses (1) important numbers in the message content, such as date and dollar amount, (2) a count of the number of messages previously exchanged between sender and receiver, and (3) a random number from a code book that sender and receiver have secretly agreed to use. The receiver confirms message origin and integrity by recomputing the test key using the message content and the agreed-upon secret information. The process is cumbersome, especially if the parties seldom exchange messages.

More-sophisticated "cryptographic" methods can protect confidentiality and evince message origin and integrity by scrambling and unscrambling data. The marvelous variety of schemes and their applications is endless. The following describes the rudiments of the two best-known cryptographic schemes.

§1.3.1 Data Encryption Standard

With the Data Encryption Standard (DES), sender and receiver use the same key (numbers agreed upon in advance) to scramble and unscramble data. Taking the agreed key, the DES algorithm (a well-known mathematical formula), and the data to be protected, the sender scrambles the data. It is now confidential because it appears to be nonsense. The sender transmits this to the recipient, who unscrambles the data using the same key and the DES algorithm.

A sender can add evidence of origin and integrity to a message with DES. She can create a message authentication code (MAC) and append it to the unscrambled text of the message. The MAC represents the product of the previously agreed-upon DES key, the DES algorithm, and specified data (or a "digest") extracted from the message text. To check message origin and integrity, the recipient recomputes the MAC using the same ingredients. If the recomputed MAC is the same as the MAC appended to the message, then the recipient knows that (unless someone stole the agreed DES key) the message came from the sender and that the message content has not been tampered with. (Note: absent circumstantial evidence and other controls, the recipient has no irrefutable evidence to prove to an outside party that the message came from the sender because the recipient has the agreed-upon DES key and the other ingredients that are necessary to forge a message.)

§1.3.2 Public Key Encryption

Under a public key encryption system, the sender has two keys, one public (which might be published in a directory as that party's public key) and one private. Mathematically, to calculate a user's private key if one knows only his public key is practically impossible. A widely known public key scheme is RSA (named for the inventors, Rivest, Shamir, and Adelman).

The origin and integrity of a message can be protected this way with RSA: The sender calculates a special digest of the message text, then scrambles it using her private key and the necessary RSA algorithm. She appends the product (sometimes called a "digital signature" in the cryptography world) to the message text. When the recipient receives the message, he (1) unscrambles the digital signature using an appropriate RSA algorithm and the sender's public key and (2) recomputes the special digest from the message text. If the unscrambled digital signature and the special digest are the same, he knows the message text came from the sender and that it is unchanged.

If the sender wishes to keep data confidential, she scrambles all of it using the appropriate RSA algorithm and the recipient's public key. The recipient can later unlock the data by unscrambling it using his private key and the necessary algorithm.

Today, except in highly controlled environments, such as a market in which all players use special equipment, cryptographic schemes can be unwieldy because of the problems in exchanging, protecting, and archiving keys. In the hands of experts, however, the schemes are powerful tools. DES is widely used in EFT, where the demand for security is high and industry standards have facilitated implementation. Inventors are creating new cryptography applications and ways to simplify implementation.[4]

[4]*See generally* Sharma, Unlocking the Secrets of Network Security Devices, Network World, Jan. 16, 1989, at 1, col. 3; U.S. Congress, Off. of Tech. Assessment, Defending Secrets, Sharing Data: New Locks and Keys for Electronic Information, OTA-CIT-310, Washington, D.C.: U.S. Govt. Printing Off. (Oct. 1987).

Chapter 2

The Applications

§2.1 FAX

A stunning array of business transactions occur electronically.

Businesses use faxes for many legal transactions, including contracts. Some of the lawsuits, involving faxes, described in this book prove that. An estimated 3 million fax machines were operating in the United States at the end of 1989, and 1.7 million were projected to be sold in 1990.[1]

Some government purchasing agents, such as the City Purchasing Director of Milwaukee, Wisconsin, accept "sealed" bids by fax. The agents either have special regulations authorizing the practice or interpret their regulations to allow it. They preserve bid confidentiality with such techniques as placing receiving fax machines in separate, restricted-access rooms.[2]

Union Pacific Railroad accepts bills of lading by fax. The received bills are not printed, but routed directly into a computer imaging system for storage, indexing, retrieval, and processing.[3]

§2.2 E-MAIL

E-mail is used mainly for informal messages. But if traders have an efficient means of communication, they will use it to make deals.

The American Gem Market System, a global videotex and e-mail network, links buyers and sellers of gems. The videotex portion lists currently offered gems. Upon electronic request, a seller will send a gem by courier to a prospective buyer for inspection. Then, if the buyer is interested, the parties negotiate and complete the sale by telephone or oth-

§2.1 [1]Markoff, Marrying the PC and the Fax Machine, N.Y. Times, May 2, 1990, at C8, col. 1 (natl. ed.).

[2]Telephone interview with Edward A. Witkowski, City Purchasing Director, Milwaukee, Wisc. (Dec. 10, 1990). The federal government has amended the Federal Acquisition Regulations to permit government contracting by fax under some circumstances. 54 Fed. Reg. 48,978 (1989).

[3]T. Smith, Fax Servers Let Union Pacific Reduce Paper, Network World, July 9, 1990, at 26, col. 1.

erwise. Because the network's e-mail feature is so convenient, final terms are often negotiated and agreed via e-mail.[1]

Internal corporate e-mail systems act as electronic conveyor belts for the internal processing of transactions. Information can be routed from terminal to terminal so managers can consider it, change it, approve or disapprove it, and delegate authority. Extensive audit trails memorialize what happens.[2] NeXT Computer, Inc., the computer maker, uses such a system.

> At Next . . . purchase requisitions are written on a computer, passed along the network for approvals, and checked against the budget. Only then is a . . . purchase order [issued].[3]

§2.3 TELEX

Telex has long been used for sending bids, acceptances, purchase orders, and legal notices, such as notices of arbitration.[1] It is especially popular in international trade. This book has space to mention only a few of the many cases dealing with telexes in commercial transactions.[2] Telex traffic is today plunging in volume because the other technologies, especially fax, are easier and cheaper to use.

§2.2 [1]Warbelow, American Gem Market System (1988) (case study prepared under supervision of Prof. B. Konsynski at Harvard Business School for class discussion, no. 9-189-088).

[2]Eckerson, Hughes Jets Through Red Tape Via E-Mail, Network World, Oct. 15, 1990, at 27, col. 4.

[3]The Third Wave According to Jobs, Bus. Week 77 (Jan. 29, 1990).

§2.3 [1]*See* Hawley, Telex Continues to Provide Service for Law Firms, N.Y.L.J., Mar. 25, 1985, at 29, col. 4.

[2]*See generally* Telex Contracts—A Comparative Study, Intl. Fin. L. Rev. 22 (May 1982).

§2.4 EDI

Worldwide, 15,000 firms use EDI.[1]

EDI quickly and efficiently conveys information between independent firms ("trading partners" in EDI speech).[2] In initial implementation, EDI replaces paper documents, such as purchase orders, transportation bookings, quotations, invoices, certificates of compliance, letters of credit, insurance claim forms, and so on. EDI might be used to convey simple, informative messages. A supplier, for example, might send its customer a shipping notice via EDI. The notice would say (in code), "I shipped eight cartons to you today via Blue Truck Line."

As trading partners advance, they swap messages in sequences, just as they would in paper trading. For example, a buyer might send an EDI purchase order message offering to buy ten widgets at $100 each. The seller can respond with an EDI purchase order acknowledgment (generically known as an application acknowledgment) that accepts the offer. At this point, a buy/sell contract exists.[3] Later, the buyer might issue an EDI purchase order change, requesting a quantity reduction to nine. The seller could accept or reject with a purchase order change acknowledgment.

ANSI X12 standards contemplate two acknowledgment types. The first addresses communication, and, if used, issues automatically upon message receipt. It could be a "transmission acknowledgment," which confirms receipt; or it could be a "functional acknowledgment," which confirms message receipt and intelligibility. The second is an "application ac-

§2.4 [1]Estimate by EDI, spread the word! *See* Seideman, Paperless Trading Rises at 35% Rate, Publisher Claims, J. Com., Aug. 9, 1990, at B2, col. 5.

[2]For a discussion devoted exclusively to EDI legal issues, including contract, recordkeeping, and antitrust issues, *see* B. Wright, EDI and American Law: A Practical Guide (1989).

[3]*See* Part V.

knowledgment," such as a purchase order acknowledgment. It responds to the prior message's content—acceptance, rejection, and so on.

An EDI message may be an instruction, which may not give rise to a contract, but does have legal consequence. A bank customer for instance may send an electronic order to its bank requesting a payment from the customer's account. Like a check, the order legally authorizes the bank to reduce the account.

As experience grows further, users abandon the paper model. They electronically relay information, such as twice-daily sales figures, that would have been impractical to exchange on paper.

Users may agree in advance (and on paper) that the seller will supply all the buyer's needs based on the buyer's twice-daily sales figures. So in this instance EDI is not used to form a contract but just to exchange data related to the fulfillment of a contract. Advanced users also simplify data movements. The automotive industry, for instance, is discontinuing the invoice document. The buyer calculates how much it owes the seller by multiplying the prices in its purchasing records against the quantities in its material receiving records. An invoice is thus no longer necessary to inform the buyer how much it owes the seller.[4]

Electronic contracting started in some industries, such as health care, with proprietary order entry systems. A supplier, such as Baxter Healthcare Corp. under its ASAP Express program, gave customers special terminals that were connected only with the supplier's order entry system. Today, the trend is to replace such systems with public standard EDI, permitting customers to link with an unlimited number of suppliers.[5]

Firms implement EDI for many reasons. It can cut costs

[4]B. Milbrandt, EDI: Making Business More Efficient 39-40 (1987).
[5]Brown, Health Care Industry Rx: Uniform EDI, Network World, Oct. 1, 1990, at 1, col. 5.

by eliminating inefficient paper shuffling and storage and redundant keying of information into computers. EDI also helps firms cut lead times and react more quickly. With EDI, companies slash inventories (and thus overhead expenses) by ordering goods only as needed. Thus, orders are smaller in quantity and more frequent. (Each order is also less valuable, and therefore less worth disputing.)

EDI is the life blood of the just-in-time campaign in manufacturing and the "Quick Response" techniques in retailing. Because it is computer readable, EDI data can more easily be extracted from such places as loading docks and retail outlets, and then analyzed. EDI can tap tremendous sources of new information that can tell a business much about consumer trends, product line profitability, and distribution channel efficiency.[6] Some large companies, such as retailing chains, have insisted that their suppliers adopt EDI.

The federal government has in place or in active development a slew of initiatives for EDI and EFT between agencies and the private sector. The Defense Logistics Agency alone reports over 20 projects for converting such transactions as requests for quotation, invoices, purchase orders, transportation orders, and shipping instructions to EDI. The General Services Administration and the Department of Veterans' Affairs have similar projects.[7]

EDI is usually implemented bilaterally between two firms, but many trading groups have exploited it as well. Since 1983 the Air Transport Association of America (ATA) has operated an on-line database and proprietary EDI system for the listing and sale of aircraft parts. Dubbed the Airline Inventory Redistribution System (AIRS), it facilitates the

[6] *See generally* A. Toffler, Powershift 95-129 (1990).

[7] McConnell, Electronic Data Interchange: Active Ingredient of Electronic Commerce, *in* A Five Year Plan for Meeting the Automatic Data Processing and Telecommunications Needs of the Federal Government, Washington, D.C.: U.S. Govt. Printing Off. (Nov. 1990).

electronic exchange of requests for quotation, purchase orders, and acknowledgments. The ATA publishes user guidelines on such matters as message response times and order cancellations.[8]

Singapore has implemented an EDI network for the exchange of international port documentation, such as ship manifests, transportation bookings, letters of credit, customs declarations, and myriad other reports and receipts. By the end of 1989, the system, called "TradeNet," boasted it had 850 of 2,200 possible subscribers and it handled 45 percent of all sea and air trade documentation through the port of Singapore.[9]

Boxmart, a global EDI and e-mail network for leasing, purchasing, and selling large cargo containers,[10] expedites contracting between container traders. Before using the system, a trader signs a paper agreement that its use of its Boxmart "electronic signature" shall "contractually bind" the trader to applicable transactions entered on the system.

Under federal sponsorship, the Information Services Institute at the University of Southern California operates an experimental automated broker. "FAST" is a facilitator between computer parts purchasers (mainly universities today) and vendors. A purchaser transmits by EDI or fax a request for quotation to FAST, which in turn electronically forwards the request to the appropriate vendors. Later, FAST delivers the responsive quotations to the purchaser, who can then, via FAST, send an electronic order to the winning vendor.[11]

[8]Air Transport Assn. of America, World Airline & Suppliers Guide (Aug. 1988 ed.).

[9]Fellow, King & Konsynski, Singapore TradeNet: A Tale of One City (Sept. 20, 1990) (case study prepared for class discussion, Harvard Business School, no. 9-191-009).

[10]Telephone interview with Geoff Ashton, Boxmart representative in San Francisco, Cal. (June 20, 1988).

[11]Telephone interview with Anna-Lena Neches, Operations Manager of FAST Parts Broker Project (Sept. 27, 1990).

§2.5 EFT AND FINANCIAL EDI

Joining the EDI movement are EFT and financial EDI. EFT, in the strict sense of interbank electronic funds, is hugely successful. The New York-based Clearing House for Interbank Payment System (CHIPS), for example, clears over $500 billion daily.[1] Financial EDI is EDI between a firm and its bank, such as an order to make an EFT.[2]

Industry has been slow to embrace EFT and financial EDI for making corporate trade payments. One reason: The volume of data in a check is small, so the savings from automation are minor. Plus, a canceled check makes a splendid receipt. An electronic acknowledgment might substitute as a receipt, but many EFT systems, such as the American automated clearing house network, permit no acknowledgments.[3] This may change.

Nonetheless, many corporate trade payments are electronic. General Motors reported in 1990 that over one-third of its eligible suppliers has agreed to take payments electronically. GM now makes 21,000 such payments per month.[4] Several states accept tax payments electronically.

A corporate trade payment involves the movement of two messages, the transfer of value ("pay Blue Co. $100") and the remittance advice ("this pays invoice #999"). A practical issue is whether the value and the remittance should move together or separately. The value transfer must cross the banking system, but the remittance could go to the payee through a VAN, in which case the payee would have to match and reconcile the two messages after they are received.

§2.5 [1]Hill & Ferguson, Introduction to EFT and Financial EDI, EDI Forum 26, 31 (1989).

[2]*Id.*

[3]Nelson, NACHA Looks at EDI, EDI Forum 36, 43 (1989).

[4]Golden, Making General Motors and America More Competitive Through Financial EDI and EFT, EDI Forum 24, 27 (1990).

Large Canadian banks have aggressively constructed an EDI/EFT payment mechanism. It keeps the value and remittance messages together. (*See* Figure 2-1.) The payor starts by sending messages to its bank. That bank verifies message authenticity, processes the messages, and forwards them to the payee's bank. The second bank checks authenticity, then credits the payee's account, and forwards the remittance message to the payee. To confirm responsibility, liability, and timing, each bank receiving a message must acknowledge it twice. First, a functional acknowledgment shows receipt; second, an application acknowledgment shows commitment to pay.[5]

FIGURE 2-1

Canadian EDI/EFT Payment System

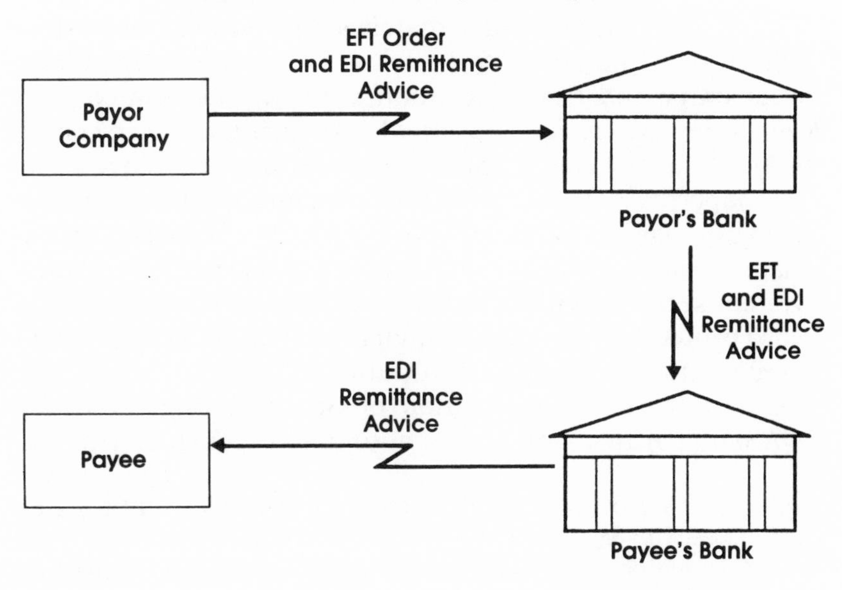

[5]Ballance & Kelso, The New Canadian EDI/EFT Payment System, EDI Forum 32 (1990).

§2.6 VIDEOTEX

Videotex, best known for consumer service (through providers such as CompuServe and Prodigy), also enables firms to sell products to remote commercial customers. A vendor might, for example, load its parts catalog onto a videotex system and permit customers, using their own computers, to browse. When one spots a product, she hits a few keys to place an order.[1]

Teamed up with Reuters Holdings PLC, the Chicago Mercantile Exchange and the Chicago Board of Trade are building "Globex," a videotex apparatus for automated trading of commodities futures and futures-options. Trading will occur interactively via terminals, in traders' remote offices, connected to a central Reuters network. Traders will enter buy and sell orders, which will be displayable on all terminal screens. When a buy order matches a sell order, the system will (in real-time) execute a trade between them. Upon both order entry and trade execution, a printer associated with each relevant trader's terminal will print a *paper* confirmation that the trader entered an order or executed a trade. The paper, which aids audit, control, and regulatory monitoring, must be retained five years. The sponsoring exchanges will set system rules and impose market surveillance. System security will include an extensive audit trail,[2] password protection, unique terminal identification features, and a segregation of support staff duties.[3]

The National Association of Securities Dealers, Inc., (NASD) operates systems for automated securities trading.

§2.6 [1]*See* Digital Equipment Corp., Digital's Use of EDI, 1 EDP Auditor J. 35, 37-38 (1990).

[2]The audit trail would permit the tracing of transactions by the time of order entry, execution, amendment, cancellation, and so forth.

[3]*See generally* Commodity Futures Trading Commn., Div. of Trading and Markets, Chicago Mercantile Exchange's Proposed Globex System (Feb. 2, 1989).

One, in use for several years, is the Small Order Execution System (SOES).[4] It provides for the electronic offer and acceptance of contracts to buy or sell small quantities of select securities. Only NASD members may participate directly, and NASD rules obligate participants to honor SOES transactions.[5]

§2.7 ELECTRONIC FILING WITH THE GOVERNMENT

The federal government has many projects for the electronic filing of regulatory documents. Technically, these projects use e-mail, EDI, or similar systems. Since the mid-1980s the Securities and Exchange Commission has been developing and pilot testing a program (EDGAR) for the electronic filing of public corporate documents, such as annual reports and proxy statements, with a view to soon requiring virtually all such documents to be submitted electronically. The Internal Revenue Service permits the electronic filing of individual tax returns, provided the taxpayer transmits via a third-party taxpreparer and manually signs a paper form to authenticate the filing. The U.S. Customs Service has for years been implementing its Automated Commercial System for the paperless filing of customs declarations. It has relied in part on its Automated Broker Interface system, which sends messages in a proprietary format, but is now evolving to EDI

[4]Another NASD system under development is PORTAL, an electronic market for the purchase and sale of designated securities on behalf of sophisticated investors. Formal securities exchanges are also automating. Trading on the Midwest Stock Exchange, for example, is almost entirely electronic. *See* Fitzgerald, All's Quiet on the Midwest Floor, ComputerWorld, Sept. 10, 1990, at 47, col. 1.

[5]Rules of Practice and Procedure for the Small Order Execution System, NASD Manual (CCH) ¶¶2451, 2465.

using the public EDIFACT standard.[1] In addition, the Department of Commerce's Bureau of Export Administration accepts export licence applications via the CompuServe e-mail service.[2]

§2.8 FUTURE APPLICATIONS

Ultimately, no transaction is immune from automation.

The Federal Judicial Center is sponsoring experiments with the electronic filing of court documents such as pleadings. The Federal District Court for the Eastern District of Pennsylvania has operated one pilot project, and another is planned for the Western District of Texas. One of the unresolved problems is how to "sign" electronic documents in compliance with Federal Rule of Civil Procedure 11.[1]

The London Insurance Market brings together underwriters and, through brokers, customers for the insurance of commercial risks. Traditionally, the placing of insurance involved the manual writing of commitments on paper slips, which presumably are legally binding. A single placement might involve multiple underwriters, each taking a negotiated portion of the customer's risk. The Market is now constructing a computer system, called LIMNET, to replace the paper slips. In the future, when an underwriter makes a com-

§2.7 [1]E. Messmer, Customs Clearance System Based on EDIFACT Hits Standards Snags, Network World, Oct. 29, 1990, at 3, col. 1.

[2]*See generally* H. Perritt, Electronic Acquisition and Release of Federal Agency Information (1988) (report prepared for the Administrative Conference of the United States).

§2.8 [1]Telephone interview with John Ours, Federal Judicial Center (Oct. 30, 1990).

mitment, the broker and the underwriter, using unique security codes, will both enter the details into LIMNET.[2]

The motion picture industry is eyeing paperless contracts in film distribution. Movie distributors and theaters routinely enter "co-op agreements" to divide the advertising expenses for each film. Heretofore, these agreements have initially been agreed to by telephone and then confirmed with formal paper contracts. Having recognized the potential for savings, industry representatives are now creating EDI messages to replace the paper contracts.[3]

To automate the lease of capital equipment, Texaco, Inc., is developing a Lease Purchase Information Trading System. Each lessor and lessee would use it to enter a series of lease contracts over a period of time. Before trading, the lessor and lessee would enter a paper agreement outlining the way in which leases may be entered. The paper agreement would contain a master lease contract form. Later, the parties would electronically negotiate and agree to terms as and when particular lease contracts are needed. Within limits, the parties could electronically amend and deviate from the master lease form.[4]

One can envision the day, not far in the future, when complex financial and corporate transactions are drafted, negotiated, edited, and executed electronically. The negotiation and closing table will be a database accessible to remote participants through computers, fax, and voice messaging. Automation will shorten the time between a transaction's proposal and its closing. The financial incentives to use such a facility will be tremendous because large transactions are

[2]LIMNET—The London Insurance Market Network, EDI Analysis (July 1990).

[3]EDI Reporter International, July 1990 at 1 (newsletter published by INPUT).

[4]Telephone interview with Mitch McKee, in-house attorney for Texaco, Inc. (July 23, 1990).

so time sensitive. Fax machines and courier services are already reducing the need for the physical presence of parties to large transactions. The trend will continue.

§2.9 RESIDUAL PAPER

Not all electronic transaction systems are completely paperless. One major oil company announced in 1990 that although it would aggressively implement EDI, it would not form "contracts" electronically. Company policy would be to have a paper "contract," such as a blanket purchase order, in place before purchasing or selling via EDI. Operative EDI messages would be mere "releases" against those blanket orders. The company would, however, continue its historical practice of forming contracts through telex. Counsel evidently felt uncomfortable with the enforceability (and perhaps the newness) of purely electronic messages.

Users of other systems may form contracts through electronic offer and acceptance messages, and later formalize the contracts with paper documents. Alternatively, they may enter paper agreements (which in the EDI community are often called "trading partner agreements") in advance of trading to confirm transaction enforceability and to fix terms and conditions.[1] A primary issue explored in this book is whether users incur any special risks by abandoning paper altogether.

§2.9 [1]*See* Part V.

Chapter 3

The Players

§3.1 INTRODUCTION

Electronic trading affects many people within an enterprise. The initial reaction, especially from attorneys and accountants, is sometimes negative. Yet as these professionals learn more about how transaction technologies function, they usually become more comfortable. Their original objections lose force. Attitudes change from (1) it cannot be done, to (2) it can be done, but there are dreadful problems, to (3) it can be done, and here is the best way to do it.

Success in electronic trading requires teamwork among

professionals with diverse skills and outlooks. It also requires education and creative thinking on everyone's part. This chapter briefly introduces the key players and their likely concerns.

§3.2 INFORMATION SYSTEMS PROFESSIONALS AND CONSULTANTS

The technical professionals are the front troops. Companies charge them with implementing and maintaining EDI and related technologies. They are also the realists, who know technology's limits. They appreciate the difficulty and expense of making computers perform as promised, and the ever-present risk of error and breakdown.

While computer professionals may not regard legal, audit, and control issues to be within their domain, they should at least be aware of the subject. A system can become much more expensive and "user unfriendly" if, after installation, it must be retrofitted with special security features and audit trails. Technicians need to include these issues in their plans and seek early and clear policies from management.

Technical professionals can be a rich source of practical ideas. If they understand control, recordkeeping, and security objectives, they can devise solutions.

§3.3 USER MANAGERS

The linchpin in the successful implementation of an electronic transaction system is the manager in charge. She must see that the system makes money for the enterprise. She could well be the manager of a sales or purchasing department.

A business manager is unlikely to know much technical detail. Her duty is to coordinate the team of technical, legal, and accounting experts with the aim of formulating balanced solutions.

The legal issues in this field present very few black and white alternatives. Most questions boil down to how much risk is economically prudent. Attorneys are ill-equipped to make decisions here, for their craft is to describe the law, not to assess a venture's profitability. A lawyer can easily advise against a risk that, at most, is worth $5000, when the business incentive to take the risk is worth $100,000. So it falls to the business manager to choose between risk and reward.

Few business managers have the luxury (or as some would say, misfortune) of a hovering lawyer or accountant to answer all legal and audit questions that arise. Therefore, managers need a sense for what is a significant legal problem and what is not. (That is why this book tries, for the most part, to speak in terms they can understand.) This sense permits managers to make the best use of limited professional resources.

This book recommends "control" over transaction systems. Computer and audit experts can list dozens of technical and organizational controls. But one is supreme and irreplaceable—manager brain power. A smart manager can do something no computer gizmo can. He can inspect an office, spot a risk, and assess it. Then he can implement a practical safeguard. For example, an alert manager supervising an office that includes a talented computer programmer would wonder whether that person could abuse the office's financial EDI system by misprogramming it. If he feels uncomfortable, the manager might erect a barrier between programmer and system. He might decree that, before installation, all financial EDI software changes must pass through the company's internal auditing department.

§3.4 ATTORNEYS

Attorneys are most comfortable when conservative. Either they want to do it the old way, or they want to see a herd doing it the new way. They sense (rightly) that if the whole world moves in a particular direction, the law will follow. Part of this book's purpose is to show that both the herd and the law are indeed accepting electronic transactions.

The common law legal systems (such as the United Kingdom, United States, Canada) are generally receptive to new, sensible ways of doing business. Commercial law seeks fairness and ease of trade. It exhibits a general preference for the substance of a transaction over its form. The American Uniform Commercial Code (U.C.C.) §1-102 provides:

> (1) [The U.C.C.] shall be liberally construed and applied to promote its underlying purposes and policies.
>
> (2) Underlying purposes and policies of [the U.C.C.] are . . .
>
> > (b) to permit the continued expansion of commercial practices through custom, usage and agreement of the parties. . . .

But there are some unanswered questions about electronic transactions. What approach should the practicing lawyer take toward these? What advice should he give the client? Too much circumspection can look very silly. One lawyer has observed:

> The typewriter, the telephone, the photocopier and the calculator were all, in their day, initially received with great

> caution. Lawyers, for example, were wary of the typewriter because they could no longer identify the source of the script in front of them in the same way they could identify a handwritten document.[1]

One who appreciates lawyers' temperaments can imagine the fear over typewriters. A handwritten document is a unique, integrated unit. It is virtually impossible to fraudulently switch the document's pages. Page switching on a typewritten document, however, requires only the lifting of a staple. So conservative nineteenth century lawyers were rational in resisting typewriters. But their judgment was pitiful, for the danger in advancing from handwritten to typewritten documents was minute. Today, it would be ludicrous for a lawyer to even wonder whether it makes any practical difference whether a business document is handwritten or typewritten.

Business attorneys have to be pragmatic in advising clients about electronic trading. Granted, the letter of the law may not precisely contemplate new methods, but the lawyer has to ask what that really means for the client's particular situation. How likely is it that a problem will emerge? If it does, how much worse off will the client be with electronic transactions than with paper? (When carefully examined, was paper really all that secure anyway?) What will the problem's magnitude be? How does the potential problem compare with the cost savings and strategic advantages the client gains with the new technology? Remember, in choosing between an electronic and a paper transaction, the risk is just economic. Neither life, limb, liberty, nor morality is at stake.

Electronic technology is flooding into business. There is no stopping it. Like a civil engineer, the wise lawyer will not

§3.4 [1]Andrews, The Legal Challenge Posed by the New Technologies, 24 Jurimetrics J. 43 (Fall 1983).

oppose it, but rather endeavor to channel and control it as necessary.

A lawyer need not be a technical expert to give sound advice. She needs to understand what the computers do much more than how. In the paper world, lawyers advise on how to use paper even though they are not forensic document experts.

§3.5 ACCOUNTANTS AND AUDITORS

Accountants (including auditors) are the watchdogs of electronic business. They prepare, review, and opine on financial statements and tax returns, and they monitor business units to ensure they are operating efficiently and in accordance with management policies and objectives. These professionals' ability to perform depends on transaction system reliability and control. One cannot judge how much money is being made or lost in a chaotic system.

Accountants may be held responsible if they pass off on systems that lack adequate controls. For example, an external auditor may be liable to company shareholders if he examines the company's financial EDI system but fails to discover that employees are fraudulently using it to siphon riches into their Panamanian bank accounts.

Within the accountant's purview can be any of the factors that might threaten a company's financial integrity. Hence, accountants may be concerned with electronic legal issues: the firm's compliance with regulations, its exposure to liability for errors, and the enforceability of its contracts with trading partners.

Accountants are control experts. They specialize in analyzing controls and devising procedures for new business systems. Some of them, especially electronic data processing

(EDP) auditors, are intimately familiar with computers. Their input in the implementation of EDI and similar systems is critical to establishing necessary control.

Electronic transaction technologies present the accounting profession with a daunting task. The audit and control of electronic systems require new methods drawn from the principles of past practices. Accountants must fast educate themselves in these new ways. They will otherwise be swept under the avalanche of electronic data that industry is generating.

§3.6 RECORDS RETENTION MANAGERS

Larger corporations and agencies have dedicated particular managers and even whole departments to records management. These develop policies for record creation, cataloging, storage, and, finally, destruction. Policies must consider legal requirements, the need for record accessibility, and the costs of record retention. In this litigious age, some companies conclude it is best to purge records systematically as soon as they are no longer required. Litigation requests for old records can be very expensive to satisfy, and old records may just as likely be damaging as helpful in court.

As explained in Chapter 6 and Part IV, the methods for retaining electronic records are significantly different from those for retaining paper. Records professionals too must reeducate themselves.

It is more efficient to address records management issues during system design rather than later. But, in the haste to make systems work, records issues are sometimes ignored. Records managers have to launch their own investigations to discover what transaction systems their companies are implementing. They are sometimes surprised to learn, for example, that their companies are sending purchase orders and invoices electronically, and disappointed that little thought has gone into data archiving.

One annoyance for records managers is that records of electronic messages can proliferate in an organization. So if in litigation a plaintiff properly asks the defendant for a copy of a certain electronic message, which was supposed to have been purged, the defendant may be hard pressed to say definitively that it has no record of the message. The message may not be in the defendant's central files, but it might still lurk on a backup tape or a user's personal diskette. Records managers are challenged to find methods of record control so that all important records can be accounted for.

PART II

PRACTICAL RISKS AND CONTROLS

Chapter 4

Customs, Business Risk, and Legal Communications

§4.1 INTRODUCTION

The particular ways legal documents are executed, delivered, and retained are governed more by custom and practical concerns than the letter of the law. Some laws, such as the statute of frauds,[1] do require some transactions to be supported by a "document," a "writing," or a "signature," but their satisfaction leaves much to interpretation.[2]

The rise of information technology throws business customs into flux and forces the trader to consciously rethink how transactions should be effected. Because the mechanics of the old routines are less applicable, he must be guided by their purposes and his own assessment of risk.

A traditional objective in negotiating an agreement is to reduce it to "writing." The writing ritual creates a record, makes the agreement more psychologically binding, and forces careful thinking. It also creates more legally useful proof, wins the protections of the parol evidence rule,[3] and satisfies the statute of frauds. Part and parcel with the writing objective is the desire for a signature, which is a legal and ritualistic symbol of finality, assent, and authenticity.

A trader in the electronic world also wants a final, binding, and authenticated record, but she must use different tools, namely, data processing controls over the initiation, transmission, and recording of electronic transactions. The trader may not be achieving her goals if, for example, she receives a simple e-mail message from a hobbyist's computer bulletin board, and records it herself on a mere personal

§4.1 [1]*See* Chapter 16.

[2]Some laws, such as government procurement regulations, provide more guidance for documenting particular transactions. The purpose might be to limit and control a contracting agent's authority. *See, e.g.,* National Institute of Municipal Law Officers Model Purchasing Ordinance §2-110 (1981) (contract for procurement by municipal government of goods or services for more than $5000 requires "formal, written contract"). Other laws mandate paper as a means of regulation. Regulations under the Controlled Substances Act, at 21 C.F.R. Pt. 1305 (1990), prescribe detailed procedures and paper forms to be used to effect sales of certain controlled substances. These procedures ensure that a tight audit trail is created for tracing the movement of dangerous pharmaceuticals.

[3]*See* §17.5.

computer floppy disk. She might do better to use more robust controls, such as a secure communications channel, and a trusted recordkeeper.[4]

§4.2 TOLERANCE OF IMPERFECT CONTROLS

One cannot dismiss an electronic transaction application just because the controls that may practically be imposed on it are imperfect. The typical controls over paper documents are imperfect too. Paper documents can rather easily be forged, misassembled, misdirected, changed, and lost.[1] No signed commercial document is guaranteed to be accepted as authentic by a court.

The means for testing the legitimacy of paper documents are less than ideal. Few paper handlers are trained or equipped to spot many types of forgeries. Although expert document examiners can, through handwriting, microscopic, and chemical analyses, discern a great deal about the origin of information on paper, their services are expensive and slow. Moreover, they are not clairvoyant and cannot guarantee conclusive or even correct results.[2]

Despite the faults of paper documents, no one would

[4]Chapters 5 and 6 discuss the authentication and recording of messages.

§4.2 [1]In international trade, the counterfeiting of bills of lading, falsification of telexes, forging of letters of credit, and fabrication of customs documents are not unusual occurrences. *See* Is Imitation Really the Sincerest Form of Flattery?, Trade Fin. 35 (May 1989).

[2]*See* A. Lipson, The Art of Advocacy: Documentary Evidence, 3—7 (1989). *See also* In the Matter of Estate of Sylvestri, 44 N.Y.2d 260, 405 N.Y.S.2d 424, 376 N.E.2d 897 (C.A. 1978) (jury may disregard expert testimony on authenticity of signature).

suggest that commerce cannot be effected with them. The advantages of doing business with paper outweigh the risks.

It is the custom in many industries, such as international shipping, to rely on simple telexes for contracting. This has proved reasonably satisfactory, but far from foolproof. Although telexes can be subjected to various controls, including "test keys," some are routinely omitted because they are cumbersome. The result has occasionally been disastrous.

In 1983, thieves sent forged telexes to Chase Manhattan Bank's London office, requesting the transfer of $13.5 million of Colombian government funds. The telexes bore the correct answerback for the Colombian central bank, but lacked a test key. Chase did not always demand test keys for such transfers, even though prudence prescribed it. The thieves made off with the money, and evidence from the ensuing investigation showed that an answerback can be forged.[3]

In a similar incident, a Swiss firm sold goods to a Dutch company based on a bank guarantee evidenced by an untested telex. When the Swiss company tried to collect on the guarantee, the bank disavowed the telex. Experts testified at trial that a telex recipient has no absolute proof of sender identity. The court concluded that, based on the facts, it was unlikely the bank had issued the telex.[4]

The lesson from these two incidents is not that telex is unsuited for contracting or that all telexes relating to legal matters should bear test keys. It is that as the value of transactions grows, the greater the need for gathering evidence, by one means or another, of who one's opposite party is. Sometimes, a test key is prudent.

For some valuable transactions, even a test key—standing alone—may be insufficient. Keys can be broken, and they

[3]Prudent Banking Practice Meets the Forged Telex, Intl. Fin. L. Rev. 24-25 (Dec. 1987).

[4]van Dort, Netherlands: Bank Guarantee by Telex, 14 Intl. Bus. Law. 173 (June 1986).

often protect only specific portions of the information in a message.[5]

Lawyers have exhibited remarkably high confidence in telex.

> Most people feel justified in believing that an answerback from the other [telex] machine appearing on their copy of the message . . . is proof positive that the message was sent to the proper recipient and that it was in fact received. It's viewed as the telex equivalent of an admission of service, and this concept of answerback integrity is an article of faith for many lawyers who use telex to send important messages.[6]

This article of faith has never been completely justified. With the old telex terminals, the machine could have run out of paper but still returned an answerback indicating receipt. With more modern equipment, a telex system may return an answerback even though a paper record is not being made on the receiving end. The terminal may be writing to a computer disk, or the message may be delivered to an electronic mailbox. In either case, there is no guarantee that an operator will retrieve and print out a message. In theory, the system in which the mailbox resides may crash and lose the message.[7]

Despite telex's shortcomings, it is routinely used for contractual correspondence, and rightly so. As with paper letters, the forging of a telex requires enough effort and the likelihood of a delivery problem is small enough that for many transactions it is a satisfactory medium. A telex is

[5]Prudent Banking Practice Meets the Forged Telex, Intl. Fin. L. Rev. 24-25 (Dec. 1987).

[6]*See* Hawley, Telex Continues to Provide Service for Law Firms, N.Y.L.J., Mar. 25, 1985, at 29, col. 4.

[7]*Id.*

widely accepted around the world as a legally enforceable business communication.[8]

§4.3 BALANCING CONTROL RISKS AND COSTS

Appendix B sets forth general guidelines for contracting with EDI and similar technologies. The guidelines establish abstract, flexible goals. The degree to which a trader should achieve those goals will differ from one implementation to another—depending on the closeness between trading partners, the value of transactions, the likelihood of dispute, and so forth.

The guidelines call for the exercise of professional judgment, which is nothing new. In paper trading, business managers and their advisors must decide whether a given agreement should be documented with a memorandum to the file, a simple letter, a registered letter, or a formal, jointly signed agreement; whether each signature should be witnessed, notarized, or backed up by a dual signature; and whether each signatory should initial every page of a document or merely sign the last. Seldom do statutes, regulations or even customs provide the professional much assurance that his decisions are correct. He always runs the risk that a deal is imperfectly documented.

Moreover, many traders are ready to absorb a few unenforceable contracts. Uncollectible debts are a business fact. Often, a modest level of direct control over communications will suffice for practical purposes. The facts and circumstances around transactions shelter them from abuse. The astute trader rarely puts much faith in a single communi-

[8]Telex Contracts—A Comparative Study, Intl. Fin. L. Rev. 22-29 (May 1982).

cation control such as an autograph. She relies much more on having obtained collateral, met the other person face-to-face, exchanged a sequence of related correspondence, spoken by telephone, checked references, and so forth. If she regularly delivers product to the other person's plant, and gets paid, she knows that she takes a small risk in making the next incremental delivery in response to a routine message.

§4.4 CUSTOMS FOR TRANSACTIONS BY CORRESPONDENCE

One might think an advantage of paper over electronic trading is that the former enjoys many well-developed customs. Although that might be true for some narrow industry segments, it is not for commerce as a whole. Paper trading knows few hard and fast rules. And the same can be said of electronic trading. The distinguishing feature of paper trading is that people have more experience with it and therefore understand it better.

§4.4.1 Paper Correspondence

Contract correspondence can be very informal. Often no attorney is involved. The parties may or may not be using standard forms or guidelines.

In theory a correspondence contract follows the sequence of offer and acceptance (e.g., a purchase order followed by a purchase order acknowledgment) or offer, counteroffer, and acceptance. In practice, however, the communications may be a jumble, and to discern precisely when the parties were bound may be impossible.

Some documents are signed, and some not. A signature might be made with pen strokes or an ink stamp. Rarely are correspondence documents notarized, and rarely are signatures compared with specimen to confirm authenticity. Firms usually have preprinted forms or letterhead to identify message origin (although little usually prevents these from being forged). The paper correspondence sender ordinarily keeps a copy. Pages in a multipart paper form are linked with staples, glue, or labels (e.g., identifying Exhibit A and Exhibit B), but some parts might be linked by little more than their logical interrelationship.

Documents are delivered by mail or courier, occasionally with a return receipt requested. A careful sender will ask for an acknowledgment of receipt, and senders may or may not return receipts. In a prudently run office written routines are established for the preparation, approval, addressing, logging, mailing, processing, and filing of correspondence.[1] These can persuasively show what happened to a document even though no one remembers it specifically. Yet many offices fail to follow these good procedures.

Agreements are commonly struck by telephone, and the wise trader confirms a telephone agreement with a letter or form. Preferably, the other party signs and returns a copy, but this does not always happen.

§4.4.2 Electronic Correspondence

As with paper correspondence, there are few absolute limits on ways to communicate and record electronic correspondence (or messages). Chapters 5 and 6 explain that the creative trader has a deep bag of tricks from which to draw methods for confirmation, record making, and control. Still,

§4.4 [1]J. Ritterskamp, Purchasing Manager's Deskbook of Purchasing Law 237 (1987).

the configuration of the technology in any particular installation can constrain the trader. An EDI message, for example, typically cannot contain much free-text; the message must primarily contain coded information.

Some industries using EDI develop implementation guidelines, but their observance varies. EDI cross-industry standards bodies, such as ANSI X12, promote generic guidelines. An automated clearinghouse such as Globex may impose very specific trading procedures. One generalization that can be made about electronic trading custom is that traders are usually expected to respond to electronic messages more quickly than paper messages.

Some deals agreed by telex are formalized later with conventional documents. The parties might subsume the telex into a longer, conventional contract. The telex's purpose was, therefore, to furnish a quick and temporary basis for reliance.

For newer technologies, a similar custom is unfolding. Agreements are commonly struck by fax, with the understanding that the original documents will be mailed. Unlike a telex, the fax contains all the intended words, but the means of communication is perceived as legally suspect. One commentator has suggested the same procedure for some valuable EDI transactions,[2] and it is natural to expect similar advice for e-mail.

Traders seem to accept the fax-then-mail procedure as part of the contracting ritual. The important thing for them is to clinch the deal quickly. A risk to recognize in commercial negotiation, however, is that the fax-then-mail procedure may invite ambiguity. The welsher could argue the fax was not the final communication and the deal was open until the original paper was mailed. The parties may need to clarify which is the operative communication.

To communicate a message a second time serves as good confirmation, but to deliver paper by mail is not necessarily

[2]Thomsen, Interchange Agreements, *in* EDI and the Law, 84 (I. Walden ed. 1989).

the most desirable method. If, for example, a buyer sends an order by e-mail, she could confirm with a fax. Better yet, the seller might send an acknowledgment back by fax or e-mail.

Double communication curbs fraud and mistake. But that is no more true for electronic communication than for paper. For many transactions, businesses see no need to communicate paper documents twice. The risk of error is too low. The same applies to some electronic transactions. Other methods are available for establishing authenticity.[3]

Some government administrative rules now recognize the efficacy of a fax standing on its own. The Federal Communications Commission permits signed petitions, pleadings, and briefs to be filed by fax, provided the signatory keeps the original. Documents signed by parties not represented by counsel must be verified, but those signed by counsel need not be.[4] The U.S. Patent and Trademark Office accepts faxes for certain signed patent application documents. They must be transmitted to the PTO's fax center, which logs and preserves transmissions.[5] Rule 5(e)(2) of the Idaho Rules of Civil Procedure now permits the court filing of certain pleadings by fax. The rule requires the court clerk to stamp the fax printout as "original" and deems the fax signature to be the required signature.[6] Still, some government rules that permit filing by fax require subsequent physical delivery of the original paper.[7]

[3]*See* §5.4.

[4]50 Fed. Reg. 19,359 (May 8, 1985), *amending* 47 C.F.R. pt. 1, §1.52.

[5]1096 Patent & Trademark Office Official Gazette 30 (Nov. 15, 1988).

[6]Similarly, government agencies, such as the Securities and Exchange Commission under its EDGAR program, permit filings to be made electronically, without requiring that original paper documents to be filed too.

[7]*See, e.g.*, Minn. Rule of Court 5.05.

§4.5 CUSTOMS FOR FORMAL TRANSACTIONS

Formal transactions do not follow the classic offer-and-acceptance routine. They consist of carefully drafted and unified documents, the negotiation, preparation, execution, and storage of which are often overseen by lawyers. Conscious of the parol evidence rule and desiring to minimize ambiguity, the lawyers strive to record all terms in the documents. Each party wishes to take original counterparts of the signed documents so that each has equal evidence.

Parties execute formal contracts with ink autographs. In critical financial transactions, lawyers will go to great effort and client expense to obtain timely original autographs. If particularly concerned with authentication, lawyers will bolster the autographs with counter signatures, signatures of witnesses, acknowledgments before notaries, bank guarantees, or the examination of authenticated, specimen signatures. In some transactions, such as commercial real estate leases, the lawyers may have signatories initial every page to preclude pages from being switched. They might even advise that signatories initial special clauses to show specific approval. The decision whether to use these extra controls is usually based only on professional judgment, not legal requirement.

Since the advent of overnight couriers, the practice of closing formal deals by circulating the closing documents from place to place rather than by convening all of the parties at a single location is more common.

§4.6 RECORDS POLICIES AND CONTROLS

Paper can retain visible symbols and marks that are easy for researchers, auditors, or courts to read. The storage of paper is intuitive—one merely drops the paper in a file. The preference is to retain the original holding the signature ink.

Paper document storage is expensive and cumbersome, however. Many archivists microfilm documents (destroying the originals). Many corporations have elaborate cataloging and retention policies that govern archive storage and purging. One objective has been to avoid keeping documents unnecessarily, on the reasoning that old documents are expensive to keep and to search, sort, and produce if requested in litigation.

Electronic traders must consider how they will archive transactions. Chapters 5 and 6 describe methods for creating reliable, credible records, which could be adopted as part of the contracting ritual. Planning is necessary to permit the easy location of particular electronic records and their selective purging when their time has expired on retention schedules.

Paper supports a host of controls and audit trails for regulating and tracing transaction initiation, processing, and accounting. Autographs can indicate approval. Ink stamps can show the fact and time of receipt and processing. Office procedures for individually reading and physically routing documents can ensure they are understood and acted upon.

Electronic transaction systems are capable of supporting similar, and often better, controls and audit trails. An "audit trail" is the presence of any record or procedure that evidences how information progressed from one storage or process to another. It might be an electronic data log, a system manual describing how transactions are changed and processed, a routine staff procedure for moving information from one place to another, a serial number attached to a message, or cross-checks of messages based on such numbers.

A practical issue, however, is that electronic trading is implemented to cut costs. The management risk is that controls—such as the routines for authorizing, inspecting, reconciling, and recording transactions—developed in a particular firm over the years will be sacrificed.

Holt Hauling v. United States Customs Service[1] forcefully demonstrates the problem. The Customs Service licensed Holt Hauling as a bonded warehouse for imported goods. Goods could enter the country "in-bond" and stay in Holt's warehouse pending duty payments. Holt was to ensure duties were paid before in-bond goods were released. Holt had traditionally tracked inventory with a paper bookkeeping system.

Then it computerized, and some intuitive controls were lost. The installed program failed to ask operators to record inventory as in-bond or not, and operators were not trained to record that information. So in-bond goods were mixed with others, and Holt released in-bond inventory without duty payments being made. When Customs discovered this on audit, it suspended Holt's license. Holt suffered greatly for failing to recognize the importance of controls when automating a paper-based system.

§4.6 [1]650 F. Supp. 1013 (Ct. Intl. Trade 1986).

Chapter 5

Trustworthiness of Electronic Messages

§5.1 INTRODUCTION

Paper and computers both impose structure, control, and durability on information. Computers are more functional, however. For messages in particular, computers are inherently superior at regulating the initiation of messages, the creation of evidence of message origin and content, and the management of message archives. But, as with paper messages, electronic message mistakes do happen. Communications can be misdirected and misunderstood; electronic errors can multiply rapidly. Some electronic transaction controls are less intuitive to understand and employ than their paper analogues.

Few detailed control and security standards exist for electronic business transactions.[1] But of course, few exist for paper transactions. In both cases businesses must rely largely on specific professional and managerial judgment. This chapter analyzes the practical concerns in transaction trustworthiness and offers examples of controls to address them. Many controls described in Sections 5.2 and 5.3 are ordinary tools of computer professionals.[2]

§5.2 TRANSACTION INITIATION

A trader must limit the ways in which it makes commitments. Binding communications should be initiated only at

§5.1 [1]ANSI X12 is reportedly at work on "commercially reasonable security" guidelines for EDI.

[2]For more information, *see* Electronic Data Interchange Council of Australia and the EDP Auditors Association, EDI Control Guide: Make Your Business More Competitive (1990); W. Powers, EDI Control and Audit Issues for Managers, Users and Auditors (1989); Hansen & Hill, Control and Audit of Electronic Data Interchange, MIS Q. 403 (Dec. 1989); S. Halper, et al., Handbook of EDP Auditing (1986).

the behest of an authorized agent, should stay within the agent's limits of the authority, and should contain only the intended information.

Paper achieves these goals with familiar techniques. To control the initiation of checks, for example, the trader can lock away the check forms. By convention, check forms are invalid unless properly signed. They can bear serial numbers and notations such as "not valid for amounts exceeding $5000" or "counter-signature required." To counteract mistakes, forms can require writers to fill in amounts twice, once in arabic numerals and once written out in words. Electronic messaging technology can employ analogous controls.

§5.2.1 Limiting Initiation Authority

§5.2.1.1 Limitation on System Access

Control over initiation starts with limits on access to the relevant system. If, for example, a buyer installs software for initiating purchases on computer X, the buyer needs to erect a fence around that software, with a gate that opens only for authorized officers. It can begin with "physical" controls, such as locking computer X in a room or installing a lock on the machine itself. It can build "logical" controls into the computer's programs to deny access to the software to users lacking a password. Passwords can be fortified with secrecy, uniqueness, and regular replacement. More sophisticated (and expensive) safeguards can identify users by scanning thumbprints or eye retinas. Access can be restricted further by requiring action from two independent users.

To deter break-ins, a computer can shut down after three unsuccessful access attempts or after idleness for so many minutes. An audit log can secretly record all access attempts.

§5.2.1.2 Delegation of Authority

In a large organization, authority to transact business is delegated to personnel in small portions and according to complex procedures. Traditionally, managers bestowed authority on subordinates by circulating documents marked with ink stamps or handwritten initials or signatures. Now computer networks can circulate authorization messages too. In the purchasing department of the City of Mesa, Arizona, for example, managers approve transactions recommended by subordinates by entering designated commands or codes into a computer system. Records of approval are stored on printouts and a secure electronic log.[1] Access controls, such as passwords, are one of the primary means of protecting the system's integrity. Secret access logs could also be employed to monitor system activity.[2]

§5.2.1.3 Automated Initiation

Some advanced firms permit their computers to initiate transactions. An inventory management program might, for instance, issue EDI purchase orders automatically when it determines inventory stocks are low.[3] Supervisors program the threshold stock level into the computer. Once the threshold is crossed, the decision to order is mechanical. This challenges the old notion of a single "agent" acting on behalf of the firm, for the computer acts on the basis of policies established and programmed by groups of people.

Transaction initiation programs must be immunized

§5.2 [1]Telephone interview with Sharon E. Seekins, Purchasing Administrator, City of Mesa, Arizona (Aug. 10, 1989).

[2]*See* §15.1 for a discussion of the law on delegating authority to agents.

[3]Hansen & Hill, Control and Audit of Electronic Data Interchange, MIS Q. 403, 407 (Dec. 1989).

from manipulation. Program changes must be approved in advance by management and audited, perhaps by an internal audit department, afterward. Without such controls, a programmer could instruct the system to divert company resources (e.g., to send supplies secretly to his brother-in-law's garage).

§5.2.2 Regulating Message Content

Human operators and programmers are a chief source of errors in electronic messages, but controls can combat errors. With proper programming, systems can automatically compare messages to predefined profiles for completeness and correctness. For example, if a purchase order cannot exceed $3000 in value, the system can be programmed either to refuse to send an order over that amount or to report any such transaction to higher management. A system can restrict the user's options in creating a message. For instance, it can require the filling of blanks in a template on a computer screen, similar to the blanks in a paper form.

§5.3 TRANSMISSION ACCURACY AND COMPLETENESS

Unlike paper documents, electronic communications can theoretically be altered during transmission without leaving a trace. For well-controlled message systems, however, that is a little like observing that a criminal, acting while the postman is at lunch, could theoretically steam open a business envelope, pull the staple from the document inside, remove pages from the document, and replace them with new pages. It is conceivable, but not likely. The risk, of course, is greater with very valuable messages, such as those for transferring funds.

Data communications technology boasts a wealth of techniques for ensuring reliable transmission:

1. A professionally operated network, supported by disaster recovery methods, can shield data from corruption or loss.
2. Communications protocols, network control and management software, and data checking and preservation techniques—when implemented by skilled professionals—can maintain data integrity, reliability, and completeness to a high degree.[1]
3. Communication through a rigid technology, such as conventional fax, makes undetectable alteration difficult and unlikely.
4. An EDI-type message can bear a hash total or line or character count, which is a sum derived from a calculation of data contained in the body of the message. Alteration of the body will throw it noticeably out of sync with the hash total or count.
5. Messages can be organized so omissions are evident. EDI messages, for example, are structured according to an arcane message syntax. In free-text messages, such as fax and e-mail, pages, paragraphs, and even lines can be numbered.
6. System security features can thwart intruders, such as "hackers." A high degree of protection is expensive, so before spending resources excessively, management should consider how likely it is that intruders would alter a substantial number of messages.
7. An altered message seldom makes sense (unless altered by a careful insider). The message is likely to

§5.3 [1]Draper, Technical Solutions, *in* EDI and the Law 96-113 (I. Walden ed. 1989).

refer to private information known only to the parties to the transaction. If the message is a fax or e-mail message written in free-text, the recipient can check it visually. An EDI recipient can automatically check messages for adherence to the prescribed EDI code and syntax. The recipient can also compare messages against a trading partner profile, which can flag unusual items (e.g., a quantity term 100 times greater than usual).

8. The recipient can return an acknowledgment that repeats or summarizes the message. If it takes a route different from the original message, the acknowledgment counteracts inadvertent communications errors and deters fraud. Similarly, the sender can transmit the message twice via two different routes.
9. The parties can employ cryptographic or similar scrambling techniques, which when fully and competently implemented can ensure message integrity to a virtual certainty. Cryptography implementation can be rather expensive and cumbersome, although advancements are occurring in the field.[2]
10. Auditors can routinely check systems for reliability and control.

Note two caveats. First, sometimes communications networks translate messages from one format to another. There is some risk of translation program error. Still, a professionally designed, tested, and maintained program can perform reliably. Second, internetworked messages (those that traverse more than one network) may be at greater risk. Control standards and audit and reporting features may vary from one network to the next. This may require users to rely

[2] *See* §1.3.

less on the networks for control and more on their own acknowledgments, redundant transmissions, or cryptography.

The cumulative effect of overlapping security features can make successful alteration of business messages difficult and rare. This is not to say mistakes and sabotage will never occur. Fax machines can drop lines inconspicuously, and EDI messages can be garbled. But, in the paper world, prestigious law firms have dropped critical numbers from documents, lawyers seal envelopes before enclosing all intended contents, the post office loses letters.

The answers for the electronic trader are the same as for the paper trader: Exercise caution. Use proven techniques and professional staff. Make quality communication a priority.

§5.4 AUTHENTICATING A MESSAGE/RECORD

Evidence of message origin and contents can be crucial. In a well-publicized lawsuit, for example, a borrower claimed that a paper letter from a creditor bank released him from liability. The crux of the dispute was that the bank claimed the letter was phony. After consulting document examiners, each side discerned forensic evidence supporting its position on the letter's authenticity.[1]

This section of the chapter compares the authentication features of paper and some potential authentication methods that could be used in electronic business.[2]

Consider the authentication of the classic paper document: The sender types information, including her identity,

§5.4 [1]Churbuck, Desktop Forgery, Forbes, 246-254 (Nov. 27, 1989).

[2]In this section, "authentication" means the ability to prove to a court the source and integrity of a message.

on a printed form (such as a purchase order) or on sheets of letterhead and second sheets.[3] She inks an autograph, staples the pages, then (keeping a copy) delivers the paper via an intermediary such as the postal service. The recipient keeps the original.

§5.4.1 The Sender's Protections

The paper sender's actions protect her from fraud. First, she can repudiate documents that lack her autograph, paper type, typewriter style, and other forensic indicia of origin.[4] Second, the staple, the difficulty of changing ink on paper, and the retained copy deter the recipient from successfully changing the document.[5] In essence the sender's precautions create a trusted record consisting of two parts—the original paper and the copy.

The electronic message sender can create a similar record with a "trusted recordkeeper." A trusted recordkeeper is any competent entity that holds or certifies a record and is insulated from the incentive and ability to falsify the record

[3]Usually a forger could create the same form, letterhead, or second sheets rather easily. Further, it is not unusual for business people to send documents printed on plain photocopy paper. Yet, for some transactions senders secure documents with special techniques, such as complex, hard to forge paper forms (like stock certificates). Automation of those transactions will require greater controls.

[4]The sender's protection is imperfect, however. If she tried to repudiate a document that has an autograph and other markings that are inconsistent with her usual autograph and markings, the recipient could still argue the sender is responsible for the document. The recipient could say that the sender, in creating the document, deliberately used a strange autograph and strange markings with the intent to permit her later to repudiate the document.

[5]None of these is perfect, however, for they depend ultimately on the sender, aided perhaps by a document expert, convincing a court (a fallible authority) that a fabricated document is fake.

or the certification.[6] The following describes three ways an electronic sender can employ a trusted recordkeeper. To be fully effective, the sender must adopt the chosen method as a regular policy.

§5.4.1.1 Notarizing Faxes

If the message starts as an autographed paper document to be transmitted by a conventional fax machine, the sender could, before transmission, identify herself to a notary (a type of recordkeeper) and acknowledge that she autographed the paper. The notary could fill in, date, stamp, and sign a certificate on the paper confirming the sender's acknowledgment, initial every page in the document, and make a notation of the acknowledgment in his official records. The sender could keep the original document after transmission.[7]

A fully authenticated fax would thus bear the sender's signature and a statement that the document has been acknowledged before a notary; it would also be supported by a note in the notary's records. So if someone tried to forge a fax by deceitfully attaching a facsimile of the sender's autograph to a printout, the sender would repudiate it by showing it was not notarized. And, if an unprincipled recipient tried to switch pages in an authentic fax, the sender could expose the fraud with her secure record of the original document. The notary's initials on each original page would deter page switching by either party.

This procedure protects the sender roughly as well as autographing, stapling, and mailing a paper letter and keeping a copy.[8] It relies in part on the notary's confirmation of

[6]The attributes of recordkeepers are considered in more detail in §6.4.

[7]*See* Appendix A.

[8]It also provides protection roughly equal to sending a message on a conventional telex, where sender and recipient each obtain a paper record bearing a telex audit trail (including answerbacks).

the sender's identity. If the notary uses conventional notary practices, he will meet the sender face-to-face, request proof of identity, and ask for affirmation of signing. A notary is generally trustworthy because he is a government official and usually liable if negligent in ascertaining identity.

§5.4.1.2 Retention of a Complete Trusted Record

The electronic sender could have a recordkeeper who is situated between the sender and recipient make a complete trusted record of each message. (*See* Figure 5-1.) Thus, the sender would privately identify herself, and deliver her message, to her recordkeeper. The recordkeeper would record the message's origin, destination, and contents, then deliver the message to the communications network for transmission to the recipient.

The procedure achieves for the sender the same purpose as autographing, stapling, and copying a paper letter or sending a conventional telex. It empowers her to repudiate mes-

FIGURE 5-1
Trusted Recordkeeper

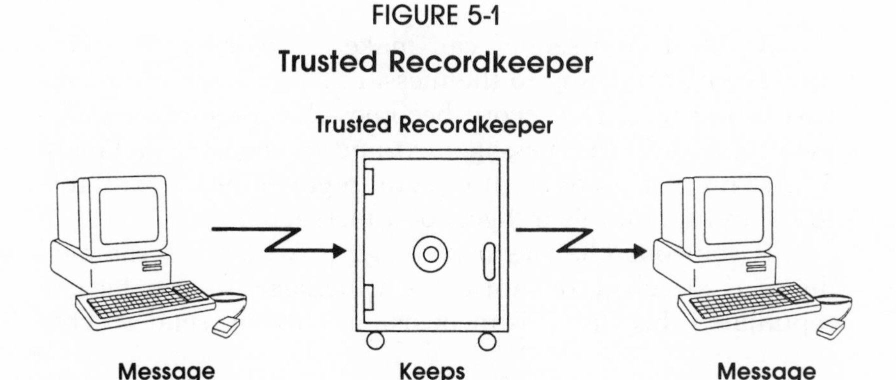

sages she did not intend to be bound to. If someone tries to enforce against her a message she did not run through her recordkeeper, she can repudiate it the same as if it were a paper letter lacking her autograph. The sender could show that she always authenticates messages through her recordkeeper and that a message not in the recordkeeper's archives is likely fake.

The sender wants a reasonably secure method for identifying herself to her recordkeeper. If it is insecure, she loses her protection the same as if she adopted an easily imitated signature (such as a typewritten "X") in paper trading. Her security measures might include passwords, cryptographic authentication, call and callback routines, or others. These would be implemented only between the sender and her recordkeeper; she would not need to make special arrangements with the recipient.

One version of the trusted recordkeeper idea is for a company to establish a central, internal office for sending faxes.[9] The office can routinely make time-stamped copies of all outgoing faxes and keep the copies, together with transmission records, in secure files.

§5.4.1.3 Scrambled Digest

An electronic sender can make a trusted record of a message by attaching to the message's text a scrambled digest of the text. The record becomes the complex arrangement of data in the message text and its digest. (*See* Figure 5-2.) Many test key or cryptographic algorithms are available to securely scramble a digest of a message.[10]

If someone changes a message to which a scrambled digest is attached, or fabricates a message, the sender can repudiate it because it is inconsistent with the sender's cho-

[9]This would be an internal recordkeeper as described in §6.4.2.
[10]*See* §1.3.

FIGURE 5-2
Scrambled Digest

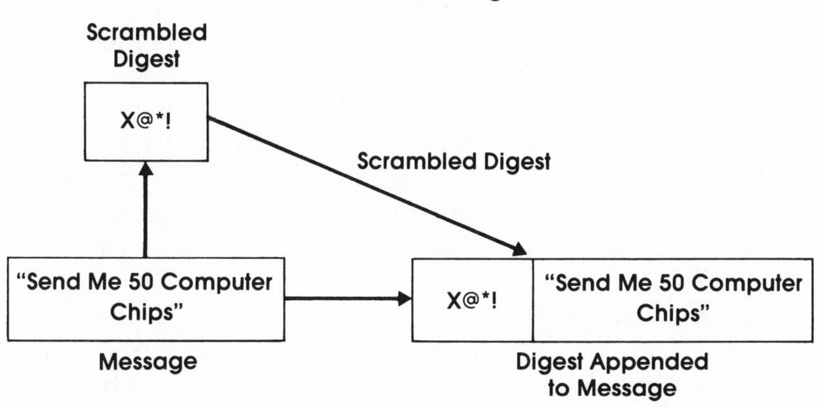

sen scrambling formula. The safeguards are roughly equivalent to signing, stapling, and delivering a paper document.

Under a scrambled digest scheme, the sender's power to repudiate a fake depends on her ability to prove the scrambling formula. Thus, before trading she must tell a trusted recordkeeper what formula she will use to scramble genuine messages. Some part of what she discloses must be a secret between her and the recordkeeper. Her recordkeeper must have confirmed and recorded her identity and the formula. Again, the sender wants a secure means for identifying herself and her formula to her recordkeeper.

As described here, a successful scrambled digest scheme needs no cooperation from the recipient—just as a successful autograph on paper does not depend on the recipient's cooperation. The scrambling formula is withheld from the recipient, and the recipient cannot necessarily read the digest.

§5.4.2 The Recipient's Protections

The classic paper letter recipient has no conclusive evidence of the letter's origin. The signature/autograph could be forged.[11] Or, the sender could have asked her janitor to sign her autograph so she could later repudiate the document. She could even have faked a notary's certificate on the letter.

Still, the autograph on stapled paper protects the recipient in two ways. First, it prevents a sender who was originally honest from changing her mind and repudiating the letter. If the sender who honestly created and autographed the letter later tries to disavow it, the recipient can (albeit with considerable effort in hiring an expert document examiner, and no guarantee of success) try to show that the sender is the originator.

Second, the paper, staple, and autograph together constitute a secure, stable object that neither sender nor recipient can easily change but that the recipient can subject to circumstantial tests. He might examine the printing and paper quality to see if they match what he expects of the sender. He could compare the message content with other information he knows about the sender (such as the type of goods she orders). He could confirm the message with an acknowledgment or telephone call to the sender. He might even compare the signature against a specimen (if by chance he has one) and act as an amateur handwriting analyst. Such circumstantial evidence might prove the origin of the message to a neutral observer, such as a court. Circumstantial evidence might even reveal that the sender who had asked her janitor to sign the message did originate it.

Let us consider electronic safeguards that can furnish the recipient the same two assurances he has in the paper world.

§5.4.2.1 Sender's Change of Mind

Message authentication is a double-edged sword. To the extent it aids the honest sender, it also prohibits her from

[11] *See* Churbuck, Desktop Forgery, Forbes, 246-254 (Nov. 27, 1989).

changing her mind. To authenticate a message, the sender must have put a record outside her control. If it is paper, she autographed and sent it. If fax, she notarized and transmitted the original. If totally electronic, she made a record with a trusted recordkeeper or a scrambling formula.[12]

In paper trading, the recipient does not know whether the sender properly autographed a letter purporting to come from her. Similarly, the electronic recipient may not know whether the sender complied with her chosen authentication scheme. But if she did, he is safe from her change of mind.[13] The sender is in fact motivated to comply because it is the means by which she protects herself from forgeries.

§5.4.2.2 A Stable Record

Electronic communication does not change the nature of the normal recipient's approach to security and proof. He still relies on circumstantial evidence—such as the sender's buying habits. Determining the optimal level of circumstantial evidence the recipient needs to feel comfortable is a matter of judgment under the circumstances.

Surprisingly, electronic communication often increases the circumstantial evidence available to the recipient. EDI, for example, adheres to a code language that requires special knowledge to write and understand. Implementation typically entails advanced coordination between trading partners. Messages often bear sequential serial numbers. Users often employ passwords.[14]

For the recipient to rely on circumstantial evidence of message origin, the message needs to be frozen in a secure,

[12]*See* §5.4.1.

[13]The telex recipient has only limited assurance (from the answerback and audit trail) that the message is authentic. But if it is, he is protected.

[14]*See* §5.5.

unchangeable record. If the message is a conventional fax that bears the notary marks suggested in Section 5.4.1.1, the printout (corroborated by the notary's record of the acknowledgment) is such a record.[15] It would be difficult for the recipient to fabricate or change it inconspicuously.[16]

The recipient of a wholly electronic message could secure a record through his own trusted recordkeeper (an entity employed but not corruptible by the recipient). Ideally, this recordkeeper would record the message contents, the time the message was received, and any related audit information from the delivering network. A recordkeeper scheme proved effective in the Iran-Contra trial of John Poindexter, the former National Security Advisor. While working in the White House, Poindexter sent an incriminating message through the White House internal e-mail system to Oliver North. A printout from a record of the message was subsequently admitted at trial. The court accepted the record as authentic and reliable because a trusted recordkeeper had made and retained it. A system operator—who was outside the control of either Poindexter or his prosecutors—had securely created the record and was able, by analyzing system audit information, to confirm to the court that the message came from Poindexter.[17] (*See* Figure 5-3.)

The authentication schemes described in Section 5.4 compensate only for the loss of the autograph, staple, and paper form or letterhead. They do not diminish the need for recipients to know their trading partners. Just as in paper trading, recipients should call to confirm message origin, send acknowledgments, and run background checks on trading partners.

[15]If the fax were sent via a telephone connection, there may also be a telephone billing record to corroborate the transmission.

[16]The same is true of a telex printout bearing an answerback and audit trail information.

[17]Transcript of Trial, at 1722-1769, United States v. Poindexter (Crim. No. 88-0080-1) (D.D.C. 1990).

FIGURE 5-3
United States v. Poindexter

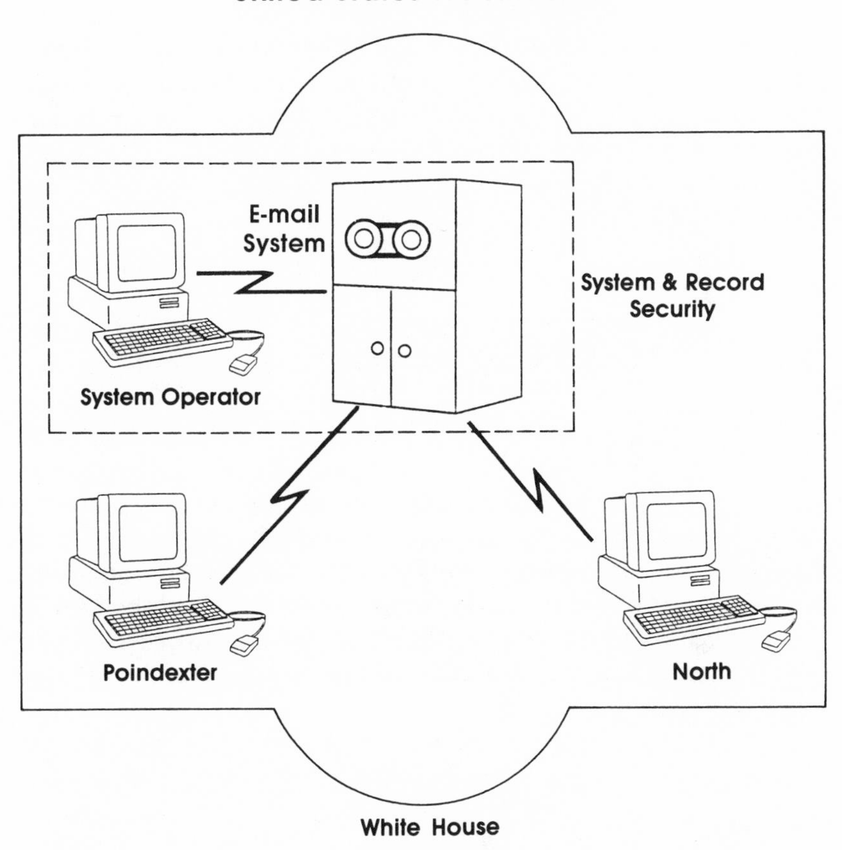

In paper trading, many devices can bolster the ordinary autograph and letterhead. The recipient can ask for autographs from two authorized agents, an attestation from a corporate secretary, or a signature guarantee from a bank. (Or even better, he can demand a letter of credit as collateral.) He can also return an acknowledgment to the purported sender's known address. Electronic traders can employ similar devices. A recipient can, for example, request through an independent route that a corporate secretary send an electronic message (again, recorded with a trusted recordkeeper) certifying that an officer did approve an indicated message. The recipient can return an acknowledgment to the purported sender's known address or expect dual messages from the sender, each via a different route. Moreover, the sender and recipient could implement a complex cryptography scheme that could provide very high assurances of message origin and integrity.[18]

§5.5 PASSWORD SYSTEMS

Secret passwords, whether used to gain access to a system or incorporated into a message's content, can provide strong circumstantial evidence of message origin. Success with a password requires that it remain secret, that it be issued by a trusted party who properly verified and recorded the user's identity, and that a secure record of the password's use is retained. If a message travels through an intermediary network, for example, the network's log of access password activity would be useful evidence of the message's origin. A

[18]Cryptography can be used to give a recipient far more protection than an autograph on paper does. The recipient can, in advance of trading, be given the mathematical formula and key necessary to ascertain the authenticity of secured messages. If the recipient is given the same formula and key the sender uses (as would be the case with DES), the recipient can theoretically fabricate a message appearing to have come from the sender. In that situation, the sender must use an additional method, such as the recording of message content with a trusted recordkeeper, if she needs to ensure she can repudiate any bogus messages generated by her recipient. If the recipient is given a formula and key that are in some way different from what the sender uses (as would be the case with RSA), then the recipient will be unable to fabricate a message purporting to come from the sender. *See* §1.3.

report from this log could be delivered to trusted recordkeepers set up for the sender and recipient respectively.

John Poindexter's Iran-Contra trial illustrates. Poindexter had sent a relevant message on the White House e-mail system. The expert system operator was able, on the basis of system audit records controlled by password security, to attribute the message and its record to Poindexter.[1] The system records were under the control of the neutral system operator rather than Poindexter or his prosecutors.

Poindexter was unable to claim that someone had framed him by stealing his password. The White House system was programmed to force each user secretly to change his password every 30 days, and users were instructed not to inform others of their passwords, or to write their passwords down.[2]

§5.6 AUTHENTICATION FOR AUDIT PURPOSES

The audit perspective on authenticity differs from the legal enforceability perspective. Each is concerned with fraud, but the nature of the fraud differs. If one trader wishes to enforce a particular transaction against another, considerable effort can be exerted to ascertain message/record authenticity. A court can, for example, hear evidence on the surrounding facts and circumstances. The opposite party will be involved, and will have relevant evidence. Any fraud that might exist is between the two trading partners.

In contrast, an auditor usually looks quickly at innumerable transactions. She has no time for a searching in-

§5.5 [1]Transcript of Trial, at 1722-1769, United States v. Poindexter (Crim. No. 88-0080-1) (D.D.C. 1990).

[2]*Id.* at 1728-1729.

vestigation into any single one. Plus, she is particularly concerned with internal fraud, where a company or its employees are stealing from taxing authorities or shareholders.[1]

Paper documents, such as invoices, serve auditors as a form of control; for an enormous mass of documents, having different letterings, sizes, colors, and formats, is expensive and tedious to fabricate. A slew of fraudulent electronic transaction records, however, could (absent appropriate controls) be generated easily. All data records appear the same, irrespective of their origin. An auditor must compensate for this added risk in some way.

A trusted recordkeeper can aid an auditor, provided the barriers protecting the recordkeeper's integrity are high enough. The auditor might also rely on other evidence held by the company—such as related payment records, bank statements, and delivery receipts—to corroborate message records. These might still be in traditional paper form, or if electronic, they could be handled through separate transaction systems or recordkeepers.

An auditor examining a totally electronic company might be at risk particularly because of the lack of evidence that obviously originated outside the company. In a large firm, it seems possible to erect sufficient internal controls (based on segregation of duties, professional internal auditors, and independent members of the firm's board of directors) to alleviate the risk. But this may not be so for smaller firms. Alternatives might be for (1) an external recordkeeper to keep whole or partial records of messages so authenticity can be confirmed; (2) senders to use cryptographic authentication, relying on trusted external parties to issue the cryptographic formulas; (3) trading partners to agree to confirm messages when requested to do so by auditors;[2] or (4) an external time-

§5.6 [1]*See* §11.1.

[2]*See* Fullerton & Evens, EDI and Auditing: Opportunity or Threat?, 2 EDI Forum 74-77 (1989).

stamping service to place secure, cryptographic time stamps on messages or records thereof.[3]

Sometimes an auditor or other examiner (such as a bank loan officer) asks for proof that a certain contract exists, expecting to receive a certified photocopy of a paper contract. If the contract is electronic, a certified printout is generally as good as a photocopy of a paper document. Any demand by the examiner that the contract bear a handwritten signature is baseless. She cannot distinguish a genuine from a fake autograph. If she needs more evidence, she should verify the contract with the other party (which is wise whether the contact is paper or electronic).

§5.7 SENDER ASSENT

Contract and other law is founded on actors manifesting an intent to commit themselves. The affixing of a signature is one recognized ritual. It separates negotiation and obligation. Yet the law is flexible in the manifestations of assent it accepts.[1] The very act of sending a message could signify assent. Logically, even the programming of a computer to automatically issue messages should suffice.

The difficulty in electronic communication is not in showing assent, but in avoiding ambiguity on what is assented to. There is little problem if data are transmitted in groups or messages analogous to documents, for a designated symbol (a "signature") could distinguish preliminary from final messages.

[3]*See* Bellcore Develops Authentication Technique for Electronic Documents, Advanced Off. Tech. Rep., Nov. 30, 1990, at 1.

§5.7 [1]*See* §15.2.

But in an interactive, "real-time" mode, the trading partners engage in a series of queries and responses, as between a customer and an automatic teller machine. A buyer might, for instance, first indicate ten widgets, and then change it to five. To clarify assent, the system might ask, "You have selected five widgets for a total of $500. Is this order correct? Enter Yes or No." The buyer would then have to enter the word "Yes" to show assent. To prove assent, the system should retain a secure record that permits reconstruction of the information displayed to the buyer and his response.

§5.8 PROOF OF DELIVERY

Paper traders rarely rely on the message delivery system itself for proof of delivery. For a special fee, the U.S. Postal Service will return a receipt, but mailers use the service for few commercial transactions. Sometimes courier services obtain delivery signatures, but not always. Sometimes services return undeliverable correspondence, but the policies and their dependability vary. Traders rely more on the return of acknowledgments, or substantive responses, from the message recipients.

Electronic message systems open a new range of proof of delivery services, but services vary widely. The X.400 standard aims to make acknowledgment practices more uniform. EDI standards support a variety of acknowledgments.

An electronic acknowledgment, if securely recorded and accurately referring to a securely recorded original message, can constitute substantial evidence of delivery. (Reliance on acknowledgments as proof of delivery requires the sender to reconcile messages and acknowledgments.) An acknowledgment sent directly from the receiver is more useful than one from the delivering network. Acknowledgment authenticity can be established with the methods used for other types of messages.[1]

When filing paper with the government, it is prudent to have an agency representative ink stamp and return a duplicate copy of the filing or at least the transmittal letter.[2] This provides strong proof that something was filed and when, but it does not precisely establish the content of the filing. (Clerks usually do not compare duplicates and originals.) For electronic filings, comparable proof can be obtained if the agency returns an acknowledgment that identifies the filing with a serial number and the filer records this information with a trusted recordkeeper.[3] Another method would be for the delivering network to keep an audit trail showing delivery.

§5.8 [1]*See* §5.4.

[2]If the document is a check in payment of taxes, the canceled check is returned.

[3]The Securities and Exchange Commission's EDGAR system, the U.S. Customs Service's Automated Commercial System, and the Internal Revenue Service's electronic return filing system all provide electronic receipts. H. Perritt, Electronic Acquisition and Release of Federal Agency Information: Report Prepared for the Administrative Conference of the United States (Oct. 1, 1988), at 90.

Chapter 6

Reliability of Electronic Records

§6.1 INTRODUCTION

Making reliable business records requires judgment in both the paper and electronic worlds. No checklist of rules is fully adequate. Success ultimately depends on professionals implementing practical systems, controls, and audit trails in a manner that will persuade an informed observer of the product's accuracy.

§6.2 WHAT AND WHEN TO ARCHIVE

An electronic message can change between the time of initiation and final disposition. Archives usually cannot be made at every point in the message's life, so which points are best?

The ideal ones would be where legally significant events occur. From the typical user's perspective, those are where the user begins or ends its control over a message. A firm is most responsible to the outside world for the messages that cross the boundary between it and that outer world. This suggests a user should keep a log of transactions as sent and received.[1]

Ideally, records would archive data in a format as close as possible to that in which they were communicated. If the format changes between communication and recording, then logically the difference should be accounted for.

These are ideals; practical considerations may intervene. Logically, it is satisfactory to record at a different point or in a different format if the intervening step(s) are controlled and covered with an accurate audit trail. This would be somewhat analogous to the accepted practice of microfilming and then destroying paper documents under controlled and documented conditions.[2]

How much data must be retained from each transaction? There are no hard rules. It depends on what information (whether message content, audit trail, or network control data) may be relevant in an inquiry and what will be persuasive. However, in the paper environment if the user must keep a document, he is expected to keep the whole document, not just parts or a summary. Recordkeeping regulations today tend to be unsophisticated relative to electronic trans-

§6.2 [1]*See also* §9.4.3. Article 10 of the International Chamber of Commerce's UNCID rules incorporate the idea that EDI users should keep data on an unmodified log. *See* §§14.2 & 15.8.

[2]*See* §10.6.

actions. Some specific regulations may fairly be interpreted to require the keeping of virtually all data for relevant transactions.[3]

§6.3 PRESERVATION OF RECORDS FROM TECHNICAL THREATS AND MISTAKES

Reliable data processing systems, in the hands of trained, well-equipped professionals, can make accurate records of electronic messages. A competent audit trail can show how the recordmakers acquired the information and recorded it. Were this not true, information technology would be a failure.

Ideally, system documentation (i.e., manuals and flowcharts showing how the system works) would precisely describe the environment and life stages of all records. The means by which data are received, altered or reformatted, and recorded would be memorialized. Logs would show who has access to systems and records and describe each record's chain of custody.

One perceived advantage of conventional documents is the durability of paper. The truth, however, is that computer records can also be durable. For one, computer records can themselves be printed on paper or written to microfilm. (Many early EDI users record data on paper for fear that other media would not be acceptable for legal or audit purposes.) Moreover, data can in principle be retained on magnetic or optical media virtually indefinitely, under appropriate conditions.

Long-term storage, however, may necessitate some rather extraordinary methods. The media may need a con-

[3]*See* §11.4.

trolled climate. Contents may need to be tested periodically for loss and transferred to fresh media. Again, the transfer process can be controlled and documented as part of the complete audit trail for the record's contents. Another preservation method is to keep two, physically separated copies. If one is impaired, the second is still available.

Irrespective of the medium, unreadable computer records are worthless. If records are in a computer language format, the archivist needs to retain the necessary computers, software, and documentation to use them. It is particularly important to be able to printout on paper because in some forums that may be the only format in which computer information is accepted. Computer technology changes constantly, and the retention of old equipment can be expensive. Data can sometimes be stored in formats that will be readable with equipment and techniques likely to exist in the future. Also, it may be possible to reformat old records so new equipment can read them. The reformatting process should be controlled and documented.

A special problem with fax records bears mention: Many conventional fax machines print on thermal paper, which yellows and deteriorates. The practical solution is to photocopy the fax onto plain paper. The copying should be done with care so that all marks are preserved, using routine, controlled, and documented procedures. Abundance of caution also advises that the original fax be attached to and stored with the plain paper copy.

§6.4 PRESERVATION OF RECORDS FROM FRAUD

Electronic records can be fabricated. Data can be falsified before being written to storage media, and if stored on magnetic media it can, in principle, be changed without leaving a trace. One practical solution, introduced in Chapter 5, is to appoint a trusted recordkeeper—an entity insulated from the incentive and ability to falsify its records. A credible party would then control data recording and storage. This is like appointing a witness to attend the signing of a will so he can attest that it occurred.

A trusted recordkeeper can furnish evidence superior to that for a multipage paper letter. When the sender prepares such a letter, she autographs it, photocopies it, staples it, places the original in the mail, and keeps the photocopy. What now prevents either sender or recipient from fraudulently switching out pages in the original or photocopy? The recipient's possession of the original deters the sender from switching pages in the photocopy. The recipient's deterrents to page switching are the sender's retention of the photocopy and the potential for a document examiner to spot a fake page from its typestyle, folds, and chemical composition. Still, page switching can happen. At bottom only the fear of a swearing match in court impedes it.[1]

The changing of a message recorded by an adequate trusted recordkeeper, however, is impossible.

§6.4.1 Common vs. Exclusive Recordkeepers

Let us consider the possible types of trusted recordkeepers.

A recordkeeper might be "common," that is, under the

§6.4 [1]Paper does not guarantee detection and deterrence of changes to messages. Ultimately the forensic analysis of changes to paper relies on judgment and guesswork. Consider, for example, a disagreement over the dollar amount on page two of a three-page, signed letter. The sender's photocopy shows \$1000. The recipient's purported original shows \$2000. The sender asserts the recipient's second sheet is fake because its typestyle, paper quality, and paper folds are different from the first and third sheets. The recipient claims the sender deliberately used different styles, quality, and folds to make the second sheet appear phony. Who is right? Judging the truth boils down to an intuitive evaluation of credibility, not the deduction of an inescapable scientific conclusion.

joint control and direction of sender and recipient. Its records would be available to both. A common recordkeeper might be an intermediary computer service provider that keeps a single archive for both of its customers. (*See* Figure 6-1.) The common recordkeeper's advantage is that both parties recognize the authority of and have access to the same record.

Alternatively, a recordkeeper could be "exclusive," that is, under the control and direction of only one party. An example might be an intermediary service provider that keeps records only for the sender, or a special recordkeeping department within the sender organization itself. An exclusive recordkeeper holds several advantages:

1. Business records are a form of valuable "property," and record ownership is easier to ascertain, transfer,[2] and regulate if only one customer is involved.

FIGURE 6-1

Common, External Recordkeeper

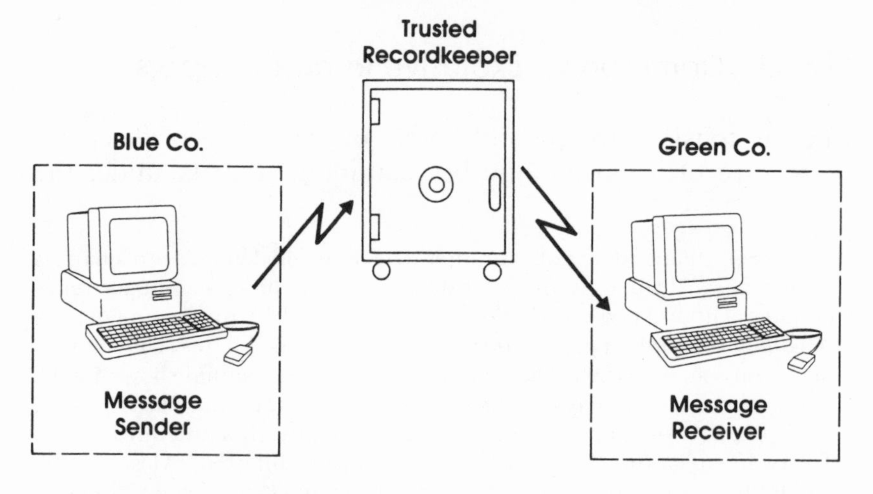

[2]An EDI user, for example, may wish to assign its accounts receivable, together with its related EDI invoice and receipt records, to a bank.

That customer need not negotiate with its trading partner over what information is retained, how, and for how long. (The record retention policies for a sender and recipient could differ greatly on any given transaction.)

2. Records cost money to maintain, and the upkeep responsibility is simplified if the records belong to only one customer. If, for whatever reason, the recordkeeper runs short of funds, that customer can pay the recordkeeper more, take possession of the records, or simply abandon them. But it need not negotiate the issue with its trading partner.
3. An exclusive recordkeeper replicates simple paper trading. When a sender mails a letter, she keeps a copy as her exclusive property. The original becomes the recipient's property. There is no common record.

Thus, the exclusive recordkeeper is generally preferable. The exception might be where a common recordkeeper is regulated by government or a trusted, well-financed association of companies. An example of a government regulated recordkeeper is a notary public who certifies and keeps records of signature acknowledgments. A notary is commissioned by the state, and laws generally provide for the preservation of notary records.[3]

§6.4.2 External vs. Internal Recordkeepers

A trusted recordkeeper could be "external," meaning independent of either sender or recipient, as an intermediary network is. Or it could be "internal" to either party—such as a special department within a company. An external rec-

[3] *See generally* W. Gilmer, Anderson's Manual for Notaries Public (5th ed. 1976).

ordkeeper could be either common or exclusive; an internal recordkeeper is necessarily exclusive. Each party could have an exclusive, internal recordkeeper. (*See* Figure 6-2.)

The design and credibility of an internal recordkeeper needs explanation. If a recordkeeper is a department within, say, the recipient, what prevents it from changing records to favor the recipient? Corporation shareholders face a similar problem. To know if employees are stealing from the firm, the shareholders must rely on books and records kept by the employees themselves. The solution is for the shareholders to expect "controls" to be implemented to stop theft and safeguard books and records. A key control is "segregation of duties"; tasks are divided among employees so each

FIGURE 6-2

Exclusive, Internal Recordkeepers

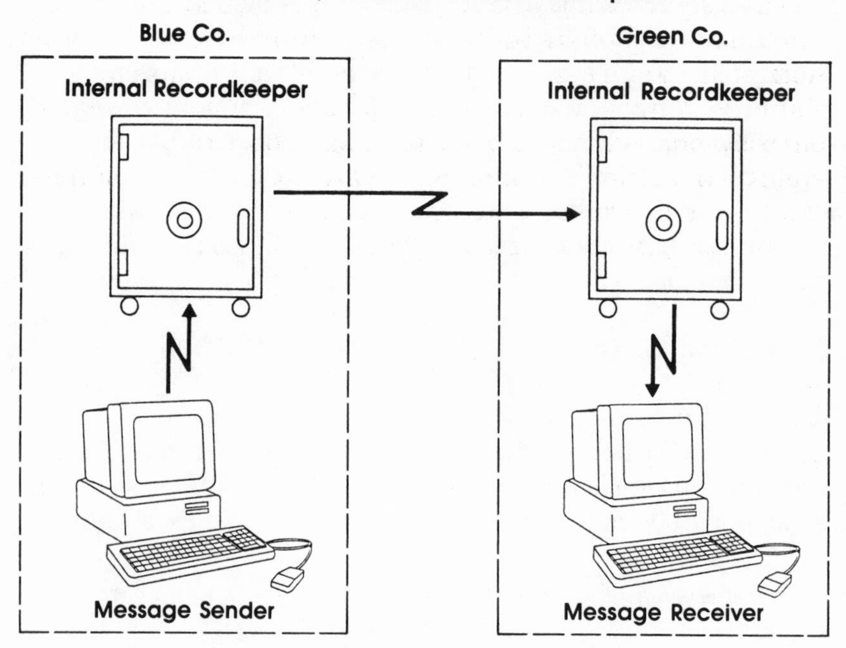

checks the other. One employee, for example, deposits receipts with the bank, while another records them in a ledger. The result: fraud involving receipts requires collusion. Competent implementation of this control, in tandem with others (such as regular audits by independent accountants), can render books and records highly reliable.

Similar controls can be imposed on an internal recordkeeper. Suppose employees in a company's legal and purchasing departments negotiate electronic transactions with other firms. The internal recordkeeper could consist of employees from elsewhere in the company, perhaps the telecommunications department.[4] Thus the duties of transaction creation and transaction recording would be segregated. Many controls could enhance record credibility:

1. Written policies and routines could be developed with the help of independent accountants.
2. Recordkeeper employees could be chosen on the basis of trustworthiness, impressed with the importance of record integrity, and trained to perform responsibly.
3. Independent internal and external auditors could regularly, perhaps even secretly, audit the recordkeeping.
4. Recordkeeper employees could report ultimately to independent members of the company's board of directors.
5. The employees could be denied access to the information, training, and software necessary to make intelligent alterations to records.
6. Records could be written to a non-rewritable medium, such as a write-once, read-many (WORM) optical disk, computer output microfilm, or even

[4]*See* Fullerton & Evens, EDI and Auditing: Opportunity or Threat?, 2 EDI Forum, 74, 76 (1989).

paper.[5] Controls such as serial numbers on storage units could prevent a forger from lifting information from one unit (such as a WORM disk), changing it, and writing it to a substitute unit.

7. Multiple, independent recordkeepers could be established within the same company. The records they keep could overlap so each is a check on the other.
8. Users could be denied precise knowledge of the location and function of the recordkeeper(s).
9. Records could be securely time-stamped with cryptographic techniques.[6]

The Iran-Contra trial of John Poindexter, a former National Security Advisor, relied on the e-mail record of an internal recordkeeper. Poindexter sent and received messages on a White House e-mail system. The system operator (in other words, the recordkeeper) kept backup copies of the messages. The operator was persuasively able to authenticate a printout of a particular message at trial because neither he nor his records were corruptible by Poindexter or the prosecutor. The operator was an "internal" recordkeeper because he and Poindexter worked for the same organization—the White House.[7]

Neither an internal nor an external recordkeeper is inherently superior. One advantage of an external recordkeeper, however, is that observers might more readily recognize its credibility. (Still, even an external recordkeeper needs to guard against fraud. Its employees could collude with its customers.) Another advantage is that it can exploit economies of scale by keeping records for many customers.

[5]WORM media and microfilm cannot easily be erased or written over once data is written to it.

[6]Bellcore Develops Authentication Technique for Electronic Documents, Advanced Off. Tech. Rep., Nov. 30, 1990, at 1.

[7]Transcript of Trial, at 1722-1769, United States v. Poindexter (Crim. No. 88-0080-1) (D.D.C. 1990).

A drawback to an external recordkeeper is that the customer's valuable records are tied to the fate of another entity. If the recordkeeper goes into bankruptcy or dissolution, the customer must work to reclaim its records. Also, the recordkeeper stands in a blackmail position. If it demands more money for its continued service of long-term records, the customer may lack bargaining power to resist. The responses available to the customer are to spread valuable records among several recordkeepers and to have appropriate contracts confirming the customer's rights. Also, these problems recede if the recordkeeper is regulated.

External records enjoy less confidentiality than internal ones. The fourth amendment's protection from unreasonable government searches may not extend to electronic records held by a third party, and the Electronic Communications Privacy Act, while providing some protections, actually empowers the government sometimes to gain secret access to external electronic records.[8] This issue's significance is less if the amount and type of information in external records is restricted. For example, a notation in a notary journal that a signatory acknowledged a document has little confidential value. Additionally, an external recordkeeper could preserve confidentiality by scrambling its archives using an appropriate form of encryption[9] and giving the customer the only unscrambling key.

The advantage of an internal recordkeeper is that it keeps records under the principal's umbrella of control and confidentiality.

A recordkeeping system can combine internal and external features. The idea of notarizing a document before faxing does that.[10] The notary is an external party who keeps one record (the notation in his official records), and the original document is another record, which the sender keeps

[8]*See* Chapter 19.
[9]*See* §1.3.2.
[10]*See* §5.4.1.1.

internally. Another internal/external combination would be for an external recordkeeper at regular intervals, such as every week, to certify and deliver all accumulated records to the customer for final storage. The recordkeeper could record data on a non-rewritable medium, such as a WORM disk, and then certify the record with a conventionally signed and notarized affidavit of authenticity.

§6.5 DESIGNING RECORDS FOR AUDIT

An audit raises special concerns. Transaction records might be subject to an audit from many quarters—internal and external financial auditors, federal or state income tax auditors, state sales tax auditors, regulatory examiners, and so forth. The sophistication of auditors and their familiarity with electronic transaction systems will vary.

The Commodities Futures Trading Commission requires that terminals for electronically trading futures contracts print out confirmations of all trades.[1] The fundamental reason: paper confirmations are easier for regulators to examine. Similarly, at least two tax authorities favor the retention of paper records of electronic transactions. HM Customs and Excise in the United Kingdom requires that, among other controls, all electronic invoices bearing value-added-tax information be summarized on printouts.[2] In addition, New

§6.5 [1]Commodities Futures Trading Commn., Division of Trading and Markets, Chicago Mercantile Exchange's Proposed Globex Trading System 12 (Feb. 2. 1989).

[2]HM Customs and Excise, Computer Audit Branch, Computer Data Interchange, Electronic Mail and Direct Transmission Systems: The Requirements Regarding Computer Data Interchange of Invoice for Value Added Tax Purposes, A Guidance Note as Supplied to Trade Organizations.

York stock transfer tax regulations encourage the retention of printouts of electronic instructions for securities transfers.[3]

Sometimes printouts are cost effective, but they are not a perfect form of evidence and control. The trend will increasingly be to store transactions on electronic media. Another trend will be that fewer detailed records of transactions will be kept and audited; auditors will rely less on records and more on the security of computer processes to verify financial results. These trends mean more tax—and other—auditors will need training in computer audit techniques and some new computer audit strategies may be needed. Yet there is no fundamental obstacle to auditors relying on computers and electronic records. If controlled with segregation of duties and other techniques, computers and their records can furnish reliable audit evidence.

Electronic transactions have not been in wide use long enough for tax and regulatory authorities to consider them thoroughly. In many instances, authorities need to develop new regulations for controlling and logging electronic transactions. The more uniformity among regulations, the better.[4]

[3]N.Y. Stock Transfer Tax Reg. §§446.1(d), 446.3(a)(2), N.Y. Tax Rep. (CCH) ¶¶57-820, 57-822 (1980). *See* Chapter 12.

[4]*See* Part IV.

PART III

LEGAL PROOF ISSUES

Chapter 7

General Proof Issues

§7.1 INTRODUCTION TO EVIDENCE LAW AND PRACTICE

Paper is a trusted medium for holding legal and audit evidence. People know how to use it, and centuries of experience have tested the application of evidence principles to paper documents. Electronic message technology seeks to eliminate the exchange of paper between trading partners and minimize the paper records each retains. Part III analyzes how the rules of evidence apply to paperless transaction records.

There are three general types of records that might be offered at trial as evidence of electronic transactions: (1) a record of the contents of an electronic message at some stage in its life, (2) a computer audit record, such as a journal noting the time at which the computer issued a message, and (3) a statistical or analytical report generated from a computer survey of a quantity of stored data.

In the classic trial, one party, the "proponent," seeks to "admit" a bit of evidence (such as a record of an invoice) to prove a point that matters in the trial. Typically the proponent must "lay a foundation" for the evidence to show its admissibility under evidence law (or the rules of evidence). The other party, the "opponent," may object if there is a basis for doing so under the law. If the judge allows admission, the "trier of fact" (normally the jury but sometimes the judge) may consider the evidence in deciding the case. A trier of fact generally decides a case only on the basis of evidence that is admitted.

Evidence is anything that demonstrates, clarifies, or shows the truth of a fact or point in question. A proponent may offer many types of evidence: documents, objects, witness testimony, and the results of practical demonstrations and scientific procedures. To be useful, evidence must persuade. But so long as it can be understood, evidence need not necessarily be communicated in any particular mode or medium to be accepted under evidence law or to be persuasive.

Aiming to ensure the usefulness of evidence and promote a fair and speedy trial, evidence law does regulate the nature and quantity of evidence that may be admitted. Evidence rules may vary from one forum to the next: federal courts, state courts, government agencies, and arbitration panels. The latter two tend to have less formal rules.

This book's evidence discussion focuses on the general principles of American evidence law, as rendered mainly in the Federal Rules of Evidence (FRE) (applicable in federal courts and some federal agencies)[1] and the common law. Some government agencies and state courts have rules that

§7.1 [1]The Uniform Rules of Evidence, which have been adopted in one form or another in most states, are similar to the FRE.

differ from these, although the concepts behind them are often similar.

Somewhat like legal triers of fact, auditors also consider evidence, such as invoice or payment records. As with legal evidence, the fundamental question for auditing evidence is whether it is persuasive in showing that a fact, such as the making of a $1000 payment, is so. In evaluating evidence, auditors do use professional guidelines, but they are less rigid and formal than the legal rules of evidence.[2]

Generally, any evidence relevant to a matter at issue may be admitted at a trial.[3] Evidence is relevant if it tends to prove that some fact of consequence is so. Logic, experience and common sense determine whether one thing tends to prove a fact or point.

A component of the relevancy requirement is that any message or record offered for admission as evidence must be *authentic*. Evidence is authentic if it is what it is claimed to be. The proponent usually bears the burden of showing in his foundation that evidence is relevant and authentic. This is done by introducing preliminary (or foundation) evidence to show the relevancy and identity of the thing offered as evidence. For example, in a trial over an international trade transaction, one party may wish to admit a paper letter of credit. To show relevance, he might offer preliminary evidence—such as the testimony of a knowledgeable witness—that this letter secured the transaction. To establish authenticity, he might show that the signature thereon is that of the appropriate bank officer. Chapter 8 examines the authenticity of electronic messages.

The opponent to relevant and authentic evidence may still object to admission under certain rules that regulate evidence. The two that most directly affect electronic transactions are the hearsay rule and the best evidence rule. Hear-

[2]American Institute of Certified Public Accountants, Statements on Accounting Standards AU (CCH) §326.02 (Aug. 1980).

[3]*See* Fed. R. Evid. 402.

say is any statement made outside a trial that is offered as evidence inside the trial to prove the matter asserted in the statement is true.[4] A simple example is a letter from *A* stating "Blue Co. made a $50,000 sale last week" if it is offered to show Blue did make such a sale. Hearsay is usually not admissible, but the rule is tricky in its application and subject to many exceptions. The proponent may be able to circumvent it by showing in her foundation that the rule does not apply or that the evidence falls within an exception. Chapter 9 explains the hearsay rule further.

The best evidence rule provides that to prove the terms of a "writing," the original writing (not a copy) must be introduced. This rule has many exceptions too, and is the subject of Chapter 10.

Despite the complexity of evidence law, many records are routinely admitted into trial with little comment or controversy. The proponent and opponent simply agree the evidence is relevant, authentic, and unobjectionable. This agreement may be struck in pretrial conferences or stipulations or may occur tacitly at trial.

Evidence might be admissible to show one fact but not another. In *Roberts v. United States,*[5] for example, the defendant was charged with stealing from an automatic teller machine (ATM). The court ruled certain electronic records from the machine were admissible to show that the transactions in question did occur. But the trier of fact could not consider them on the question whether the transactions were unauthorized, for the records logically bore little connection to that issue. The unauthorization issue had to be covered with different evidence, namely, testimony from the holders of the accounts from which funds were drawn.

In developing a case at trial, a proponent may have to show a chain of conditional facts to prove an ultimate fact by inference. For example, a proponent might show that a

[4] *See* Fed. R. Evid. 801(c).

[5] 508 A.2d 110 (D.C. App. 1986).

programmer successfully instructed computer X to reject orders over $1000 and that the price of a green widget, as listed in computer X, is $2000. The trier of fact could then infer that computer X accepted no orders for green widgets.

§7.2 THE STRENGTH OF EVIDENCE

Evidence rules regulate admission, but they generally do not determine whether evidence will be believed. Admissibility is decided by the judge.[1] Believability or "weight" is normally decided by the trier of fact. Experience and logical analysis of the particular situation are the best guides to knowing what is credible. The auditing profession has developed some noncompulsory presumptions to aid in evaluating credibility:

> a. When evidential matter can be obtained from independent sources outside an entity [i.e., the firm being audited], it provides greater assurance of reliability for the purposes of an independent audit than that secured solely within the entity.
>
> b. The more effective the internal control structure, the more assurance it provides about the reliability of the accounting data and financial statements.
>
> c. The independent auditor's direct personal knowledge, obtained through physical examination, observation, computation, and inspection, is more persuasive than information obtained indirectly.[2]

In evaluating the utility of evidence in court, attention must be given to the logical connection between it and the

§7.2 [1]*See* Fed. R. Evid. 104(a).

[2]American Institute of Certified Public Accountants, Statements on Accounting Standards AU (CCH) §326.19 (Aug. 1984).

point it is offered to prove. "Direct" evidence has a strong and immediate connection. "Circumstantial" evidence is less strong; it requires the trier of fact to draw inferences to believe that the evidence proves the point. For example, the EDI recipient's unmodified data log of the messages he received is direct evidence for determining what EDI information had reached him. But that log is only circumstantial evidence of what a sender had transmitted to the recipient. To determine from the log what was transmitted requires knowledge of the existence and function of the communication link between sender and recipient and the drawing of inferences from that.

The precise boundary between direct and circumstantial evidence is indefinite, but the distinction is useful. Circumstantial evidence of something is less valuable than direct evidence of the same thing. (The auditor's indirect observation is less valuable than her direct observation.) Lower value evidence is less persuasive with the trier of fact and more likely to be excluded from trial under the many evidence rules.[3]

The more circumstantial the evidence, or the greater the inferences the trier of fact must leap through, the less the weight. To illustrate, suppose the trier of fact must consider conflicting evidence on the same fact—the time a fax was transmitted. The incoming fax printout has been lost. The sender testifies she transmitted in the morning and kept a notation to that effect. The recipient claims it was in the afternoon, as that was when his communications center called to say the fax had arrived. The evidence, however, indicates (1) the recipient's communications center often is remiss or slow in calling when a fax has arrived, (2) the recipient was sometimes out of his office on the day in question, and (3) the communications center often fails to leave a message

[3]*See* Huber, Hunt & Nichols, Inc. v. Moore, 67 Cal. App. 3d 278, 136 Cal. Rptr. 603 (1977) (computer printout inadmissible where the printout may cause confusion and its probative value is low).

for the recipient if it calls while he is out. The inferences the trier of fact must tolerate to believe the recipient are considerable, and the trier could justifiably believe the sender.

The weight the trier assigns also depends in part on whether it suspects error or deceit. Suppose, for example, in another dispute over the time a fax was sent, the sender, a notorious liar, testifies she transmitted in the early morning. The recipient's printout is available, however, and the time stamp on it shows 2:00 p.m. The recipient's fax machine is in an independent print shop, which owns and operates the machine, located down the street from the recipient's office. The trier of fact might reasonably accord more weight to the time on the printout and conclude that the fax was sent at 2:00 p.m.

The proponent may take extra steps when introducing evidence to convince the trier of its credibility. He may, for example, show the record was created under conditions that make mistakes unlikely. In *United States v. Greenlee*[4] the government offered Internal Revenue Service (IRS) computer records indicating the defendant filed no tax return. To bolster the evidence, the government tried to show it could not have failed to record a return if one had been filed. Officials testified that on receipt all returns are broken into groups of 100 and assigned individual control numbers. An employee records certain information from each return, including the taxpayer's social security number, in a computer, and then another repeats the step to catch errors. A third employee recounts the 100 returns to preclude loss. Finally, the computer information is compared with Social Security Administration data for conflicts in social security numbers. The government apparently succeeded in showing that the IRS records were believable because the court permitted it to admit the records and convicted the defendant for failure to file a return.

[4]380 F. Supp. 652 (E.D. Pa. 1974), *aff'd,* 517 F.2d 899 (3d Cir. 1975), *cert. denied,* 423 U.S. 985 (1975).

The opponent can introduce her own evidence to refute the original evidence. Consider *Judd v. Citibank*[5] in which a court disbelieved a computer record. A customer sued her bank, seeking repayment of ATM withdrawals from her account. The bank claimed the withdrawals had been made using her ATM card and secret password. It introduced a printout from the machine's log and testimony on the machine's reliability (although the bank's witness acknowledged the machine can suffer mechanical malfunctions). Then, to contradict the printout, the customer presented her own testimony that she had made no withdrawals along with a letter from her employer to the effect that she was at work when the withdrawals occurred. The court, viewing the suit as a credibility contest between the customer and the machine, sided with the customer, suggesting it is good public policy in a close call to accord greater credibility to people than machines.

Any technique making records more reliable and relevant to points at trial will aid both their admissibility and weight. Thus "controls" that insulate records from possible error and dishonesty are desirable.[6] Further, records creating evidence that is less likely to be circumstantial are more valuable. This is the basis for the practical observation in Section 6.2 that it is preferable to make data recordings as close as possible to the stage in processing at which legal rights are affected. Such recordings more directly reflect the data at its critical state.

Nevertheless, a secure and credible audit trail can shrink the inferences needed to link a distant record and a legally significant stage in processing. Suppose, for instance, that computer X is designated as the place for legal receipt of purchase orders by a company. For technical reasons, the company chooses to pass the received orders to computer Y before recording them. It is easier to conclude that the mes-

[5]107 Misc. 2d 526, 435 N.Y.S.2d 210 (Civ. Ct. 1980).

[6]*See* the auditing presumptions above and §§6.3 & 6.4.

sages computer Y recorded are the ones the company received if a useful audit trail (including perhaps time and sequence numbers stamped onto messages by computer X) shows the messages' passage between the computers.

§7.3 THE ADMISSION OF ELECTRONIC RECORDS GENERALLY

As explained in Chapters 8-10, computer records are often admitted into evidence, although some are rejected. From a legal policy standpoint, few disagree that relevant information from reliable computer records may be admitted.[1]

Computer record reliability depends on the controls around the data in the records—from the data's inception, to their recording, to their ultimate retrieval. In simple form, the data controls in an electronic messaging system might be analyzed as follows:

1. Controls over original data input, which ensure transaction originators are identified and message contents are accurate and complete.
2. Controls over transmission to preserve message contents and provide proper delivery and processing.

§7.3 [1]*See* §2.716, Sixth Recommendation, Manual for Complex Litigation (5th ed. 1982):

> Computer-maintained records kept in the regular course of business and printouts prepared especially for litigation should be admitted if the court finds that reliable computer equipment and techniques have been used and that the material is of probative value.

Although this version of the Manual has been superceded by the Manual for Complex Litigation, Second, which devotes less attention to the admissibility of computer records, this concise statement of policy is still true.

3. Controls over record creation, indexing, and storage.
4. Security features throughout the system to preclude intentional tampering with messages and records.[2]

Each area has the potential for weakness. Systems can be poorly designed or programmed. Users can be ill-trained or neglectful. Errors in electronic transactions are ultimately traceable to human mistakes in system design, programming, operation, or security. The points at which humans are directly involved in an information system are especially ripe for error.

Any computer record offered in court could have flaws.[3] However, a careful analysis of the control and security features in a system can help a court evaluate record reliability. There is a policy debate, however, over how the job of analyzing control and security should be handled.

At one extreme courts would take a very skeptical view, requiring that as a condition to admission the proponent lay an extensive foundation to show reliability, meticulously tracing data from their origin, through all the stages of processing, to their final archive. The proponent would have to spend the time and money to marshall one or more computer experts to test the relevant programs and testify on the details of their function.

At the other extreme the law would allow admission with rather little foundation on reliability by the proponent—perhaps just a showing that the circumstances suggest reliability. It would then permit (but not require) the opponent to attack the weight of the evidence by probing control and security weaknesses in the relevant system. To challenge the evidence at trial, the opponent could have obtained the necessary information about the system through pretrial discovery procedures that permit the parties to learn

[2] *See* Chapters 4-6 for a discussion of practical controls.
[3] The same is true of any manual record.

facts pertinent to the litigation. The opponent would have to spend its resources probing the issue.

Courts generally required exhaustive foundations for microfilm and general computer records when they were first offered as evidence decades ago. Courts later relaxed such requirements as more businesses adopted the technologies and experience with them grew.

The current trend among courts is to accept general business computer records with relatively little foundation establishing reliability. This effectively creates a presumption of reliability for computer business records. One consequence is that if record reliability is to be questioned in court, the opponent must take the initiative.[4] Another is that the technology's use is encouraged because users are assured that their records will not be unduly difficult to admit in court.

Some argue for a more complete foundation by the proponent.[5] Among the rationales put forth are these: The proponent has access to more information about the controls and security for the relevant systems.[6] Business computer systems have too much potential for error to be presumed reliable. And, "it is simple in most cases to alter a computer record or even the system program that produces the record. . . ."[7]

The debate has been framed in terms of the authenticity requirement, the hearsay rule, and (to a lesser extent) the best evidence rule, each of which is discussed in the following chapters. None of these three principles is perfectly suited

[4]Peritz, Computer Data and Reliability: A Call for Authentication of Business Records under the Federal Rules of Evidence, 80 Nw. U.L. Rev. 956, 958 (1986).

[5]*See id.* at 958-961, 999; Lynch & Brenson, Computer Generated Evidence: The Impact of Computer Technology on the Traditional Rules of Evidence, 20 Loy. U. Chi. L.J. 919, 927-928 (1989).

[6]This will not always be true, especially where computers link across the boundaries of multiple firms.

[7]Lynch, above, at 927.

for analyzing electronic evidence. In the presence of this new medium, the distinctions among the legal principles blur. Courts mix them. Thus, the following analysis with each in a separate chapter is artificial.

The crux of the policy debate today is how to judge accuracy and reliability. Traditionally it concerned the reliability of records in a self-contained computer system. Now, the advent of electronic business transactions has complicated the debate by adding a new issue: the authenticity of electronic messages (i.e., their origin and integrity) that originated in external systems. In addition, the debate's importance grows because electronic information is becoming ever more pervasive in business.

Despite the debate about how the rules should be applied, a practical observation holds for each of the evidence principles discussed in Part III: Appellate courts tend to afford trial courts considerable discretion in applying the principles to particular situations. The close call is left to the judge on the scene.

Chapter

8

Authentication of Electronic Evidence

§8.1 INTRODUCTION

To be admitted as evidence, an electronic message or record must first be authenticated, or identified. Authentication is a function of the relevance requirement; unidentified evidence cannot be relevant. The proponent must show the judge that the evidence is what she says it is.[1]

Usually, however, even after the judge allows admission

§8.1 [1]*See* Fed. R. Evid. 901(a).

of the evidence, the trier of fact remains free to believe or disbelieve its authenticity. Thus, if the proponent of a fax printout establishes its authenticity for admissibility purposes, the opponent can still offer evidence to persuade the trier of fact that the printout is fake.

Electronic message authentication can pose challenges. A conventional paper letter unites a message and its record in a single, durable medium. Authentication of the letter thus deals with the message and the record simultaneously. Electronic message identification, however, splits into two inquiries: (1) What is the genuine message? and (2) Is this an authentic record of that message?

§8.2 WHEN AUTHENTICITY IS A PRACTICAL ISSUE

For many business disputes, the question of message and record authenticity will be a minor issue. Rather, the crux of disputes will be the interpretation and implication of message contents. The opponent to evidence can confirm from his own records the authenticity of the messages and records introduced by the proponent.

Courts discourage meaningless contests over authenticity (especially in civil trials), and tests of evidence are expensive and time consuming for both sides. Through pretrial discovery procedures, parties can review record authenticity and determine whether it is an issue. The parties can then agree through pretrial conferences, stipulations, or even tacit understandings that evidence is authentic.

The authenticity of some business messages will be questioned, however. A classic example comes from a report from The Netherlands.[1] A Swiss corporation sold equipment

§8.2 [1]van Dort, Netherlands: Bank Guarantee by Telex, 14 Intl. Bus. Law. 173 (June 1986).

allegedly believing a large Dutch bank had, by a telex to a Swiss bank, guaranteed payment. When the seller tried to collect on the guarantee, however, the Dutch bank denied having issued the telex. At trial, an expert witness testified that, absent special security measures, means do exist by which one telex user can masquerade as another. (This implied that the telex answerback scheme is not highly secure.) Another witness stated that it is banking custom for binding telexes to be secured with test keys.[2] The telex in question bore no test key. Arguing that the telex was phony, the Dutch bank presented evidence that only its main branch issued telex guarantees, and that it was standard practice for the branch to use test keys and to confirm guarantees by mail. Based on this, the court judged the bank not responsible for the telex.

§8.3 TECHNIQUES FOR ESTABLISHING AUTHENTICITY

The message evidence proponent might show (or lay the foundation for) authenticity with virtually any type of preliminary evidence—the testimony of witnesses on the circumstances surrounding the message, the internal characteristics of the message itself, or a demonstration of the process producing the message.[1] The critical characteristic of authenticating evidence is that it be persuasive.

A mere statement of origin in a communication is usually insufficient to establish authenticity, however. For purposes of admitting communications into evidence, courts expect more of a foundation, with the stated goal of pre-

[2] *See* §§1.1.3 & 1.3.
§8.3 [1] *See* Fed. R. Evid. 901.

venting fraud.[2] The simple presence of an autograph on a paper document, purporting to be from a certain person, cannot by itself authenticate the document. The proponent must introduce evidence that the autograph is genuine—such as a comparison to a specimen autograph or the testimony of an expert document examiner who scientifically analyzes the fingerprints on, or the paper and ink constituting, the document.[3]

Under Federal Rule of Evidence (FRE) 901(b)(4) the authentication of evidence may come from its "[a]ppearance, contents, substance, internal patterns, or other distinctive characteristics, taken in conjunction with circumstances." The associated Advisory Committee Note states: "Thus a document or telephone conversation may be shown to have emanated from a particular person by virtue of its disclosing knowledge of facts known peculiarly to him; . . . similarly, a letter may be authenticated by content and circumstances indicating it was in reply to a duly authenticated one." Hence, forensic reference to an autograph or the physical characteristics of paper and ink is not the only way to establish message authenticity.

A conventional letter can be authenticated solely from circumstantial evidence. In *United States v. Eisenberg,*[4] for example, a letter was authenticated from (1) its location when found, (2) the odd address and return address on the accompanying envelope, and (3) the letter's contents, which correctly referred to private facts known by the alleged originator. Similarly, in *United States v. Grande*[5] a paper invoice was authenticated by testimony that it (1) was in the customary form, (2) was paid by the appropriate party, (3) purported to be for a job that was indeed done, and (4) listed charges that conformed to the agreed rate.

[2]McCormick on Evidence, §218, 687 (Cleary ed., 3d ed. 1984).

[3]McCormick, above, §221, 691 n.13.

[4]807 F.2d 1446 (8th Cir. 1986).

[5]620 F.2d 1026, 1035 (4th Cir.), *cert. denied,* 449 U.S. 830, 449 U.S. 919 (1980).

For purposes of admissibility, the so-called reply doctrine supplies an authenticity presumption for some messages. If one message is shown to have been issued, then a return message that indicates it is in reply to the first can be authenticated solely from its contents.[6] Thus, in *United States v. Weinstein*[7] a telex was authenticated as a communication from the defendant by the fact that it replied to a prior letter addressed to the defendant. Similarly, evidence that a mailgram confirmed the contents of a telephone conversation with a person having a recognized voice was sufficient to authenticate the mailgram in *Milner Hotels v. Mecklenburg Hotel*.[8]

Under the FRE, one way of identifying technological evidence is to present "[e]vidence describing a process or system used to produce a result and showing that the process or system produces an accurate result."[9] The applicable Advisory Committee Note explains that this rule is designed especially for computer business records. Thus, competent testimony identifying, describing the function of, and confirming the accuracy of a computer system that produced a message or record is sufficient to authenticate the message or record. It is not necessary to bring the computer system itself into the courtroom for a demonstration. In practice, courts seldom cite this rule as the basis for electronic record authentication. They have focused more on whether the evidence qualifies under the business records exception to the hearsay rule.[10]

One method for authenticating physical evidence, such as a specific computer tape on which a message was recorded, is to present testimony describing its chain of cus-

[6]McCormick, above, §225, 695-696; 7 Wigmore, Evidence §2153 (Chadbourne rev. 1978).

[7]762 F.2d 1522 (11th Cir. 1985), *cert. denied,* 475 U.S. 1110 (1986).

[8]42 N.C. App. 179, 256 S.E.2d 310 (1979).

[9]Fed. R. Evid. 901(b)(9).

[10]*See* Chapter 9.

tody.[11] Such testimony proves the object is as the proponent claims by tracing who possessed it over time since its origin.

The following sections consider the authentication of electronic message evidence as two separate inquiries—one into the message contents and the other into the message record.

§8.4 AUTHENTICITY OF ELECTRONIC MESSAGE CONTENTS

To admit electronic message contents into evidence or, ultimately, to prove their authenticity to the trier of fact, the proponent generally must show origin and integrity. He must show who or what originated the message and whether its contents are complete and in the form intended, free from error or fabrication. Business managers, technicians, and auditors are familiar with this issue. They too are concerned with message authenticity, for bogus messages are operational and security threats. Managers and technicians are likely, to one degree or another, to have practical and technical controls in place to prevent creation of phony or flawed messages.

In a trial where authenticity is disputed, the proponent's challenge is to marshall persuasive evidence to show the message to be genuine. Evidence that a message recipient/evidence proponent might put forth includes parts or all of the following: (1) testimony on, and procedures manuals documenting, the recipient's policies for screening messages and returning acknowledgments, (2) a log showing whether an acknowledgment for the message in question was returned and when, (3) evidence that the contents of and circum-

[11]*See* Fed. R. Evid. 901(b)(1). Authentication can be established by "[t]estimony that a matter is what it is claimed to be."

stances surrounding the message conformed to what was expected from the alleged sender, and (4) qualified testimony on the communication link's reliability in maintaining message integrity.[1]

A purported message sender/evidence opponent might employ similar techniques to disavow a message. In the Dutch-Swiss telex case described previously, the Dutch bank's consistent policy when issuing telex guarantees was to transmit only from its main branch (which presumably was equipped for recording and securing telexes), and to use test keys and mail confirmations. The receiving Swiss bank, on the other hand, assumed that an insecure telex was authentic, failing to require a test key or to confirm the telex with an acknowledgment. The Dutch bank, possessing better controls and thus the better evidence, prevailed when the dispute erupted.

The question concerning computer message authenticity is in truth an extension of an issue previously encountered in computer evidence cases—the authenticity of data input into a computer. In *Victory Memorial Hospital v. Rice*,[2] for example, a hospital tried to admit computer records of medical services performed for a patient. The records derived from information on paper forms (such as laboratory test reports) that had been keyed into the computer. The patient questioned the data's trustworthiness before it was entered into the computer. To establish the data's authenticity, the hospital (1) produced a sample of the original forms and matched them to the records in issue and (2) introduced testimony on the reliability of the hospital's procedures for collecting the data and entering it into its system. The court held that the hospital had laid a sufficient foundation for the records' admission, noting that the patient could still argue to the jury (the trier of fact) that the records were flawed and that it should therefore accord them little weight.

§8.4 [1]*See* §5.3.

[2]143 Ill. App. 3d 621, 493 N.E.2d 117 (Ill. App. 2d Dist. 1986).

§8.5 AUTHENTICITY OF ELECTRONIC RECORDS

The second issue is the authentication of the message record. As with other computer records, message record authentication could be established by a witness testifying on (1) the procedure used to create the record and (2) the record's chain of custody after creation.

Computer records cases often mix the authenticity issue with the hearsay-rule/business-records-exception analysis discussed in Chapter 9. In *United States v. Jones* the court stated that for a computer record to qualify under that exception, a witness must "be able to identify the record as authentic and specify that it was made and preserved in the regular course of business."[1] Most cases emphasize the hearsay inquiry over the authenticity inquiry.

In the electronic messaging context, a qualified witness could describe the circumstances surrounding a message record's creation and the record's chain of custody. Generally, such a witness would not need personal knowledge of the information in the record or to have participated in its creation. She would need some knowledge of the recordkeeping process, however.[2] A prime candidate for such a witness would be a manager in charge of the applicable data processing or communications system. At trial, the witness would identify

§8.5 [1]554 F.2d 251, 252 (5th Cir.), *cert. denied*, 434 U.S. 866 (1977). *See* United States v. Vela, 673 F.2d 86, 90 (5th Cir. 1982), *reh'g denied*, 677 F.2d 113 (5th Cir. 1982), in which the court stated that the defendant's demand for greater authentication of the computer records than was given at trial went "beyond [the hearsay/business records exception] and its reasonable purpose to admit truthful evidence." *See also* McCormick, above, §314, at 885 n.6, opining that the FRE 901(b)(9) inquiry into trustworthiness duplicates the business records exception inquiry.

[2]McCormick, above, §312, 881 (speaking as to business records generally). *See* §8.6.

the system and its general function and might also describe the procedure for indexing and storing records.

A possible objection to an electronic message record is that the recordkeeper could have fabricated it (or permitted fabrication). A court might justifiably be unconvinced of record authenticity if it recognizes an ability and a strong incentive to falsify records. As explained in Chapter 5 and 6, the employment of a trusted recordkeeper can help verify record authenticity. In *United States v. Poindexter,*[3] for example, it seemed particularly plausible that a record of the electronic message at issue was authentic because it was controlled by a neutral party—the e-mail system operator. The Fifth Edition of the first *Manual for Complex Litigation,* which is noted for its conservative approach to computer evidence, suggested that the level of scrutiny a court applies to computer business records may be relaxed where they were created by a disinterested party.[4] More extensive proof of authenticity may be in order, however, when the circumstances hint at the potential for fraud or a lack of care by the recordkeeper.

§8.6 EXTENT OF FOUNDATION

An issue in laying the foundation for an electronic message or its record is the qualification of the foundation witness. Witnesses separate into two categories: A lay witness generally testifies from first-hand knowledge; an expert witness is someone with special knowledge, skill, experience, or education who can help the trier of fact understand the evi-

[3]*See* §§5.4.2.2 & 5.5.
[4]Manual for Complex Litigation 123 (5th ed. 1982).

dence or determine a fact. Use of an expert at trial often entails extra effort and expense.

A computer-records-foundation witness need not necessarily be a computer expert. In *United States v. Linn*[1] the director of communications for a hotel authenticated a computer printout showing a telephone number called from a room and the time, even though the witness could not explain the technical process by which the record was generated. The witness' personal knowledge of the record's source, and her ability to show the records qualified as business records (discussed in Chapter 9), satisfied the court.

American Oil Co. v. Valenti[2] examined whether the foundation for a computer printout summarizing a current account between a vendor and customer could come from testimony by the sales manager who supervised the account. He knew about the computer's function from his receipt of monthly reports from it and from his work with the computer's operators, but he had no direct experience with the computer. Noting that a few other courts required a lower standard, the court ruled the witness must have "some working acquaintance with the methods by which [the] records are made."[3] Acknowledging it was "an extremely close question" whether this sales manager satisfied the standard, the court ruled he did, given his knowledge of the account and the recordkeeping procedures employed.

One scholar argues that courts are too lax with computer records. He contends that courts should require proponents to show, with expert testimony under an analysis like that in FRE 901(b)(9) (evidence describing a process and showing its accuracy), that the systems producing the records yield accurate results.[4] In practice, however, courts seem to pre-

§8.6 [1]880 F.2d 209 (9th Cir. 1989).

[2]179 Conn. 349, 426 A.2d 305 (1979).

[3]426 A.2d at 311.

[4]Peritz, Computer Data and Reliability: A Call for Authentication of Business Records under the Federal Rules of Evidence, 80 Nw. U.L. Rev. 956 (1986).

sume that if businesses rely on the records in the ordinary course of their affairs, then the means by which the businesses process and record the data under their control is accurate.

This presumption is realistic. In *United States v. Linn* for example, the computer records at issue were mere telephone records created by a neutral party, the hotel. The court permitted the proponent to authenticate the records with testimony from a lay witness who knew little about the recordkeeping system's technical functions. To have required technical proof of the means by which data accuracy was maintained in a system the hotel used daily would have been a waste of time. It is very unlikely that as a result of such an inquiry the court would have concluded that the recorded telephone numbers and times were doubtful. The hotel obviously had an incentive to make its system accurate.

United States v. Poindexter[5] seemed to rely on the same presumption of accuracy in allowing an e-mail record into evidence. A system operator, a computer expert, authenticated a record from the internal e-mail system regularly used by the White House staff, but he only described the rudiments of what the system did. He did not tell how the system functioned or vouch for how well it performed. There was no showing, in a technical sense, that the system yielded accurate results.[6] Neither the proponent nor the opponent of the evidence asked searching technical questions about the potential for the system to make inaccurate records.[7]

[5]*See* §5.4.2.2.

[6]*Compare* Fed. R. Evid. 901(b)(9).

[7]Transcript of Trial, at 1722-1814, United States v. Poindexter (Crim. No. 88-0080-1) (D.D.C. 1990). These observations are based on the trial transcript. It is conceivable that during a pretrial event, such as a deposition of the system operator, the parties explored the capacity of the system's hardware and software to produce accurate records. Nevertheless, given the regularity with which this system was relied on by the White House staff, it is doubtful either party made much effort to examine this subject.

Indeed, in the absence of a serious allegation that the system was suspect, such an examination of the White House e-mail system would have been a meaningless exercise. In accepting the e-mail record, the court was correct in presuming that the system produced accurate results. People used the system daily for important communications, so the circumstances suggested its records were accurate.

An issue may arise from the translation or reformatting of message data between origination and final recording. In EDI implementations, electronic messages are commonly "translated" into EDI standard format immediately before being sent, and translated out of that format after being received. Some data, particularly that dealing solely with the communication process, may be discarded. The final record of a transaction may therefore be considerably different in form from the actual message.

If this process occurs in the ordinary course of business and free of circumstances indicating carelessness, then a complex technical foundation for the admission of resulting records seems unjustified. Virtually all the leading computer evidence cases have overcome a similar electronic translation problem; they accepted human-readable printouts of machine-readable data stored on magnetic tape. In each such case, computer had to translate stored data in order to make a printout, but few if any of the cases have considered the possibility that the translation could be distorted. The implicit assumption seems to have been that printing is a routine process likely to be accurate.[8]

Still, the careful recordkeeper will be able to account for message translation. Evidence of a competent implementation of, and a robust audit trail (computer logs and documentation) for, this process would be useful if a court did put the proponent to the task of explaining its accuracy.

[8]*See, e.g.,* Transport Indemnity Co. v. Seib, 178 Neb. 253, 132 N.W.2d 871 (1965).

Chapter

9

The Hearsay Rule and Electronic Messages

§9.1 INTRODUCTION TO THE RULE

The classic evidence analysis of computerized records falls under the hearsay doctrine. Electronic message records also should be examined under this doctrine. Hearsay is any statement made outside a trial, which is offered as evidence in the trial to prove the matter asserted in the statement is true.[1] Consider for example *A*'s statement to *B:* "Blue Co. produced 2000 widgets today." The statement was made outside court, so *B*'s testimony in court on what *A* said would generally be hearsay if offered to show that 2000 widgets were made. Likewise, if *A* stated in a fax that Blue Co. produced 2000 widgets, the fax would be hearsay if offered to show the statement was true.

As a rule, hearsay is inadmissible as evidence at trial. The rule's purpose is to enhance the reliability and completeness of courtroom evidence. Hearsay's chief perceived danger is that the declarant, *A*, might not have been accurate, sincere, or completely truthful when he made the statement. Our justice system prefers that *A* himself testify in court about widget production. He would then take an oath to tell the truth, speak in the presence of the trier of fact, and be subject to cross-examination. In a sense, the law's disfavor of hearsay is analogous to the auditor's disfavor of indirect observations. Evidence filtered through any intermediary is prone to error and distortion.[2]

Not all out-of-court statements are hearsay, however. If a statement is offered to show simply that it was made, rather than that it was *true,* it is not hearsay. Thus a message or document having a legal effect is not hearsay if offered in court to show the effect. For instance, it is not hearsay for *B* to testify she heard *A* say to her, "I accept your offer to sell widgets." What matters here is not whether *A* was truthful or sincere in what he said but whether he spoke the legally effective words to accept an offer. Another example: a paper purchase order acknowledgment from *C* is not hearsay if entered into court to show the legal event of accepting an order. The document is not admitted to prove that in her

§9.1 [1]*See* Fed. R. Evid. 801.
[2]*See* §7.2.

heart *C* wanted to sell something, but to prove that *C* issued the legally potent document.[3]

Beware of the double hearsay problem. It would be hearsay for *C* to testify that *B* told her that *A* said, "I accept your offer to sell widgets." The purpose would be to show that what *B* said (i.e., that *A* spoke the words) was true. The hearsay lies in *B*'s statement.

§9.2 EXCEPTIONS TO THE RULE

If applied vigorously, the hearsay rule would exclude much useful evidence from trials. Therefore, modern evidence law restrains the rule's effect. Exceptions to the rule permit admission of hearsay evidence where the circumstances suggest it is trustworthy. The following introduces three exceptions particularly applicable to computer records.

§9.2.1 Business Record Exception

The most important exception derives from the traditional common law hearsay exception afforded regularly kept records. At common law, a record manually written to a journal was excepted from the hearsay rule if the record was made (1) as an original entry in the regular course of a business, (2) within a reasonable time after the occurrence of the event being recorded, and (3) by someone, with personal knowledge of the event, who is not now available to testify.[1] Accordingly, courts accepted accounting journals to show business debts, rather than requiring employee testimony.

The exception is today articulated in various ways under

[3]McCormick on Evidence §249, at 732-733 (Cleary ed., 3d ed. 1984).
§9.2 [1]McCormick, above, §306, at 872.

the evidence law of many jurisdictions: Federal Rule of Evidence (FRE) 803(6), the identical state Uniform Rule of Evidence 803(6),[2] state common law decisions, and the Uniform Business Records as Evidence Act[3] (applicable in some states). This book refers to it generically as the "business records exception," and focuses primarily on its expression in FRE 803(6).

FRE 803(6) excepts from the hearsay rule:

> [a] memorandum, report, record, or data compilation, in any form, of acts, events, conditions, opinions, or diagnoses, made at or near the time by, or from information transmitted by, a person with knowledge, if kept in the course of a regularly conducted business activity, and if it was the regular practice of that business activity to make the memorandum, report, record, or data compilation, all as shown by the testimony of the custodian or other qualified witness, unless the source of the information or the method or circumstances of preparation indicate lack of trustworthiness. The term "business" as used in this paragraph includes business, institution, association, profession, occupation, and calling of every kind, whether or not conducted for profit.

Thus, a record can generally qualify for the business records exception if (1) it reflects someone's personal knowledge, (2) it is made in the regular course of business, at or near the time the recorded event occurred, and (3) the business regularly makes such records.

Two rationales support the exception. First, records kept in the ordinary course of business are likely to be reliable. Because businesses keep records for serious purposes, they are likely to be careful, and the systematic and routine accumulation and storage of information is less prone to error than casual recordmaking.[4] Second, it would be impractical

[2]Unif. R. Evid., 13A U.L.A. 728 (1986).

[3]9A U.L.A. 506 (1965).

[4]*See* Fed. R. Evid. 803(6), Advisory Committee Note.

to call as witnesses all who had a role in preparing a large organization's records. Few would be likely to remember relevant details. It is more expedient for the court simply to rely on the record.[5]

The exception does not apply if there is reason to believe the records are untrustworthy. Under the FRE, the burden of showing untrustworthiness falls on the opponent to the evidence,[6] although one scholar disputes whether that is fair when computer records are at issue.[7] Records signaling the possibility of untrustworthiness are those that have been made and controlled by people having a motive to fabricate or those (i.e., records, but not printouts thereof) that have been prepared specifically for trial.[8]

The absence of a record of an event from relevant business records may be used to show the event never happened. That evidence would itself usually be hearsay, were it not for a component of the business records exception. FRE 803(7) excepts from hearsay:[9]

> [e]vidence that a matter is not included in the memoranda, reports, records, or data compilations, in any form, kept in accordance with the provisions of [FRE 803(6)], to prove the nonoccurrence or nonexistence of the matter, if the matter was of a kind of which a memorandum, report, record, or data

[5]*See* Stegemann v. Miami Beach Boat Slips, Inc., 213 F.2d 561, 563 (5th Cir. 1954).

[6]In re Japanese Elec. Prod. Antitrust Litig., 723 F.2d 238, 288 (3d Cir. 1983), *rev'd for other reasons sub nom.* Matsushita Elec. Indus. Co. v. Zenith Radio Corp., 475 U.S. 574 (1985). *But see* Byrd v. Hunt Tool Shipyards, Inc., 650 F.2d 44, 46 (5th Cir. 1981).

[7]Peritz, Computer Data and Reliability: A Call for Authentication of Business Records under the Federal Rules of Evidence, 80 NW. U.L. Rev. 956, 960 (1986). His view is that the proponent is likely to be better capable of obtaining information on trustworthiness.

[8]*See* United States v. Glasser, 773 F.2d 1553, 1559 (11th Cir. 1985). *See also* Manual for Complex Litigation 123 (5th ed. 1982).

[9]*See* United States v. De Georgia, 420 F.2d 889 (9th Cir. 1969) (absence of auto rental record in rental company database admissible).

compilation was regularly made and preserved, unless the sources of information or other circumstances indicate lack of trustworthiness.

§9.2.2 Public Records Exception

A separate hearsay exception applies to public records, which under FRE 803(8) include:

> [r]ecords, reports, statements, or data compilations, in any form, of public offices or agencies, setting forth (A) the activities of the office or agency, or (B) matters observed pursuant to duty imposed by law as to which matters there was a duty to report, . . . unless the sources of information or other circumstances indicate lack of trustworthiness.

This applies to records of public agency activities—not documents, such as tax returns, filed by private parties with agencies. The reasons behind the exception are (1) records created by officials having a duty to create them tend to be reliable, (2) public agencies rely on such records, and (3) it is impractical in many cases to call on public officials to testify about their agencies' affairs.

If given a choice, the evidence proponent may prefer using the business records exception over the public records exception. A public agency seems to fit the liberal definition of "business" in FRE 803(6), and a public record could be considered a "business" record. The public records exception requires showing the record covers an agency's specific activities or was made under some report-making duty. This may require more effort than simply showing the record was kept in the regular course of "business." But the boundary between the two exceptions is unclear. In *United States v. Orozco*[10] the trial judge had admitted government computer

[10] 590 F.2d 789, 793 (9th Cir. 1979), *cert. denied,* 439 U.S. 1049 (1978).

records under the business records exception, but the court of appeals preferred to consider them admissible under the public record exception.

FRE 803(10), analogous to Rule 803(7), excepts from hearsay a certification from public officials showing the absence of information in a public record. Under this exception, the court in *United States v. Neff*[11] permitted admission of a certificate, based on a computer record search, stating that the defendant had not filed a tax return.

§9.2.3 Residual Exception

The FRE contain a "catch-all" hearsay exception, articulated in Rules 803(24) and 804(b)(5). Excepted from the hearsay rule is:

> [any] statement not specifically covered by any of the [other exceptions in FRE 803 and 804] but having equivalent circumstantial guarantees of trustworthiness, if the court determines that (A) the statement is offered as evidence of a material fact; (B) the statement is more probative on the point for which it is offered than any other evidence which the proponent can procure through reasonable efforts; and (C) the general purpose of these rules and the interests of justice will best be served by admission of the statement into evidence.

This pliable standard, if broadly construed, could nullify much of the hearsay rule. Courts are split over how liberally this type of exception should be read.

It is particularly well-suited for accommodating new forms of trustworthy evidence.[12] *Palmer v. A. H. Robins Co.*,[13] a state court case applying the common law of evidence, upheld the admission of computer records under the "gen-

[11] 615 F.2d 1235 (9th Cir.), *cert. denied*, 447 U.S. 925 (1980).
[12] Fed. R. Evid. 803(24), Advisory Committee Note.
[13] 684 P.2d 187, 202 (Colo. Sup. Ct. 1984).

eral hearsay exception" at common law, which is roughly equivalent FRE 803(24) and 804(b)(5).

Courts have occasionally used this exception to admit records that fail to strictly qualify under the business records exception. *Karme v. Commissioner*[14] admitted foreign bank records where the records appeared sufficiently trustworthy, but the foundation witness was technically unsuitable under the business records exception.

§9.3 APPLICATION TO COMPUTER BUSINESS RECORDS GENERALLY

Classic computer evidence involves business records from a self-contained computer system controlled by the evidence proponent. The recorded data were input by human operators, who had obtained information from their own observations or those of others. A printout offered to prove the truth of information in the computer could suffer from four possible sources of inaccuracy: (1) the person with personal knowledge may not have been the one entering data, (2) the person entering data may have made mistakes, (3) the processing and storage programs—which reflect their programmers' judgment and biases—manipulated and changed the data, and (4) the printout could be a distortion of the information on the records.

The considerable case law explaining the hearsay rule's application to classic computer records indicates that the rule has not presented an insurmountable barrier to relevant and useful computer business records. Still, it does threaten the computer evidence proponent when she fails to lay the proper foundation or the circumstances show untrustworthiness.

[14] 673 F.2d 1062, 1064-1065 (9th Cir. 1982).

§9.3.1 Application of the Business Records Exception

Computer evidence proponents routinely use the business records exception to vault over hearsay problems. The Advisory Committee Comment to FRE 803(6) confirms that the term "data compilation" in that provision embraces computer records. And one state court has opined that the medium on which records are stored is irrelevant to the exception. The key is whether the records were created and maintained under circumstances that suggest reliability.[1]

There is disagreement, however, in defining what "foundation" the proponent must lay to show reliability. The precise standards vary from jurisdiction to jurisdiction. Early cases tend to require more extensive testimony on the source of computer input and the function and reliability of systems than later cases do.[2]

In *Transport Indemnity Co. v. Seib,*[3] the most famous computer evidence case, the court considered the admissibility under the Uniform Business Records as Evidence Act (a statutory articulation of the business records exception) of a computer record of insurance premium data. Under an insurance contract, the defendant owed the plaintiff premiums calculated from a formula using past premium payments by the defendant and claims payments by the plaintiff. The plaintiff was suing for payment. The issue was how much was owed.

Apparently, relevant data gathered by the plaintiff's personnel had been fed into a computer, calculated, and stored on tape. At trial the plaintiff offered a printout, which showed earlier premium and claims payments, together with the sums due based on the formula. The plaintiff's director of accounting, the official who oversaw the printout's prepa-

§9.3 [1]Brandon v. State, 272 Ind. 92, 396 N.E.2d 365 (1979).
[2]*See* McCormick, above, §314, at 886, n.9.
[3]178 Neb. 253, 132 N.W.2d 871 (1965).

ration, testified on how information had been entered and stored on the computer and how the tape record had been regularly made and used in the plaintiff's business. The witness also recomputed the amounts owed to confirm the accuracy of the sums on the printout. The court held a proper foundation had been laid for the printout's admission into evidence.

In *King v. State ex rel. Murdock Acceptance Corp.*,[4] another famous business records exception case, the plaintiff offered into evidence a printout of electronic records showing the amount due on a promissory note. The plaintiff's officer in charge of the computer accounting system testified on the source of the records, the type of computer used, and the means by which data were controlled and fed into the computer. Without hearing testimony from the individuals who made the original entries, the court held the printouts admissible

> if it is shown (1) that the electronic computing equipment is recognized as standard equipment, (2) the entries are made in the regular course of business at or reasonably near the time of the happening of the event recorded, and (3) the foundation testimony satisfies the court that the sources of information, method and time of preparation were such as to indicate its trustworthiness and justify its admission.[5]

Under this standard, the proponent arguably has a considerable burden of showing system trustworthiness. The court held the plaintiff carried its burden and allowed admission of the printouts.

At issue in *United States v. Russo*,[6] a criminal trial of a physician, was the admissibility of a printout of a statistical analysis of claim reports previously submitted by physicians to an insurance company. The company had recorded the

[4]222 So. 2d 393 (Miss. 1969).
[5]*Id.* at 398.
[6]480 F.2d 1228 (6th Cir. 1973), *cert. denied,* 414 U.S. 1157 (1974).

reports in its computer system and later generated the analysis as a routine function of business. At trial, the prosecution offered the printout to show what claims the defendant had submitted. The defendant asserted that only the original claim reports could prove that. But because the company auditors and actuaries regularly used such analyses, and because the prosecution had presented extensive evidence of the controls employed to ensure the accuracy and reliability of the information in the computer, the court sustained the admission under the business records exception.

The defendant in *Russo* also argued that the analysis was not calculated within a reasonable time after he filed the reports with the insurance company. The court observed, however, that a record on magnetic tape was made when each report was submitted and it was immaterial that the analysis was created later.

United States v. Scholle[7] is sometimes cited for the proposition that computer evidence requires a foundation more extensive than that for manual business records. Besides the requirement that the computer records be kept in such a way that procedures and motives suggest trustworthiness, the opinion stated that, as part of the proponent's foundation, "the original source of the computer program must be delineated, and the procedures for input control including tests used to assure accuracy and reliability must be presented."[8] The printout at issue represented a compilation and digest of data on illegal drugs seized in different places over a period of time. Because the data came from scattered computer files, the printout could have reflected programmer biases and distortions of the underlying information. The appellate court, unsure whether the proponent had laid a satisfactory foundation, decided that any shortcoming went to the weight rather than the admissibility of the evidence. It assented to the printout's admission. Thus, the court's apparent require-

[7]553 F.2d 1109 (8th Cir.), *cert. denied,* 434 U.S. 940 (1977).
[8]*Id.* at 1125.

ment for an extensive, technical foundation seems to be toothless, and maybe just meaningless.

Some more-recent and less ambiguous cases declare that the foundation for computer business records requires no special, technical examination of the relevant computer system. *United States v. Vela*[9] concerned the admission of electronic records of a criminal defendant's long distance telephone charges, as retained by the telephone company, a neutral party. The foundation was established with testimony from the telephone company record custodian. He explained that computers automatically register the dialing of numbers on electronic tapes. The information is then transferred onto billing tapes, from which bills are calculated and printed. According to the custodian, the company retains microfiche copies of the bills, and the copies offered into evidence came from those microfiche.

The witness vouched for the process' general reliability and confirmed that the company made and relied on the records in its regular course of business. But the defendant objected, challenging the records' reliability on the ground that the witness could not identify the types of computers used or verify the particular computers' working conditions.

The appellate court sustained the records' admission. It observed that the proponent had sufficiently established that the records were trustworthy by showing they were made and relied upon by a neutral business. The court criticized the idea, originally expressed in the old *King* opinion discussed previously, that the proponent must show that the computers were "standard" equipment. "The failure to certify the brand or proper operating condition of the machinery involved does not betray a circumstance of preparation indicating any lack of trustworthiness."[10] The court maintained that the defendant's contention that the computers might have been unreliable goes to the evidence's weight,

[9]673 F.2d 86, *reh'g denied,* 677 F.2d 113 (5th Cir. 1982).
[10]*Id.* at 90.

not its admissibility.[11] Thus, the court suggested that after the records were admitted the opponent could argue to the trier of fact that they were not reliable and therefore should not be believed.[12]

Originally, at common law the business records exception applied only to "original entries." Thus, there was once a question whether an entry on a consolidating ledger could be admitted if the first entry was in a journal or daybook. The modern view is to except from hearsay all records kept in the ordinary course of business, irrespective of whether they contain the "original entries."[13] The rationale is that second-generation records can be considered convenient and trustworthy.

This issue emerges in the computer record context where data have been transferred from one file or magnetic tape to another before being offered at trial. If the transfer occurs as a normal part of business recordkeeping, then the business records exception should normally cover the hearsay problem when the record is admitted. This seems to have been the reasoning in *Vela,* where the original record was recorded on one tape, it was transferred to a second, the bill was calculated and printed onto paper, the company kept an archive on microfiche, and the copy brought to court was a reproduction from the fiche.[14]

[11]*See also* United States v. Jones, 554 F.2d 251 (5th Cir.), *cert. denied,* 434 U.S. 866 (1977) (foundation witness for telephone records need not be person preparing records or even establish for certain who prepared them; must only identify the record as authentic and made and preserved in the regular course of business).

[12]*See also* People v. Lugashi, 205 Cal. App. 3d 632, 252 Cal. Rptr. 434 (1988) (admission of computer records under the business records exception does not require testimony from computer expert as to computer's technical reliability). *See generally* Brockett, Evidence and Trial Advocacy: The Erosion of the Hearsay Objection to Computer Generated Evidence, 26 Crim. L. Bull. 357 (July-Aug. 1990).

[13]McCormick, above, §307, at 874.

[14]An alternative basis for overriding a hearsay objection to trans-

Appellate courts accord trial courts considerable discretion in judging trustworthiness under the business records exception. In *Esco v. Kitchens Construction, Inc.,*[15] the plaintiff, in a suit to collect on paper invoices it had sent the defendant, offered into evidence a computer printout from its records of the invoice contents. The defendant objected, alleging that the paper invoices derived from information different from that represented in the printout. The appellate court declined to overturn the trial court's decision to admit the printout under the business records exception, noting that the trial court had considered two witnesses' testimony on the procedures used to prepare the computer evidence.

In reported computer hearsay cases where an admission was denied, the issue has usually been decided on the proponent's failure to lay a satisfactory foundation. The court in *United States Fidelity & Guaranty Co. v. Young Life Campaign, Inc.,*[16] rejected computer printouts of an insurance premium account because the foundation witnesses were neither the custodians nor the preparers of the records. They could not testify on the circumstances under which the records were made, the controls used to ensure accuracy, or whether the records were relied on in the regular course of business. In *People v. Bovio*[17] the court disallowed admission of a computer-generated bank statement because the proponent failed to lay a foundation similar to that required in the old *King* case discussed previously. Foundation testimony showed that the statement was made in the regular course of business, but did not indicate whether the computer equipment was standard, the processing methods were trustworthy, or how data were processed through the computer.[18]

---

ferred data might be the photocopy statutes, such as the federal statute at 28 U.S.C. §1732 (1988). *See* §§10.3 & 10.6.

[15]106 N.M. 753, 750 P.2d 114, 117 (1988).

[16]42 Colo. App. 298, 600 P.2d 79 (1979).

[17]118 Ill. App. 3d 836, 455 N.E.2d 829 (1983).

[18]The requirement, originally articulated in King v. State ex rel. Murdock Acceptance Corp., 222 So. 2d 393 (Miss. 1969), that a computer

§9.3.2 Should Foundations Be More Extensive?

Some scholars, notably Professor Rudolph Peritz, criticize the relaxed foundation requirements that courts in more recent cases, such as *Vela,* have applied to computerized business records.[19] Professor Peritz endorses as the more appropriate standard §2.716, Sixth Recommendation, of the *Manual for Complex Litigation* (5th ed. 1982), which directs that before admitting any such record into evidence the proponent must establish that the record is reliable. To do that, the proponent must, among other things, (1) show the record is the product of standard industry computing practices and (2) have an expert testify that the computer program functions reliably and accurately.[20]

The *Manual,* which has been rewritten as the *Manual for Complex Litigation, Second* (1985), seems to have liberalized its stance since Professor Peritz wrote the article ex-

---

be "standard" is losing meaning. *See* Comment, Admitting Computer Generated Records: A Presumption of Reliability, 18 J. Marshall L.R. 115, 146 (1984).

[19]Peritz, above.

[20]The Sixth Recommendation provides:

> Computer-maintained records kept in the regular course of business and printouts prepared especially for litigation should be admitted if the court finds that reliable computer equipment and techniques have been used and that the material is of probative value. The court should therefore require, well in advance of trial, that (a) the offering party demonstrate that the input procedures conform to the standard practice of persons engaged in the business or profession of the party or person from whom the printout is obtained; (b) in the case of a printout prepared especially for trial, the offering party demonstrate that the person from whom the printout is obtained relied on the data base in making a business or professional judgment within a reasonably short period of time before producing the printout sought to be introduced; (c) the offering party provide expert testimony that the processing program reliably and accurately processes the data in the data base; and (d) the opposing party be given the opportunity to depose the offeror's witness and to engage a witness of its own to evaluate the processing procedure.

pressing his opinion. Section 21.446 still assigns to the proponent "the burden of laying a proper foundation by establishing [the] accuracy" of the record, but, unlike its predecessor, it does not detail how that must be done. Nor does it preclude a court from determining that computer records are likely to be reliable simply because they are kept and relied upon in the ordinary course of business.[21]

In footnote 81 under §21.446,[22] the revised *Manual* suggests that an appropriate foundation standard for computer evidence is FRE 901(b)(9). This Rule permits the authentication of evidence that was created by a complex process; it requires the proponent to describe the process and show that it produces an accurate result. Professor Peritz argues that authentication under FRE 901(b)(9) requires the comprehensive foundation prescribed in the old Fifth Edition of the *Manual.*[23]

Professor Peritz believes the federal courts have improperly relegated the examination of record trustworthiness to a question of weight rather than admissibility.[24] He argues (1) that it is unfair to place the burden of showing unreliability on the evidence opponent, and (2) that computer systems are complex and prone to error and security breaches. Therefore, computer record proponents should have to establish reliability with expert testimony.[25]

Other authorities also suggest a more extensive foundation may be necessary for computer records, but only when the computer acts as more than a mere information routing, storage, and retrieval device.[26] When a computer has ana-

[21]This seems to be a popular approach among courts, as illustrated by the *Vela* case discussed previously.

[22]Manual for Complex Litigation, Second, §21.446, at 60-61 (1985).

[23]Peritz, above, at 984-989.

[24]*See* United States v. Scholle, 553 F.2d 1109 (8th Cir.), *cert. denied,* 434 U.S. 940 (1977); United States v. Vela, 673 F.2d 86, *reh'g denied,* 677 F.2d 113 (5th Cir. 1982).

[25]Peritz, above, at 990-999.

[26]People v. Mormon, 97 Ill. App. 3d 556, 422 N.E.2d 1065, 1073 (1981),

lyzed, computed, or summarized data, the process of establishing the resulting printout's trustworthiness is different than establishing a paper record's trustworthiness. The process is more like authenticating the results of a technical process, which generally entails having a qualified expert testify on its reliability.[27] The special foundation is necessary to guard against what might be called "programmer hearsay," the threat that the programmer's biases and judgment in screening and interpreting information may distort the results.[28] The point at which a computer ceases to do routing and sorting and begins to do analysis and computing is indistinct.

In spite of these arguments by critics, the mainstream view seems to be that, so long as the link between an event and its transcription into business records is a process that a business regularly relies on, no special foundation is necessarily required.[29] If the proponent shows the record was made and relied on in the regular course of business, the trial court may (but is not required to) presume that the entire record creation process is reliable. This allows the record to be admitted without expert testimony on the process' reliability. The rationale is that even though a programmer can

---

aff'd, 92 Ill. 2d 268, 442 N.E.2d 250 (1982); A. Lipson, Art of Advocacy: Documentary Evidence, 2—15-27 (1989 and Oct. 1989 Supp.).

[27]Lipson, above, at 5—6 (Oct. 1989 Supp.).

[28]Programmer hearsay might be understood this way. Suppose units of data, *X, Y,* and *Z,* reside in a computer's database. One programmer designs software to analyze and summarize the data. Based on this programmer's biases and judgments in designing the software, the result of the analysis and summary of *X, Y,* and *Z* is *R.* But if a different programmer had designed the software, the result might be *T.* Thus, the result of a computer summary, analysis, or computation reflects the type of potential distortion the hearsay rule is intended to avoid. *R* and *T* are each hearsay because they are out-of-court statements offered in court to show that they truly reflect *X, Y,* and *Z.*

[29]*See* People v. Lugashi, 205 Cal. App. 3d. 632, 252 Cal. Rptr. 434, 440 (1988) (specifically considered and respectfully declined to follow Professor Peritz's position).

make mistakes and inject biases into a system, the programmer's job is to write software that creates accurate records. If a business relies on the programmer's work, it is likely the records are reliable. This likelihood of reliability is satisfactory to justify admission of the records under the business records exception. The opponent can still attack the credibility (weight) of the evidence with questions and rebuttal evidence.

United States v. Vela[30] illustrates the mainstream view. There, even though the computerized telephone data underwent considerable processing and reformatting before reaching the final archive, the appellate court held that the trial court was not required to hear an expert vouch for the process' reliability.[31]

The outcome in *Vela* is clearly correct. The records came from the telephone company, a disinterested and responsible party. The company has a strong, independent incentive for its telephone records to be reliable. Common experience shows these records are usually correct. To have required the proponent to have technicians testify in detail about the computers' operating conditions would have been pointless. Even the *Manual*'s Fifth Edition supports this conclusion; it acknowledges the necessary foundation may be less if a disinterested party makes the records.[32]

Significantly, the appellate court in *Vela* stated it could reverse the trial court's judgment only if that court had abused its discretion. That is a reminder that trial judges enjoy considerable freedom in applying the hearsay rule.

[30]673 F.2d 86, *reh'g denied,* 677 F.2d 113 (5th Cir. 1982).

[31]*See* Comment, Admitting Computer Generated Records: A Presumption of Reliability, 18 J. Marshall L. Rev. 115, 146-147 (1984), which argues there is no sound reason for requiring circumstantial guarantees of trustworthiness beyond a showing that the records are relied on as business records.

[32]Manual for Complex Litigation 123 (5th ed. 1982).

§9.4 APPLICATION TO ELECTRONIC MESSAGE RECORDS

In the classic case, computer evidence originates as information in noncomputer form, such as words on a delivered paper purchase order, which an operator then keys into the computer. Or a user observes some event, such as the delivery of cash, and enters a record of that into the computer. A legal event occurs outside the computer, and then a human records it in the computer.

An automated electronic transaction is different. A purchase order, offering to buy goods for example, is delivered through a computer system. The legal event and the recording occur entirely inside the system and without human action.

§9.4.1 No Hearsay in Legally Operative Message

As explained in Section 9.3, the classic computer record has four sources of error: (1) the observer, (2) the data entry clerk, (3) the programmers of the processing and storage program, and (4) the programmers of the retrieval and printing program.

Fully automated electronic transactions eliminate the first two sources of error, since there is no human intervention. (Note the implication for record reliability. The leading source of errors in computer records is the human entry of data. Businesses know this, and a primary justification for EDI is a reduction in data entry errors.)

An electronic message is, at the point it effects a legal event, not hearsay if offered in court to show that event. As with a paper purchase order, an electronic order introduced to show that the sender obligated itself to buy something is not offered to prove the truth of the information in the order. It is offered to show that the order existed.

United States v. Sanders,[1] a prosecution of a pharmacist who had submitted fraudulent Medicaid vouchers, supports this proposition. The pharmacist delivered the vouchers as paper documents to a computer service bureau he had hired. The service bureau entered the information from the pharmacist's (and others') vouchers onto computer tapes, then submitted the tapes to a state agency to elicit payment for the vouchers. The state agency retained its own computer records of these submissions, and the prosecution sought to admit these records into evidence. The pharmacist objected, arguing that the agency's records were inadmissible hearsay.

The court acknowledged that computer records are inadmissible if they are themselves mere accumulations of hearsay. This case's import lies in the court's analysis as to whether the statements on the tapes from the *service bureau* were hearsay. Significantly, the court did not apply the business records exception to those statements. Rather, it held they were not hearsay because they were *admissions* under FRE 801(d)(2)(C). That rule provides, "A statement is not hearsay if . . . (2) [it] is offered against a party and is . . . (C) a statement by a person authorized by the party to make a statement concerning the subject. . . ." The court considered the service bureau the pharmacist's agent because the pharmacist had hired it to make his submissions. Thus, the court reasoned, the statements on the tapes were admissions by the pharmacist speaking through his agent. A business records analysis under FRE 803(6) was not unnecessary.

The court could have gone farther. The electronic vouchers were not hearsay just because they were admissions. They fell entirely outside the definition of hearsay because they were not offered to prove the truth of the matter asserted in them. Rather they were offered only to show that they were

§9.4 [1]749 F.2d 195 (5th Cir. 1984).

communications—just as a typical paper invoice is—that effected a legal event (i.e., giving notice of debt).

Sanders is an electronic messaging case. The service bureau's submission of tapes was a primitive form of EDI (a tape-to-tape exchange), and each voucher reflected therein was an EDI invoice (a structured electronic message giving notice of a debt).

Michaels v. Michaels[2] is another case supporting the proposition that an electronic message is not hearsay if offered only to prove that it was stated. The court sustained a telex printout's admission into evidence, over a hearsay objection, on the ground that the telex contents were not offered to prove their truth. The telex indicated the interest of one party in pursuing a business transaction. It was admitted to show how another party reacted upon learning of this interest.

§9.4.2 Programmer Hearsay

An electronic message can be manipulated and distorted after the time it effects a legal event. An EDI invoice, for example, can be translated, condensed, broken into pieces for entry into various parts of a database, and so forth after its receipt. The way in which this occurs depends on programmer decisions, which can infect the system with biases and judgment errors. Thus, resulting records can be hearsay.

The ideal electronic message recordkeeping system would avoid this "programmer" hearsay altogether. It would keep a record of all transactions exactly as sent and received. This is effectively what conventional telex and fax do. They print unchangeable records upon transmission receipt. In principle, there is no reason e-mail or EDI systems cannot do the same on magnetic or optical media. An unmodified log could be made of data exactly as it exists when it effects

[2]767 F.2d 1185, 1201 (7th Cir. 1985), *cert. denied*, 474 U.S. 1057 (1986).

a legal event. Usually, that time would be when the data enter or leave a party's system. The admission of a direct printout from this log into evidence to prove only what was sent and received should not raise a hearsay issue. (Authenticity would still have to be established, however.)

United States v. Boyd[3] supports this position. The court there dismissed a hearsay objection to the admission of sound recordings of conversations about illegal gambling. The court reasoned that the conversations were admitted not to prove the truth of their contents but to show that they were uttered. The court did not mention the possibility of hearsay from the distortion the tape recorder could have made in converting sound waves into magnetic tape records and later reversing the process.[4] The court rightly implied that the recording represents the original sound waves directly enough to preclude distortion by the tape recorder's engineers (the analogue to computer programmers).

Another relevant case, *Stark v. State of Indiana,*[5] involved the introduction of a transaction record from an automatic teller machine (ATM). The machine made the record automatically when used. The defendant objected to the record, arguing that because it did not represent the knowledge of any person it was not admissible under the business records exception. The court summarily dismissed the objection and upheld the record's admission. A logical basis for the holding is that the defendant was right, the business records exception did not apply. Nevertheless, the record was admissible because it was not hearsay. First, the ATM user's statement in punching the machine's keys—"These are my identification devices, and I request so much cash"—was not hearsay because it was not offered to prove its truth but to prove it was stated. Second, the machine's record so directly reflected

[3]566 F.2d 929, 937 (5th Cir. 1978).

[4]*See also* United States v. Gutierrez-Chavez, 842 F.2d 77 (5th Cir. 1988).

[5]489 N.E.2d 43 (Ind. 1986).

the user's statement that no appreciable distortion could have occurred; no clerical or programmer hearsay was present. The absence of intervention by a human in the record's creation actually eliminated hearsay.

But what if an electronic message is not recorded immediately and exactly as received, and thus is distorted? An EDI invoice, for example, might be translated after receipt and before recording. What do the cases say when "programmer hearsay" does exist? As explained earlier, the mainstream cases[6] view the business records exception as overcoming the problems of programmer hearsay so long as the programmer's purpose was recordmaking in the ordinary course of business.[7] A recipient's routine translation of an EDI invoice is conceptually no different from the translation and manipulation of computer data present when the telephone company in *United States v. Vela*[8] converted logged information from one tape to another or calculated telephone bills.

Within its discretion, a trial court could deny admission of an electronic message record if it finds reason to question the trustworthiness of a record creation process. This might occur, for example, where the recordkeeper has an incentive and the ability to fabricate records. Obviously, users would be well-advised to promote trustworthiness by imposing controls on recordkeeping systems.

§9.4.3 Conclusion

Electronic business messages appear to raise no new hearsay problems. In fact, they reduce hearsay concerns. First, a legally operative electronic communication itself is not hear-

[6]*See* §9.3.2.

[7]Arguably a photocopy statute could allow admission of such a record over a hearsay objection. *See* §10.3.

[8]*See* §9.3.2.

say if offered in court to show that it was sent.[9] Second, electronic transactions remove some or all human intervention between the receipt of communications and their entry into a computer. A direct, complete record, such as a data log, of electronic messages appears not to constitute hearsay if the messages themselves are not hearsay.

"Programmer" hearsay can be an issue if the record does not directly reflect the messages, but typically the business records exception can allow admission of such a record. Nonetheless, where the incentive and possibility for fraud appear great, a trial court might deny admission on the ground that the circumstances indicate untrustworthiness. From this perspective, the ideal electronic transaction record would be a log of data, exactly as sent and received, which is subject to controls against falsification and error.

[9]*Accord* Bradgate, Evidential Issues of EDI, *in* EDI and the Law 13-14 (I. Walden ed. 1989, London).

Chapter

10

The Best Evidence Rule and Electronic Messages

§10.1 INTRODUCTION

The "best evidence rule" may require a special plank in the proponent's foundation when he attempts to admit electronic evidence at trial. Since the rule is rooted in the days when written information was assumed to be on paper, it is better understood as the "original document rule." It provides, "In proving the terms of a writing, where the terms are material, the original writing must be produced unless it is shown to be unavailable for some reason other than the serious fault of the proponent."[1] So the rule disfavors the admission of copies of and testimony about the contents of writings when those contents are at issue. The rule evokes interesting questions when applied in the electronic messaging environment, where legal communications are not necessarily embodied in any particular recording.

The rule reflects recognition of the substantial affect in meaning that a variation in a document's words can have. Like the hearsay rule and auditors' presumptions for evaluating evidence,[2] it favors direct observation. It aims to curtail error and, to a lesser extent, fraud; it also regulates the introduction of potentially misleading evidence in the form of extracts or summaries of writings. The best evidence rule may apply to information affixed on things other than paper, provided it is the information itself that is at issue. Thus, the Federal Rules of Evidence (FRE) version covers any "writings" or "recordings," both of which are defined to "consist of letters, words, or numbers, or their equivalent, set down by handwriting, typewriting, printing, photostating, photographing, magnetic impulse, mechanical or electronic recording, or other form of data compilation."[3]

§10.2 THE RULE'S GENERAL APPLICATION

The best evidence rule applies to the *contents* of a writing or recording. It is triggered when the proponent tries to prove

§10.1 [1]McCormick on Evidence §230, at 704 (Cleary ed., 3d ed. 1984).

[2]*See* §7.2.

[3]Fed. R. Evid. 1001(1).

what the writing said, rather than the identity, existence, or delivery of a writing.

The rule does not apply to an effort to show external facts that just happen to be recorded in a writing. For example, if the proponent wishes to prove that Blue Co. was open for business on May 28, she could show that with testimony, even though there might be a written record of the fact somewhere. The rule does not in this case require that an "original" written record be produced.

The rule generally does apply when a proponent wishes to introduce the terms of a document that is central to a case, such as a contract, deed, or bill of lading.

If multiple copies of a writing exist, the one, or more, deemed "original" depends on which affected the rights at issue. If *A* printed a legal notice with a typewriter, then photocopied it, signed the photocopy, and sent it to *B*, the original notice would be the photocopy. The photocopy is the document delivered to effect the legal act of giving notice. It is immaterial that a typewritten copy was made first.[1]

FRE 1001(3) defines the " 'original' of a writing or recording" as "the writing or recording itself or any counterpart intended to have the same effect by a person executing or issuing it." Thus, if a party types a document, makes two photocopies and signs each of the three with the intent that it be an original, then each is a counterpart original. Formal contracts customarily contain clauses confirming that multiple counterparts are being created with the intent that each be an original.

An issue with early telegrams was which record of the telegram—the piece of paper the sender handed to the telegraph carrier for transmission or the piece of paper delivered by the carrier to the recipient—was the "original." The general rule seemed to be that it depended on which record was the subject of the controversy, based on the applicable

§10.2 [1]McDonald v. Hanks, 52 Tex. Civ. App. 140, 113 S.W. 604, 607 (1908).

substantive law. In *Anheuser-Busch Brewing Co. v. Hutmacher*[2] the defendant sent a telegram (for which it had paid the transmission costs) stating it would pay the plaintiff to perform certain services. The defendant later reneged. When the plaintiff sued, the dispatch the plaintiff received was deemed the central document, for that was the one on which he relied.[3] Contrast that to *The Western Union Telegraph Co. v. Hopkins*[4] in which a customer sued the telegraph company for failure to transmit a message. The court deemed the paper handed to the operator the original because that was the one instructing the company about what to do.

§10.3 THE RULE'S EXCEPTIONS

The best evidence rule prefers the original document over "secondary" evidence of it, but the rule is generally not one of exclusion. A proponent is excused from presenting the original writing if she shows, as part of her foundation, that one of the many spacious exceptions applies. If excused, the proponent can introduce certain secondary evidence, such as a copy or testimony from an informed witness, to show the writing's contents. The FRE version includes these exceptions:

1. ***FRE 1003.*** A duplicate of the original is always admissible to the same extent as the original unless there is a genuine question as to the original's au-

[2]127 Ill. 652, 21 N.E. 626, 628 (1889).

[3]The court suggested the result would have been different if the plaintiff had paid for the transmission costs. The telegraph company would then have been considered the plaintiff's agent; and therefore, the plaintiff would have been deemed to have relied on the paper the defendant delivered to the operator.

[4]49 Ind. 223, 227 (1874).

thenticity or it would be unfair under the circumstances to admit the duplicate.

2. ***FRE 1004(1).*** If all originals are lost or destroyed (and, if the proponent lost or destroyed them, he did not act in bad faith), then secondary evidence is permitted.
3. ***FRE 1004(2).*** Secondary evidence is permitted if the original cannot be obtained through judicial procedures—such as when the original is in the hands of a third party who is beyond the court's jurisdiction.[1]
4. ***FRE 1004(3).*** Secondary evidence is admissible if the original is in the opponent's hands and he, after notice, does not produce the original.
5. ***FRE 1004(4).*** Secondary evidence is permitted if the writing is not closely related to a controlling issue in the trial.
6. ***FRE 1005.*** The contents of a government record or filing (including "data compilations") may be proved by certain types of copies.
7. ***FRE 1006.*** Summaries of voluminous writings or recordings may be admissible if the writings or recordings are available to the opponent.
8. Although not part of the FRE, the federal photocopy statute is effectively another exception to the best evidence rule in the FRE. It provides:

> If any business, institution, member of a profession or calling, or any department or agency of government, in the regular course of business or activity has kept or recorded any memorandum, writing, entry, print, representation or combination thereof, of any act, transaction, occurrence, or event, and in the regular course of business has caused any or all of

§10.3 [1]*See* United States v. Taylor, 648 F.2d 565 (9th Cir.), *cert. denied,* 454 U.S. 866 (1981), in which a photocopy of a fax printout was admitted where efforts to obtain the sender's "original" had failed.

> the same to be recorded, copied, or reproduced by any photographic, photostatic, microfilm, microcard, miniature photographic, or other process which accurately reproduces or forms a durable medium for so reproducing the original, the original may be destroyed in the regular course of business unless its preservation is required by law. Such reproduction, when satisfactorily identified, is as admissible in evidence as the original itself in any judicial or administrative proceeding whether the original is in existence or not and an enlargement or facsimile of such reproduction is likewise admissible in evidence if the original reproduction is in existence and available for inspection under direction of court. . . .[2]

In addition, some authorities hold that satisfaction of the business records exception to the hearsay rule[3] also overcomes any best evidence rule objection.[4]

Many courts recognize a hierarchy of secondary evidence. Thus, if an exception excuses production of the original, then a more direct copy is preferred to a less direct one, and copies of writings are preferred to testimony describing the writings.[5] The FRE do not recognize a hierarchy in this way. Under FRE 1003, if a "duplicate" is admissible, and more than one exists, then any of them may be admitted. Other secondary evidence generally must come in under the

[2] 28 U.S.C. 1732 (1988). Many states have adopted similar photocopy statutes. *See* the Uniform Photographic Copies of Business and Public Records as Evidence Act, 14 U.L.A. 145 (1949).

[3] *See* Chapter 9.

[4] D. Bender, Computer Law 5—76 (1989). *See* United States v. Miller, 500 F.2d 751, 755 (5th Cir. 1974), *rev'd on other grounds*, 425 U.S. 435 (1976) (best evidence rule inapplicable to record qualifying under former federal Business Records Act, the broadly worded statutory predecessor to FRE 803(6)). *Compare* State v. Loehmer, 159 Ind. App. 156, 304 N.E.2d 835 (1973) (sustained introduction of computer printout over best evidence objection on ground that printout fell within very broadly worded statute permitting admission of public records).

[5] McCormick, above, §241, at 720-722.

Rule 1004 exceptions. If a Rule 1004 exception applies, then any type of secondary evidence is admissible, with no preference among the different types.

§10.4 APPLICATION TO COMPUTER RECORDS

Historically, the best evidence rule's application to computer records has received only modest attention. The rule's explanation in this context has been relatively brief and inexact. In practice, courts dealing with computer evidence seem to subordinate the best evidence rule's theoretical requirements to inquiring whether the evidence is reliable under the hearsay/business records analysis.

The rule's federal version does specifically mention computer data. FRE 1001(3) states, "If data are stored in a computer or similar device, any printout or other output readable by sight, shown to reflect the data accurately, is an 'original.'" The relevant Advisory Committee Note states, "practicality and usage confer the status of original upon any computer printout."

Presumably FRE 1001(3) means that an accurate printout is an original of the particular computer record from which the printout is made. If the record itself is a duplicate of something else, then the printout is also a duplicate of that other thing. It is illogical to think that a duplicate of *X* could be fed into a computer and printed out as an original of *X*. Unfortunately, the rule is unclear here.

What is an accurate printout? A program must interpret the codes on an electronic record to print them out as alphanumeric characters. When printed, the information might have any number of manifestations, each reflecting some bias. For example, the printout of an EDI invoice could be a direct repetition of the EDI data in the structured and coded format in which it was communicated. Or it could be a representation of the invoice's information, in the format of a conventional paper invoice, with each portion of information translated into English and set into a space on the document as though a printed form had been filled in with a typewriter. The difference can influence the impression and emphasis made to a jury. Presumably a trial court must consider this potential for bias, and even distortion, in judging a printout's "accuracy."

Many computer records might be considered duplicates of other things. FRE 1001(4) defines a "duplicate" as "a counterpart produced by . . . electronic re-recording . . . or by other equivalent techniques which accurately reproduces the original." Again, determining whether a record is a duplicate entails a judgment on what is an "accurate" reproduction.

With some exceptions, the best evidence rule has played only a small role in computer evidence cases. In the seminal case *Transport Indemnity Co. v. Seib*[1] information from paper documents had apparently been fed into a computer. The court held that information on a tape created by that computer was admissible under the business records exception to the hearsay rule. But it did not consider whether either the initial paper documents or the data on the tape were the original writings at issue. The court permitted the information on the tape to be admitted in the form of a printout. It implicitly assumed that the printout was identical to the information on the tape, and it did not mention the best evidence rule. The court's approach is consistent with FRE 1001(3) (adopted some years later), which deems an accurate printout to be an "original" of data in a computer.

In another early case, *King v. State ex rel. Murdock Acceptance Corp.*,[2] the court said it followed the best evidence rule when it admitted a printout from a computer record. The court considered the printout the best evidence available

§10.4 [1]178 Neb. 253, 132 N.W.2d 871 (1965).
[2]222 So. 2d 393, 398 (Miss. 1969).

of the computer record's contents. This approach seems to grow from the idea that the best evidence rule ranks evidence in a hierarchy. It requires a court in its discretion to judge which evidence is "best," second best, and so forth, and then to favor evidence at the top of the hierarchy.

In *Schiavone-Chase Corp. v. United States*[3] the proponent sought to admit computer printouts of billing lists. These derived from paper documents that the opponents' agents had signed but that had been destroyed under a routine record destruction program. The opponents objected to the computer records. The appellate court affirmed the admission, stating, "In view of the circumstance that the computer lists constitute the best evidence that is available now, . . . as well as the fact that the plaintiffs did not present any conflicting evidence, it was the trial judge's opinion that the interests of justice would be served by accepting the computer lists. . . ."

In *Ed Guth Realty, Inc. v. Gingold*[4] a taxpayer tried to admit computer printouts of statistical data on property values. Aided by an expert witness who explained the procedures used to collect the data from many sources, the taxpayer sought to establish an equalization rate relevant to tax assessment. Apparently, the printouts did not directly reflect all the data that had been collected. The tax authority (the opponent) objected that the printouts were not the best evidence of the data, but the court held the printouts were summaries of voluminous records admissible under a best evidence exception for summaries equivalent to FRE 1006.

The government in *United States v. Sanders*[5] had charged the defendant with submitting false claims for Medicare reimbursement to a state agency. It offered as evidence a printout, made specially for trial, from the agency's computer records showing the history of the claims the defendant

[3]553 F.2d 658 (Ct. Cl. 1977).
[4]34 N.Y.2d 440, 315 N.E.2d 441, 358 N.Y.S.2d 367 (1974).
[5]749 F.2d 195 (5th Cir. 1984).

had submitted. The defendant objected, claiming, in effect, that they were not properly handled under the best evidence rule. He characterized the printouts as data summaries that should be governed by FRE 1006 (part of the federal courts' best evidence rule provisions) and that necessitate special jury instructions on the use of summaries. Observing that the printouts represented a complete rather than a selective listing of all information in the computer on the matter at hand, the court rejected the claim. It saw no consequence in the printout having pulled all the relevant information into a single, structured unit.

The best evidence rule has occasionally been invoked to exclude computer evidence from admission at trial. In *State v. Springer*[6] a witness who had examined a printout that constituted a bank's official record of credit cards it issued testified about the printout's contents. One reason the court excluded the testimony was that the best evidence rule required production of the printout itself. In truth, this well-known case adds little to the understanding of the best evidence rule's application to electronic evidence. It merely holds that if information appears on paper (the printout), the paper itself is preferred to testimony about the paper.

One commentator suggests that any information derived from a data base search must, to be admitted under the best evidence rule, be in the form of a printout (if obtainable).[7] Under this view, testimony by a computer operator about what he saw is unacceptable if a printout can be obtained.

Citing the best evidence rule, *Harned v. Credit Bureau of Gillette*[8] excluded a recapitulation of computer records of invoices owed for propane gas deliveries. The original invoices were probably still in existence, but the proponent had made no attempt to obtain them or account for their

[6]283 N.C. 627, 197 S.E.2d 530 (1973).
[7]D. Bender, Computer Law, 5—72-73 (1989).
[8]513 P.2d 650, 652 (Wyo. 1973).

absence. The court seemed to consider the invoices central to the dispute; it disallowed admission of the computer records, or of their recapitulation, in place of the invoices. This holding seems contrary to many other cases that have upheld the admission of computerized business records. Using the logic of *Harned,* both of the famous *Transport Indemnity* and *King* cases could have considered the paper documents underlying the computer records to have been central to those cases and therefore excluded the computer printouts under the best evidence rule. The *Transport Indemnity* court, however, made no inquiry into whether the underlying documents were available. *King* did note that the underlying paper records were available, but it permitted the computer records anyway.[9]

§10.5 APPLICATION TO ELECTRONIC MESSAGES

The best evidence rule could spawn confusion with electronic messages. First, the rule's federal version applies to an original "writing" or "recording."[1] In paper communication, the writing and recording are the same thing. Similarly, with telegraphic communication the legally operative communications (the order handed to the carrier and the dispatch delivered to the recipient) were embodied in paper. A purely electronic message, however, exists independent of any particular recording. Thus there is some potential ambiguity.

Second, FRE 1001(1) defines both "writings" and "recordings" as "letters, words, or numbers, or their equivalent, set down by handwriting, typewriting, printing, photostating, photographing, magnetic impulse, mechanical or electronic recording, or other form of data compilation." This

[9] 222 So. 2d at 397.
§10.5 [1] Fed. R. Evid. 1002.

suggests some degree of permanent recording is necessary to invoke the rule. But for paperless electronic messages (exclusive of fax and telex) there may be no original document in the sense of letters or words being "set down" somewhere. The legally effective communication is only a temporary, dynamic, and changeable set of impulses traveling from one machine to another.[2] The machines might "set down" one or more records (with varying durations) of those impulses before, during, or after transmission, but the records are not the messages themselves.

Under at least federal law, the best interpretation is that the best evidence rule does not apply to purely electronic messages. The same interpretation applies to oral conversations that happen to be recorded. In *United States v. Gonzales-Benitez*[3] defendants claimed, on best evidence grounds, that the trial court erred by permitting an eyewitness to testify about certain conversations that had been recorded. "They claim[ed] that since the conversations were recorded on tapes, the tapes themselves, and not testimony of one of the participants, were the 'best evidence' of the conversations."[4] The appellate court dismissed the claim.

> The appellants simply misconstrue the purpose and effect of the best evidence rule. The rule does not set up an order of preferred admissibility, which must be followed to prove any fact. It is, rather, a rule applicable only when one seeks to prove the contents of documents or recordings. Fed. R. Evid. 1002. Thus, if the ultimate inquiry had been to discover what sounds were embodied on the tapes in question, the tapes themselves would have been the "best evidence."

[2]The electronic message itself is the "legally effective communication" because that is the source of the expression the sender expects the recipient to read and rely on to understand the sender's intent. The fact that the recipient may alter or record the message after receipt does not change this conclusion. Any record of or change to the contents after receipt is under the recipient's control, not the sender's.

[3]537 F.2d 1051 (9th Cir.), *cert. denied,* 429 U.S. 923 (1976).

[4]*Id.* at 1053.

> However, the content of the tapes was not in itself a factual issue relevant to the case. The inquiry concerned the content of the conversations. The tape recordings . . . would have been admissible as evidence of those conversations. But testimony by the participants was equally admissible and was sufficient to establish what was said.[5]

Analogously, in a dispute over an electronic message, the issue will be what were the message's contents, not what were the contents of any of the recordings of the message. Therefore, the best evidence rule will not exclude any of the recordings made of the message.

An alternative, and less persuasive, interpretation of the best evidence rule is that it can apply to a purely electronic message. Under this interpretation, the message itself is the "original" writing, even though that original is lost or destroyed (through the fault of no one) as soon as it reaches its destination. Hence, under FRE 1004, any secondary evidence of the message, such as any recording of it, is admissible.

Under a third interpretation, which may apply in some state courts, the best evidence rule would impose a hierarchy on the available records of an electronic message. If there were more than one record, the more direct one would be preferred to the less direct. But the rule would be flexible enough to permit admission of at least one of the available records. Under this interpretation, the rule's purpose is to secure the "best *obtainable* evidence."[6] The rule is not one of exclusion, but rather one establishing a preference when more than one version of written or recorded evidence is available. Trial courts applying this interpretation should be accorded considerable deference when they decide to admit evidence over a best evidence objection.[7] Thus, application of this third interpretation boils down to a judge's sense of justice under the circumstances.

[5] *Id.* at 1053-1054.
[6] McCormick, above, §237, at 715.
[7] McCormick, above, §243, at 723.

Recognize that under each of these three interpretations of the best evidence rule, if there are any records of an electronic message, at least one record should be admissible. It would be very difficult to rule that all of the available records must be excluded. Thus, the rule should not be a significant concern for electronic message users.

Keep in mind that the analysis of conventional fax or telex may be different because paper exists on both ends of those communications. Fax and telex may well be analyzed the way the telegram was.[8] The received paper is the original for purposes of showing what the recipient relied on. Another way to view fax and telex is that the paper on each end is a counterpart original. Each piece of paper would then be equally admissible under the best evidence rule. To clarify that the sender intends for the paper on each end to be a counterpart original, the sender could include a clause in the document to that effect. And, because thermal fax printout paper yellows quickly, a fax sender may desire to state that any complete photocopy of the printout is also a counterpart original.[9]

§10.6 APPLICATION TO RECORDS TRANSFERRED BETWEEN MEDIA

An additional best evidence issue involves the transfer of archive data from one medium to another. Sometime after the user has made a message's "final" record, she may wish to transfer it. It might be economical, for instance, to transfer from magnetic tape to microfilm.

Logically, if the best evidence rule does not apply to an inquiry into what the contents of a particular telecommuni-

[8] *See* §10.2.
[9] *See* Appendix A.

cated message were, then the later transfer of message archives from one medium to another should raise no best evidence issues. Nonetheless, it could sometimes be that an inquiry in court would focus on the contents of a particular recording, such as a fax printout or a file on a disk.

The process of transferring a recording from one medium to another is roughly analogous to transferring original paper records to microfilm or optical storage. If one attempts to introduce the new records into evidence, the best evidence objection would be that they are not the original recording. Evidence law has proved reasonably accepting of the microfilming process, so long as it is properly controlled to ensure accuracy. The most well-recognized control is for the transfer to take place in the regular course of business. This ensures that decisions on what is recorded and how are made for business reasons only and not to affect parties' rights in litigation. Commentators argue rather persuasively that the same treatment should apply to the transfer of paper documents to optical storage.[1]

§10.6.1 Photocopy Statutes

The basis for overcoming a best evidence objection to information transferred between media varies from one jurisdiction to another. Of primary importance are the federal photocopy statute and its state counterpart, the Uniform Photographic Copies of Business and Public Records as Evidence Act.[2] These acts do not distinguish among types of

§10.6 [1]*See* R. Williams, ed., Legality of Optical Storage: Admissibility in Evidence of Optically Stored Records (1987) (the true issue is not whether optically stored evidence will be admitted but what foundation must be laid to permit admission). *See also* Skupsky, The Legal Status of Optical Disk and Electronic Imaging Systems, ARMA Records Mgmt. Q. 56 (Jan. 1986).

[2]*See* §10.3.

media so long as the media provide for accurate reproduction.

Courts seem to take a pragmatic approach to the transfer of information from one medium (such as computer tape) to another (such as paper). One commentator argues that the famous *Transport Indemnity*[3] court properly read the business records exception to the hearsay rule to permit the admission of the computer record at issue (which was on computer tape), but that it logically needed some additional authority to admit that record's printout. This commentator suggests that additional authority "might be application of a photographic copy statute,"[4] which permits admission of "facsimiles," made for trial, of reproduced business records.[5] Nevertheless, the *Transport Indemnity* court seemed to have implicitly adopted the more direct and practical rule now embraced in FRE 1001(3): An accurate printout of a computer record is an "original" of that record.

People v. Mormon[6] involved evidence of an automobile rental agreement that had undergone a series of media transfers. At the time of rental, a rental company employee filled out a form contract and simultaneously keyed the information into a computer. The computer data was later converted to microfilm. (The original contract was lost.) Months later, when the rental agreement became relevant to a criminal trial involving a passenger who had been in the rented car, the company placed information from the microfilm record onto a blank rental form to recreate the paper original. The appellate court sustained the recreation's admission because the computer records qualified under the business records exception to the hearsay rule. The court considered the microfilm a reproduction falling within the Illinois photocopy

[3]178 Neb. 253, 132 N.W.2d 871 (1965).

[4]D. Bender, Computer Law, 6—80 (1989).

[5]*See* §10.3.

[6]97 Ill. App. 3d 556, 422 N.E.2d 1065 (1981), *aff'd*, 92 Ill. 2d 268, 442 N.E.2d 250 (1982).

statute (very similar to the federal photocopy statute quoted in Section 10.3). It deemed the document brought to court a "facsimile" under the photocopy statute, and thus ruled the document admissible in lieu of the microfilm. The court did not mention the best evidence rule, but it cited *Transport Indemnity* for the proposition that reproductions (such as printouts or facsimiles) based on original business records are admissible.

§10.6.2 Best Evidence Rule Exceptions

An alternative route around a best evidence rule objection might be one of the rule's many generous exceptions, such as those approving duplicates or other secondary evidence in FRE 1003-1006.[7] *United States v. Taylor*[8] upheld the introduction of a photocopy of a fax of a letter. Noting that subpoenas had been issued without success to obtain the sender's initial letter, the court approved the photocopy's admission under FRE 1004(2), which permits secondary evidence if the original is unobtainable through available judicial procedure. (The court did not rule on which document was the "original.")

A best evidence rule exception is not needed, however, if the new record itself is considered an original. A second or later generation record of data may be either an original or secondary evidence depending on the purpose for which it is offered at trial. If the purpose is to show what the recipient's many records themselves said, then each of the recipient's records is an original. *United States v. Russo*[9] illustrates. At issue were claims for payment of medical services, originally reflected on paper reports, submitted by a physician to an insurance company. The reports had been

[7]*See* §10.3.
[8]648 F.2d 565 (9th Cir. 1981), *cert. denied,* 454 U.S. 866 (1981).
[9]480 F.2d 1228 (6th Cir. 1973), *cert. denied,* 414 U.S. 1157 (1974).

entered into the company's computer system. Sometime later, in the regular course of business, the company ran a statistical analysis of the reports submitted during a year by this physician and others. The physician objected when the government sought to admit this statistical analysis in his criminal trial. The court sustained admission, calling this analysis, which was two steps removed from the original reports, an "original record" of the insurance company.[10]

§10.6.3 The Search for Reliability

Ideally, where a record's contents are at issue, the transfer of those contents from one medium to another creates a copy that corresponds directly to the original's contents, as a photocopy or microfilm copy corresponds directly to the original paper document. Yet that is not necessarily what happens in a computer environment. The Fifth Edition of the *Manual for Complex Litigation* explains an example of what might happen as computer data are transferred from a database to paper:

> Sometimes . . . data are randomly recorded in the computer in the sequence in which events occur or in which information is received, rather than as organized bundles relating to specific customers or transactions. When directed to do so, the machine will collect and print out all the data relating to a particular transaction or customer. Such a printout is not a visual counterpart of the machine record but, rather, a compilation of scattered, related information.[11]

If properly controlled, the transfer to a new medium can create useful evidence. The Fifth Edition of the *Manual* suggests trial judges should have considerable leeway to grant

[10] *Id.* at 1241.

[11] Manual for Complex Litigation 123 (5th ed. 1982). (Footnotes omitted.)

or deny admission of such transferred data. Their judgment is guided by a search for reliability.

> [T]his evidence should not be rejected merely because it is not a visual counterpart of the machine record; but the court must carefully consider whether the reliability of this evidence has been compromised in any way.[12]

Such trial court discretion makes sense considering information technology's flexibility and the possible confusion it raises with the best evidence rule.

Considering the foregoing, the central advice for users transferring evidence between media is (1) do it in the ordinary course of business, (2) use techniques designed to ensure accuracy, (3) document the process so it can later be explained, and (4) mark the new records so the identity of each unit of evidence can readily be determined.

[12] *Id.*

PART IV

RECORDKEEPING AND INTERNAL CONTROL

Chapter 11

General Recordkeeping and Control Requirements

§11.1 INTRODUCTION

Without transaction records, bills go unpaid, assets are lost, investors flee, and businesses collapse. Equally as indispensable is internal control: the presence of procedural safeguards to ensure transaction authorization, correctness, completeness, efficiency, and consistency with management policies. Internal controls deter, detect, and correct errors and fraud, and permit management and auditor oversight of business.

This chapter considers the application to electronic commerce of a host of laws that require recordkeeping and internal control for business and government transactions. The practical lesson from this and the following two chapters is this: Electronic transaction users should make their recordkeeping and control policies rational and explicit. As explained, the presence of thoughtful, written policies on record creation, retention, and destruction and on internal control can rebut charges of unlawfulness. Further, the very act of writing can force users to consider the issues deliberately and thus be more likely to address them soundly. Policies are especially persuasive if based on industry standards, provided any exist.

Electronic message systems differ from their paper counterparts in the manner in which recordkeeping and control policies are implemented. Automation changes some comfortable habits. To retain a paper invoice, for example, one simply inserted it in a file, knowing it would remain readable there for years. Retention of an EDI invoice, however, requires the recordmaker to think ahead as much as seven or more years to consider what resources will be available in the future to retrieve and understand the record. He may need to provide specially for the retention of hardware, software, and system documentation. This type of problem has for years plagued taxpayers that keep accounting ledgers on computer, but it has now worsened because electronic messaging is enlarging the volume of electronically retained data. The recordmaker must also consider which format (whether EDI code or English) and medium (magnetic tape, optical disk, paper, and so forth) is best.

Internal control over paper systems relies in part on manual procedures, such as the physical movement of paper from one clerk's desk to the next, and visual audit trails on paper in the form of words, signatures, ink stamps, and control numbers. In contrast, internal control over computer systems relies on such devices as system access barriers and the professional development, testing, maintenance, and backup of software.

Electronic data processing stories about losses due to inadequate internal control are not uncommon. In one, a graduate student stole between $100,000 and $1 million in merchandise from a telephone company by placing transfer orders through the company's computerized inventory system. Logging onto the system from outside the company, the thief requested nighttime deliveries to remote receiving docks, where he intercepted the merchandise. He obtained passwords and learned how to fool the system simply by questioning employees and retrieving documentation from a waste bin.[1] More stringent computer security measures would have denied the thief this information.

In another case, the Bank of New York suffered a $5 million loss as the result of a computer system outage that halted its government securities trading business. The bank lacked an adequate backup system.[2]

Electronic trading changes the patterns of information exchange between companies. Goods may be ordered in

§11.1 [1]A. Bequai, White Collar Crime: A 20th Century Crisis 15 (1978); R. Soble & R. Dallos, The Impossible Dream: The Equity Funding Story: The Fraud of the Century 197 (1975); Allen, Embezzler's Guide to the Computer, Harv. Bus. Rev. 79 (July-Aug. 1975).

[2]Betts, Bank Blames Nightmare on Software Flop, ComputerWorld, Dec. 16, 1985, at 1, col. 3.

smaller quantities. Expected response times may be compressed dramatically. Certain information exchanges may be eliminated entirely. Some trading partners, for example, are discarding the invoice (the traditional accounting document against which trade payments are made) and instead are regulating payments with information from purchase orders, price catalogs, and delivery notices. Fewer people may be involved in transactions as clerks are eliminated. The consequence of all this is that controls need to be more automated, quickly carried out, and preventive in nature. The reduction of staff makes controls based on numerous people watching over one another—such as through the segregation of duties—more difficult. Companies must thoroughly reassess controls as they migrate away from paper.[3]

Laws set some standards for recordkeeping and control. Their satisfaction in the paper world involved rather well understood practices, using a rigid medium. Computer technology, however, is so abundantly flexible and computer applications are evolving so rapidly that generally-accepted recordkeeping and control practices have not been fully developed. Even when innocent at heart, the user risks having her ad hoc practices judged irresponsible or even deceitful.

It might be tempting in EDI practice, for instance, for the recipient of a message to save, as the only record of the message, a brief reference in a database, while deleting the original message contents from the system. For operational purposes, the database reference may appear to be the only record needed. If the message had been on paper, however, the user instinctively would have kept the paper, with all its contents. In the eyes of a retrospective critic, this EDI user could appear to be losing information. Her practice may appear remiss and unlawful.

Well-considered recordmaking and control policies can help overcome any appearance of impropriety.

[3]EDI Council of Australia and the EDP Auditors Assoc., EDI Control Guide: Make Your Business More Competitive 4 (1990).

§11.2 COMMON LAW REQUIREMENTS

§11.2.1 Agency Law

An agent is one who legally undertakes to perform a task on behalf of another (known as the "principal"). An example might be the business manager of a small firm. The manager looks out for the firm's affairs, guards its assets, and binds it to transactions, such as agreements to buy supplies. Another example of an agent might be an inventory management company that undertakes to receive, warehouse, and ship goods for another company.

§11.2.1.1 Recordkeeping and Control Generally

General agency law obligates an agent to keep accounts, or records, for money and other property entrusted to him.[1] So if the business manager is given $5,000 to buy supplies, he must keep records to show what he bought and how much he paid and to whom; this might logically include, in either a paper or automated environment, the retention of copies of purchase orders and invoices. The law's obvious purpose is to permit the principal to audit the agent.

Failure to keep records could make the agent liable to the principal.[2] The agent has the burden of proving what happened to assets, and she is liable for their value if she cannot carry the burden.[3]

§11.2 [1]Restatement (Second) of Agency §382 (1957); Adkins v. Moody, 228 Ark. 175, 306 S.W.2d 333 (1957).

[2]Kennard v. Glick, 183 Cal. App. 2d 246, 7 Cal. Rptr. 88 (Dist. Ct. App. 1960). *See* §13.2.1.

[3]*Id. See also* Alexopoulos v. Dakouras, 48 Wis. 2d 32, 179 N.W.2d 836 (1970) (failure to account for funds makes agent liable for conversion).

What type and quality of records must be made? The question is particularly apt in an electronic trading environment, where there are so many different means for and degrees of recordkeeping.[4] First, agency law requires the agent to take such receipts as are customarily taken in business transactions and to act reasonably in view of the prevailing business customs.[5] Thus, agency law does not prescribe precisely how transactions, such as EDI invoices, are recorded and accounted for, but it does impose an obligation on agents using EDI to act rationally. For a company using EDI, determining what is acceptable is not entirely easy because prevailing customs are few.

Second, implied within the obligation to keep accounts is the duty to control the recordkeeping process, so that records are accurate and reliable.[6] A rational and explicit policy on recordkeeping and control would make it difficult for someone to second guess an agent's choices.

Although not necessarily agents, some organizations holding the records of others may be liable for negligently losing those records. One court held a hospital liable to a patient for losing his medical records.[7] The damage allegedly suffered was an inability to sue a physician for malpractice. The court did not speak in terms of agency law, but simply negligence. Noting that regulations and industry practice prescribed hospital retention of the patient records at issue, the court held the hospital owed a duty to exercise reasonable care in keeping them. The same type of duty might apply to a government agency with whom a person has filed information or a financial institution that might be expected to keep customer transaction records. If the recordholder is using electronic data processing (EDP) systems, then presum-

[4]*See* §5.4 and Chapter 6.

[5]Restatement (Second) of Agency §382 comment a (1957).

[6]*See* Chapter 6.

[7]*See* Fox v. Cohen, 84 Ill. App. 3d 744, 406 N.E.2d 178 (1980).

ably it must institute appropriate EDP controls to protect records.[8]

§11.2.1.2 Preservation of Assets

An agent who undertakes a job is bound to perform it.[9] A custodian of assets must keep them safe.[10] If the custodian, an inventory management company, for example, is buying, selling, and storing inventory, it must take precautions against theft of the inventory. In an EDP context, the very assets an agent/custodian, such as a data processing manager, is hired to keep are records and information. Electronic transaction systems also control and safeguard underlying assets such as funds and goods. It follows then that agents using electronic systems must implement controls to prevent asset loss and system abuse.

An investment banker or lawyer is an agent of her client and obligated under general agency law to protect the client's assets entrusted with her. One such asset may be sensitive financial information. Thus, such an agent must take steps to preserve confidentiality. This might mean, for example, avoiding fax transmissions (1) to machines that are exposed to many users, (2) via insecure VANs where operators can view the transmissions, or (3) in extreme cases, that are not encrypted.

The precautions an agent could use to make records and preserve assets are endless. How far must he go? Agency law generally holds the agent liable only for his negligence, or failure to exercise the requisite standard of care. The law defines that as the "standard of care and . . . skill which is

[8] *See* Burk & Winer, Failure to Prepare: Who's Liable in a Data Processing Disaster?, 5 S.C. Computer and High Tech. L.J. 19 (1989).

[9] Restatement (Second) of Agency §377 (1957).

[10] Restatement (Second) of Agency §422 (1957).

standard . . . for the kind of work which [the agent] is employed to perform and, in addition, to exercise any special skills that he has."[11]

Accordingly, to adapt this standard to an information systems manager, the manager must use the talents of an average computer professional (plus any special talents it has) to devise and implement protections for the principal's assets. Those protections might include the hiring, training, and supervision of competent staff and consultants, the acquisition and maintenance of adequate computing resources, the deployment of security measures such as passwords and physical locks to prevent outsiders from exploiting the principal's information, and the preparation for contingencies such as data processing disasters. Resources always being limited, the manager must balance recordkeeping and control needs with the attendant costs. Whether it has exercised the requisite care is determined from all the facts and circumstances.

In a general sense, the foregoing reading of the law applies equally to corporations serving as data processing managers for other firms[12] and individual officers acting as data processing managers. But as a practical matter, the risk of an officer actually being held liable to her firm is limited, as explained below.

§11.2.2 Corporate Law

Most larger businesses are organized as corporations—legal entities, owned by shareholders, that possess and manage assets. To protect shareholder interests, the law requires corporations to keep records. Section 16.01 of the Revised Model Business Corporation Act (1984) for instance provides:

[11]Restatement (Second) of Agency §379 (1957).

[12]*See* Part VI for a discussion of the duty of computer service providers to customers.

> (b) A corporation shall maintain appropriate accounting records. . . .
>
> (d) A corporation shall maintain its records in written form or in another form capable of conversion into written form within a reasonable time.

The Act's official comments explain:

> The word "appropriate" is used to indicate that the nature of the financial records to be kept is dependent to some extent on the nature of the corporation's business. . . . "Appropriate" records are generally records that permit financial statements to be prepared which fairly present the financial position and transactions of the corporation.

The implication is that the records must be systematic, auditable, and subject to controls to make them reliable,[13] but the law leaves the corporation considerable discretion in choosing how to do that. Shareholders can obtain legal relief if records are inadequate, however. At the demand of a minority shareholder in *Neese v. Richer*[14] the trial court ordered a corporation to obtain and pay for an independent audit of its books. The court grounded this ruling on its finding that the corporation's books and accounting procedures were sloppy, incomplete, and disorganized. The corporation also had to pay the shareholder's attorneys fees involved in pressing for the audit even though the audit revealed no dishonesty.

Under corporate law, directors and officers occupy a special fiduciary relationship to their corporation and its shareholders, which is similar to an agent/principal relationship. Another case championing minority shareholder rights, *Backus v. Finkelstein,*[15] confirmed that corporate

[13]*See* Dunn v. Acme Auto & Garage Co., 168 Wis. 277, 169 N.W. 297, 301 (1918).

[14]428 N.E.2d 36 (Ind. Ct. App. 1981).

[15]23 F.2d 357, 364 (D. Minn. 1927).

officers must maintain accurate accounts, in an orderly, intelligible manner, and preserve important records. Management's failure in that case to keep adequate records, together with the court's suspicion that management had defrauded shareholders, rendered management personally liable to shareholders for certain damages.[16]

The lesson for the management of companies implementing electronic transaction systems is that adequate means must be installed to record transactions, such as purchases, and log them into the companies' accounting systems.

Corporate directors and officers have an affirmative obligation to look after the corporation's interests, and they can be liable for neglecting the obligation. In principle, they could, for example, be accountable if a great percentage of corporate records was lost due to management's failure to consider reasonable EDP storage practices. Further, if a company came to rely on its EDP system to the point that a breakdown crippled it, management could be liable if it was blind to the need to control the system and ensure its proper functioning. Nevertheless, managers are expected under the law to balance the benefits, costs, and administrative burdens in making records and establishing controls.

The precise wording of the standards that govern managers varies from state to state. Yet it is clear that the law affords directors and officers considerable latitude in choosing between one degree of records and control and another. First, absent fraud or disloyalty, executives are liable only if they fail to exercise "ordinary care" in fulfilling their du-

[16]Sometimes the scope of the job of a particular officer, such as a treasurer, can specifically include recordkeeping, and that officer can be held liable for defaulting on that duty. *See* Atlantic Acoustical & Insulation Co. v. Moreira, 348 A.2d 263 (Me. 1975) (under the facts, the court found treasurer had not breached duty).

ties—in other words, only if they are negligent.[17] Reasonable decisions are unlikely to be challenged.

Second, under the "business judgment rule" directors and officers making a business decision are presumed to have "acted on an informed basis in good faith and in the honest belief that the action was taken in the best interests of the company."[18] This presumption severely handicaps a plaintiff trying to prove negligence. A showing that management failed to make an informed decision (in other words, that it was ignorant), however, can overcome the business judgment rule presumption.[19]

Third, proving damages can be very difficult for a plaintiff. In *Barnes v. Andrews*[20] a defendant director did little to inform himself about the corporation's affairs, nor did he query the president for details about the business. The company foundered due to the president's mismanagement. The court determined the director did violate his fiduciary duty of care. But assessing damages against him was another matter.

> [W]hen a business fails from general mismanagement . . . or bad judgment, how is it possible to say that a single director could have made the company successful, or how much in dollars he could have saved? [T]he plaintiff must show that, had [the defendant] done his full duty, he could have made the company prosper, or at least could have broken its fall. He must show what sum he could have saved the company.[21]

[17]Sections 8.30(a) and 8.42(a) of the Revised Model Business Corporation Act (1984), for example, direct each director and officer to discharge his respective duties "with the care an ordinarily prudent person in a like position would exercise under similar circumstances" and "in a manner he reasonably believes to be in the best interests of the corporation."

[18]Aronson v. Lewis, 473 A.2d 805, 812 (Del. 1984).

[19]Smith v. Van Gorkom, 488 A.2d 858, 872 (Del. 1985).

[20]298 F. 614 (S.D.N.Y. 1924).

[21]*Id.* at 616-617.

The plaintiff won no damages in that case.

Few cases have held corporate directors or officers liable for mismanagement in the absence of some disloyalty by the defendants or fraud.[22] One that has, however, is *Selheimer v. Manganese Corp. of America*[23] in which directors were assessed for allowing the proceeds of a financing to go to an unprofitable, old facility when it had been represented to investors that those proceeds would go to a new facility.

It appears there are no reported court decisions holding directors or officers accountable for "simple" negligence—even negligence involving absolute inattention and ignorance—in such a routine (nonfinancial) decision as how to keep records or whether to protect a computer facility from disaster.[24] One dated case even held corporate directors not liable for failing to insure corporate property that later burned.[25]

In sum, corporate directors and officers owe a duty of care to their corporations and shareholders in implementing, controlling, and protecting electronic transaction systems. But, unless fraud or disloyalty are present, the threat of suffering a money judgment for disappointing that duty seems limited. Still, an allegation that executives had breached their duty could be detrimental when coupled with other claims. Explicit and rational record retention and control

[22]Bishop, Sitting Ducks and Decoy Ducks: New Trends in the Indemnification of Corporate Directors and Officers, 77 Yale L. J. 1078, 1099 (1968).

[23]423 Pa. 563, 224 A.2d 634 (1966).

[24]Nevertheless, the threat of liability in an extreme case exists. Corporate officer insurance carriers agreed to pay a utility $27.4 million plus attorney fees in connection with alleged "gross mismanagement, wasting assets and other misconduct that resulted in the closing of the company's . . . nuclear power plant . . . by federal regulators." It was "alleged that management . . . ignored warnings from various sources that the plant's problems, including operators asleep on the job, would force regulators to close it." Geyelin & Goel, Philadelphia Electric Co. Will Get $27.4 Million in a Settlement, Wall St. J., Oct. 31, 1990, at B10, col.3 (s.w. ed.).

[25]Charlestown Boot & Shoe Co. v. Dunsmore, 60 N.H. 85, 87 (1880).

policies can refute charges that management failed to consider these issues.

§11.3 FOREIGN CORRUPT PRACTICES ACT

In 1977 Congress enacted the Foreign Corrupt Practices Act (FCPA) to stem corporate bribery of foreign government officials. Among the devices Congress chose to achieve its end were sweeping recordkeeping and control requirements for most larger companies. The rationale was that if a company were to keep detailed records and adhere to rigorous controls, slush funds for bribes would be difficult to create and hide. The Act is misnamed, however, since its recordkeeping and control provisions apply to all public companies, irrespective of whether they conduct foreign business. Congress' motives in enacting the law extended beyond just curtailing bribes and included the protection of investors from the abuse of corporate assets.

The FCPA, which is incorporated into the Securities Exchange Act of 1934, covers every company having securities registered, or filing reports, under the 1934 Act (so-called publicly held companies). Under the FCPA, such a company must "make and keep books, records, and accounts, which, in reasonable detail, accurately and fairly reflect the transactions and dispositions of assets of the" company.[1]

Additionally, such a company must

> devise and maintain a system of internal accounting controls sufficient to provide reasonable assurances that—
>
> (i) transactions are executed in accordance with management's general or specific authorization;

§11.3 [1]15 U.S.C. §78m(b)(2)(A) (1988).

> (ii) transactions are recorded as necessary (I) to permit preparation of financial statements in conformity with generally accepted accounting principles or any other criteria applicable to such statements, and (II) to maintain accountability for assets;
>
> (iii) access to assets is permitted only in accordance with management's general or specific authorization; and
>
> (iv) the recorded accountability for assets is compared with existing assets at reasonable intervals and appropriate action is taken with respect to any differences.[2]

The FCPA also warns that "[n]o person shall knowingly circumvent or knowingly fail to implement a system of internal accounting controls or knowingly falsify any book, record or account" described above.[3] In keeping with modern business practices, the 1934 Act defines "records" very broadly to include "accounts, correspondence, memorandums, tapes, discs, papers, books and other documents or transcribed information of any type, whether expressed in ordinary or machine language."[4]

The government enforces the FCPA through administrative investigations and proceedings by the Securities and Exchange Commission (SEC), civil injunctive actions by the SEC, and criminal actions by the Justice Department.[5] At least two lower courts have held, however, that the FCPA's recordkeeping and control provisions cannot be enforced through a private lawsuit by investors.[6]

[2] 15 U.S.C. §78m(b)(2)(B) (1988).

[3] 15 U.S.C. §78m(b)(5) (1988).

[4] 15 U.S.C. §78c(37) (1988).

[5] *See* §13.2.3 for a discussion of a criminal action under the FCPA.

[6] Lewis v. Sporck, 612 F. Supp. 1316, 1326-1334 (N.D. Cal. 1985); Eisenberger v. Spectex Indus., 644 F. Supp. 48, 50-51 (E.D.N.Y. 1986). Two commentators have suggested, however, that failure to keep records and institute controls could give rise to a tort (negligence) action in favor of injured investors. The law might look to the FCPA for standards to judge recordkeeping and control measures. Burk & Winer, Failure to Prepare: Who's Liable in a Data Processing Disaster?, 5 S. C. Computer & High Tech. L.J. 19 (Feb. 1989).

§11.3.1 Interpretation

Publicly held companies implementing electronic trading systems must consider the FCPA. The FCPA applies to all corporate financial and accounting systems, whether manual or electronic and whether dealing with internal or external transactions. The practical extent to which companies must keep records and maintain controls under the FCPA is subject to debate, and practices vary considerably among companies. In an authoritative speech on the FCPA, which the SEC noted officially in the Code of Federal Regulations,[7] SEC Chairman Harold M. Williams stated that

1. inadvertent recordkeeping and control errors would not be the subject of enforcement actions; and
2. the standard for judging compliance would be reasonableness under the circumstances.

This approach accords businesses considerable discretion in designing and implementing recordkeeping and control programs for EDP systems.

In *SEC v. World-Wide Coin Investments, Ltd.*,[8] the first case finding a violation of the FCPA's recordkeeping and control provisions following a trial, the court opined:

> It does not appear . . . Congress . . . intended that the statute should require that each affected [company] install a fail-safe accounting control system at all costs. It appears that Congress was fully cognizant of the cost-effective considerations which confront companies as they consider the institution of accounting controls and of the subjective elements which may lead reasonable individuals to arrive at different conclusions. Congress has demanded only that judgment be exercised in applying the standard of reasonableness. The size of the business, diversity of operations, degree of centralization of fi-

[7] 17 C.F.R. pt. 241 (1989), referring to 46 Fed. Reg. 11544 (1981).
[8] 567 F. Supp. 724 (N.D. Ga. 1983).

nancial and operating management, amount of contact by top management with day-to-day operations, and numerous other circumstances are factors which management must consider in establishing and maintaining an internal accounting controls system.[9]

In 1988 Congress amended the FCPA to provide that "reasonable assurance" and "reasonable detail" (the standards fixed in the FCPA provisions quoted previously) "mean such level of detail and degree of assurance as would satisfy prudent officials in the conduct of their own affairs."[10] The legislative history of the amendment suggests the standard allows for a consideration of costs, among other factors, in determining the level of compliance a company undertakes.[11] Still, the FCPA does not appear to have an exclusion for "immaterial" lapses in recordkeeping and control—which would permit ignoring matters that are small relative to the company's size.

The prudent officials standard is similar to the ordinary care standard for officers and directors under general corporate law.[12] Yet it does not appear to be subject to the protective shield of the business judgment rule, and the showing of pecuniary damages is not necessarily critical for the government to bring an action under the FCPA. So, in enforcing the FCPA, the government is free of some of the burdens a shareholder has when suing under corporate law.[13]

§11.3.2 Application to Particular Civil Cases

SEC enforcement of the FCPA per se has not been vigorous. Historically, SEC investigations into books and controls is-

[9] *Id.* at 751.

[10] 15 U.S.C. §78(m)(b)(7) (1988).

[11] H.R. Conf. Rep. No. 100-576, 100th Cong., 2d Sess., *reprinted in* 1988 U.S. Code Cong. & Admin. News 1547, 1950.

[12] *See* §11.2.2.

[13] *See* §13.2.3.

sues have been appended to other fraud and misleading securities-reporting inquiries. The following are enforcement actions that illustrate the types of abuses the FCPA remedies.

The court in *World-Wide Coin* found:

> [T]he internal recordkeeping and accounting controls of World-Wide [have] been sheer chaos. . . . For example, there has been no procedure implemented with respect to writing checks: employees have had access to presigned checks; source documents were not required to be prepared when a check was drawn; employees have not been required to obtain approval before writing a check; and, even when a check was drawn to "cash," supporting documentation was usually not prepared to explain the purpose for which the check was drawn. [T]here has been no separation of duties in the areas of purchase and sales transactions, and valuation procedures for ending inventory. [E]mployees have not been required to write source documents relating to the purchase and sale of . . . inventory. Because of this total lack of an audit trail with respect to these transactions and the disposition of World-Wide's assets, it has been virtually impossible to determine if an item has been sold at a profit or a loss.[14]

In response to these infractions, the court ordered a full accounting of the company to determine to what extent executives were liable to the corporation for misappropriated assets.

A few FCPA civil lawsuits have dealt specifically with computerized records systems. In *SEC v. National Business Communications Corp.*[15] the SEC charged that a company and certain officers failed (among other things) to segregate duties adequately among accounting and bookkeeping employees, to guard against unauthorized access to the com-

[14]567 F. Supp. at 752.

[15]SEC Litig. Release No. 11223, Sept. 19, 1986, *reprinted in* 36 SEC Docket (CCH) 801 (Oct. 7, 1986), and SEC Litig. Release No. 11229, Sept. 26, 1986, *reprinted in* 36 SEC Docket (CCH) 887 (Oct. 15, 1986).

pany's computerized business records, and to record the identities of persons making changes to those records. The company was enjoined from further violations of the securities laws, and the officers were barred from serving as officers of publicly held companies. In another suit, *SEC v. Saxon Industries,*[16] the SEC charged Saxon with a variety of securities laws violations revolving around the falsification of books and records. One of the allegations was that Saxon had programed its computer to add false figures automatically to inventory levels. Saxon consented to the entry of an injunction against further securities law violations.

A FCPA bookkeeping violation can result from the recording of sales when customer communications do not amount to an obligation to buy. In *In the Matter of DSC Communications and Delmar G. Cartwright*[17] the SEC brought an administrative action against DSC and its vice president for filing misleading disclosure statements with the Commission[18] and failing to keep accurate books and records. The problem's origin was the improper recording of equipment sales. Although preliminary arrangements had been made for the sales, the customers were not obligated to buy until they issued purchase orders and other conditions were fulfilled. DSC recorded the sales even though the conditions were unmet. One customer had even given the vice president a letter disavowing any obligation to buy, but the vice president discarded it. DSC and the vice president settled the charges and agreed to take steps to prevent similar errors.

[16]Civil Action #82-5992 (S.D.N.Y., Sept. 9, 1982), *as reported in* G. Lynch, Assoc. Dir. Div. of Enforcement, SEC, Enforcement of the Accounting Provisions of the Foreign Corrupt Practices Act of 1977, *reprinted in* F.C.P.A. Rep. 273 (W. Hancock ed. 1983).

[17]Securities Exchange Act of 1934 Release No. 34-26434, Admin. Proc. File No. 3-7115, Jan. 9, 1989, *reprinted in* 42 SEC Docket (CCH) 859 (Jan. 24, 1989).

[18]In addition to the FCPA requirements, the Securities Exchange Act of 1934 obligates publicly held companies to periodically file detailed and accurate financial disclosure statements.

The practical implication for companies implementing EDI and other electronic order entry systems is that the systems should be designed to recognize sales only after all the preconditions to legal obligation have been satisfied. A trading partner agreement can establish those preconditions.[19]

These cases suggest the threat of legal challenges for recordkeeping and control shortcomings may be greater under the FCPA than under general corporate law.[20] Again, a practical response would be for electronic traders to adopt and implement explicit and rational record and control policies.

§11.4 OTHER REGULATIONS

Assorted recordkeeping and control regulations protect state interests within regulated industries such as banking and transportation. For illustration, this section examines a selection of recent or anticipated regulations or policy statements addressing EDP recordkeeping and control. The specificity of regulation and the intensity of oversight vary from industry to industry. Enforcement of these regulations most often comes as administrative proceedings within the applicable regulatory agencies.

For electronic transaction systems, in many cases the full significance of these regulations lies in their implications. It would seem, for example, that implicit within any record retention rule are requirements for controls to ensure record accuracy and disaster recovery capacity and the keeping of hardware, software, and system documentation for data retrieval and comprehension. Also implied may be some requirement to retain documentation so systems can be au-

[19]*See* §Part V.
[20]*See* §11.2.2.

dited. These regulations often do not state the standards against which choices are judged, but rational, articulated decisions by companies that seek to stay within the regulations' purposes are less likely to be questioned. Here, too, written corporate policies defining and explaining choices would be prudent.

§11.4.1 Oversight of Government Contractors

To permit oversight of government contractors, Federal Acquisition Regulation (FAR) subpart 4.7[1] prescribes policies, procedures, and time periods for the retention of certain contractor records. FAR 4.703(d) provides that if covered information

> is maintained on a computer, contractors shall retain the computer data on a reliable medium for the time periods described. Contractors may transfer computer data in machine readable form from one reliable computer medium to another. Contractors' computer data retention and transfer procedures shall maintain the integrity, reliability, and security of the original computer data. Contractors shall also retain an audit trail describing the data transfer. For the record retention time periods prescribed, contractors shall not destroy, discard, delete, or write over such computer data.

Presumably, this contemplates that a contractor with relevant EDI or other electronic data will capture and store it in some systematic way. Once stored, the data must be preserved in the form originally stored, although it can be transferred to new media, provided the transfer is done reliably and is traceable with an audit trail.

When the government originally proposed amending this regulation, it appeared to contemplate that contractors, to

§11.4 [1]54 Fed. Reg. 48982 (1989), *amending* 48 C.F.R. ch. 1, §4.703(d).

maintain data integrity, would keep the original media on which records were made. Some contractors objected, pointing out that prudent data processing practices often require the transfer of data from one medium to another.

§11.4.2 Regulation of Financial Institutions

As part of its supervision of national banks, the Office of the Comptroller of the Currency (OCC) has issued a circular advising national banks of the importance of data processing disaster recovery or contingency plans.[2] It calls for "off-site backup of critical data files, software, hardware, documentation, forms and supplies, as well as alternative means of processing information." It requires annual board of director review and approval of management's handling of contingency planning.

Recognizing the importance of outside EDP service providers to many banks, the OCC has alerted banks to the need to keep abreast of their providers' financial condition.[3] Some providers to the banking industry have failed, leaving a number of banks ill-prepared to continue their daily operations. The OCC has also warned banks against signing long-term agreements with providers that do not adequately protect the banks' interests. Among other things, the OCC suggests that when negotiating such contracts banks insist on reducing oral claims and promises to writing and establishing in contracts ways to implement and test contingency plans.[4]

In 1985 the OCC even sanctioned one service bureau,

[2]Comptroller of the Currency, Admr. of Natl. Banks, Banking Circular 177 (Revised) (Apr. 16, 1987), Fed. Bank. L. Rep. (CCH) ¶59,335.

[3]Comptroller of the Currency, Admr. of Natl. Banks, Banking Circular 187 (Jan. 18, 1985), Fed. Bank. L. Rep. (CCH) ¶59,336.

[4]Comptroller of the Currency, Admr. of Natl. Banks, Banking Bulletin 87-3 (Feb. 12, 1987), Fed. Bank. L. Rep. (CCH) ¶59,337.

which had been providing computer services to banks, for its financial instability and weaknesses of internal control. The OCC required the service bureau to provide the OCC audited financial information, furnish certain information to the banks it serves, adopt a disaster recovery plan, establish appropriate internal controls, and provide adequate liquidity, in advance, when operating losses are identified.[5] The action reflects the OCC's insistence that companies furnishing bank recordkeeping and transaction services be financially responsible.

The OCC has also instructed banks about maintaining the security of bank information systems. Noting the critical role EDP systems play in banking today, the OCC recommends the imposition of appropriate controls on systems, such as physical security, segregation of duties, computer access controls, and regular audits.[6]

Regulations under the federal Investment Company Act[7] require investment companies to keep extensive records, and the SEC has approved retention of such records on electronic media.[8] Under these regulations, the companies must "reasonably safeguard" the records, which may include keeping separate backup records, and be "ready at all times" to produce the records. These regulations do not specify in detail the protection measures that must be instituted, but they do imply that disaster recovery and other security plans need to be in place.[9]

[5]Comptroller of the Currency, Admr. of Natl. Banks, Cease and Desist Order Entered Against National Bank EDP Provider (Apr. 30, 1985), [1984-85 Transfer Binder] Fed. Bank. L. Rep. (CCH) ¶86,238.

[6]Comptroller of the Currency, Admr. of Natl. Banks, Banking Circular 229 (May 31, 1988), Fed. Bank. L. Rep. (CCH) ¶59,338.

[7]17 C.F.R. §§270.31a-1, 270.31a-2 (1989).

[8]17 C.F.R. §270.31a-2(f) (1989).

[9]Burk & Winer, Failure to Prepare: Who's Liable in a Data Processing Disaster?, 5 S.C. Computer & High Tech. L.J. 19, 33 (1989).

§11.4.3 Regulation of Automated Commodities Trading

In connection with the development of automated commodities trading systems such as Globex, the Commodities Futures Trading Commission (CFTC) issued an interpretation of its record retention regulations under the Commodity Exchange Act.[10] The regulations require self-regulatory organizations such as the Chicago Mercantile Exchange and the Chicago Board of Trade (Globex sponsors) to keep certain records pertaining to their supervision of commodities markets.[11] The CFTC interpreted these to cover records of

> the steps taken to identify vulnerabilities in [each electronic trading] system, to establish safeguards that address such vulnerabilities, and otherwise to ensure the system's technical accuracy, reliability, and ability to operate as intended. The information contained in such documentation may relate to such aspects as the physical environment of the system, the system's capacity, the operating system software, data integrity, access controls, user guidance, systems testing, internal controls, and contingency plans, among other things.

The CFTC said that retention of these materials could assist it in assessing the ability of the self-regulatory organizations to fulfill their oversight responsibilities.

Separately, the CFTC contemplates individual Globex terminals printing out paper confirmations of all trades. The reason for recording on paper rather than some other medium is that paper records are easier for market auditors to examine.[12]

[10]Interpretative Ruling, 55 Fed. Reg. 17932 (1990).
[11]17 C.F.R. §§131, 151 (1989).
[12]*See* §6.5.

§11.4.4 Regulation of Transportation Carriers

For certain railroads, Interstate Commerce Commission regulations prescribe the keeping of extensive transaction and financial records, including books of account and checks, receipts, vouchers, records, and memoranda in support thereof.[13] These railroads and certain other carriers, such as motor and water carriers, must retain specified records for prescribed periods, and under conditions that protect the records from fires, floods, and deleterious climate.[14] The regulations allow the retention of records on computer media such as tapes and disks, but on the conditions that

> [e]ach machine-readable form of media shall be accompanied by a statement clearly indicating the type of data included in the media. This statement shall be executed by a person having personal knowledge of the facts contained in the records. The records shall be indexed and retained in such a manner as will render them readily accessible. The company shall have facilities available to locate, identify and reproduce legible paper copies of the records.[15]

Query whether anyone has "personal knowledge" of the information in purely automated electronic (such as EDI) transaction records. Perhaps it would be more realistic to require the execution of a statement that the records accurately reflect transactions sent and received at a certain place during a stated period. As electronic messages become more the norm, regulations such as these may need clarification. Depending on the potential for abuse, requirements for special recordkeeping controls, such as the segregation of duties, may be warranted.

[13] 49 C.F.R. pt. 1201, subpart A, General Instruction 1-3 (1989).
[14] 49 C.F.R. §1220.0 et seq. (1989).
[15] 49 C.F.R. §1220.3 (1989).

§11.4.5 Customs Regulations

The federal Tariff Act of 1930, which governs customs declarations for the import and export of merchandise, requires importers to retain extensive records.[16] The U.S. Customs Service has proposed that Congress amend the Tariff Act, which now speaks in terms of "documents," to better accommodate electronic business practices and to clarify the law's application to computer data. Customs may need also to revise its regulations pertaining to record retention and control to make them more precise.[17] As they stand now, these regulations simply and inflexibly require the retention of all relevant computer media and programs for five years. They do not seem to contemplate the reuse of temporary media or the controlled transfer of data from one medium to another.

§11.5 OVERVIEW OF REQUIREMENTS FOR PUBLIC ADMINISTRATORS

In principle, the need for government entities to keep records and maintain control of transaction systems is as great as for commercial firms. Often recordkeeping and control requirements for public organizations are explicitly set forth in constitutions, charters, statutes, and regulations. The Federal Manager's Financial Integrity Act of 1982, for example, directs the head of each executive agency to maintain a system of accounting and internal control so as to permit adequate financial disclosure of the agency's activities and proper management of the agency's assets.[1] In addition, an-

[16] 19 U.S.C. §1508 (1988).
[17] *See* 19 C.F.R. §162.0 et seq. (1990).
§11.5 [1] 31 U.S.C. §3512 (1988).

other statute states, "The head of each Federal agency shall make and preserve records containing adequate and proper documentation of the . . . essential transactions of the agency and designed to furnish the information necessary to protect the legal and financial rights of the Government. . . ."[2] The California Financial Integrity and State Manager's Accountability Act of 1983[3] exemplifies a state statute setting similar recordkeeping and control objectives. Installation of electronic trading systems will raise the same need for reassessment of recordkeeping and control practices for government entities as it raises for commercial firms.

The National Archives and Records Administration (NARA) has developed state-of-the-art regulations on electronic records management by federal agencies.[4] The regulations give rather detailed guidelines for creating, using, preserving, and disposing of electronic records. They contemplate each agency developing thorough and systematic programs for the training of EDP users, the documentation of systems, the labeling of records, the safeguarding of data, and the scheduled destruction of records or the delivery of records to the NARA for permanent retention.

One federal initiative in this area may influence practices in the private sector. The Computer Security Act of 1987 appoints the National Institute of Standards and Technology to set security standards and guidelines for federal government computers. The standards' purposes will be to control the loss, alteration, or disclosure of data and the misuse of systems.[5] Because the federal government is the world's largest user of computers, these standards and guidelines could influence private-sector computer design and security practices. Computer vendors will have to make products for the

[2]44 U.S.C. §3101 (1988).
[3]Cal. Govt. Code §13400-13407 (West Supp. 1990).
[4]36 C.F.R. pt. 1234, *as revised by* 55 Fed. Reg. 19216 (1990).
[5]15 U.S.C. §278g-3 (1988).

government that conform to the standards, so they are likely to make all their products conform.

The Computer Security Act also requires each federal agency to establish a plan for the security and privacy of its computer systems. The level of security for each system need not be excessive; it need only be "commensurate with the risk and magnitude of the harm resulting from the loss, misuse, or unauthorized access to or modification of the information contained in such system."[6]

[6] 40 U.S.C. §759 note (1988).

Chapter 12

Tax Recordkeeping

§12.1 INTRODUCTION

Corporate tax laws require taxpayers to retain financial records. Government auditors review them to confirm income, deductions and other items reported on tax returns.

> [A federal corporate income tax] audit normally starts with the tax return and verifies, on a selective basis, the figures

> which are used to determine the tax liability. This process usually involves the general ledger, accounts receivable, accounts payable, fixed asset and similar types of accounting records. The fundamental procedure is to trace the amounts on the tax return back through the accounting records to the source documents, continuously checking accounting techniques and classifications for compliance with the [Internal Revenue] Code.[1]

Historically, "source documents," such as invoices, checks, and check stubs, were written on paper. What types of records do (or should) the laws require for paperless source documents?

As explained in Chapters 5 and 6, paper documents exchanged between firms afford auditors a trusted and convenient form of evidence and control. An auditor knows that some small percentage of these documents may be fake, but he can usually assume that—absent conspicuous clues to the contrary—most documents are genuine. Wholesale forgery of a large, assorted heap of documents is very difficult.

Also, in a major criminal investigation, paper's forensic qualities can reveal whether particular documents have been fabricated. In one exemplary case, the Internal Revenue Service's (the IRS or the Service) criminal forensics laboratory scientifically proved that several notebooks of documents were forged. On their face the documents indicated, and the taxpayer claimed, that they were made in 1978 and 1979. But a chemical analysis coupled with a review of ink manufacturer records disclosed that the ink on the documents was not marketed until a year or so later.

Nevertheless, paper is an imperfect means of control. Expert document examination is very expensive and time consuming. An informed IRS employee "acknowledges that most of what he calls mom-and-pop cases are handled in the

§12.1 [1]Roberts, Working with the IRS, Tax Adviser 366, 368 (June 1971).

field without the benefit of world-class expertise."[2] Electronic methods can provide recordkeeping and control that equals or exceeds paper methods.[3]

§12.2 FEDERAL INCOME TAX RECORDS GENERALLY

Section 6001 of the Internal Revenue Code of 1986 (the Code) obliges income taxpayers to keep such records and comply with such regulations as the federal tax authorities deem necessary to show whether the taxpayer is liable for tax. Treasury regulations elaborate:

> ***§1.6001-1(a)*** generally mandates that the taxpayer "keep such permanent books of account or records . . . as are sufficient to establish the amount of gross income [or] deductions" of the taxpayer.
>
> ***§1.6001-1(d):*** "The [IRS] district director may require any person, by notice served upon him, to make such returns, render such statements, or keep such specific records as will enable the district director to determine whether or not such person is liable for [the applicable] tax."
>
> ***§1.6001-1(e):*** "The books or records required by this section shall be kept at all times available for inspection . . . and shall be retained so long as the contents thereof may become material in the administration of any internal revenue law."[1]

[2]Hershey, Tax Sleuths Turn to Technology, N.Y. Times, Mar. 28, 1990, at C1, col. 3 (natl. ed.).

[3]*See* Chapters 5 & 6.

§12.2 [1]For policy reasons, and by custom, many tax advisors recommend (subject to many exceptions) that tax records be kept for 7 years, although no particular regulation specifies that time period. *See* D. Skupsky, Recordkeeping Requirements 69 (1988).

Federal income tax laws generally do not impose a particular system of accounting on taxpayers.

> It is recognized that no uniform method of accounting can be prescribed for all taxpayers. Each taxpayer shall adopt such forms and systems as are, in his judgment, best suited for his needs. However, no method of accounting is acceptable unless, in the opinion of the [IRS] Commissioner, it clearly reflects income. . . . Each taxpayer . . . must maintain such accounting records as will enable him to file a correct [tax] return.[2]

Generally speaking, federal income tax regulations are understood to require taxpayer retention of:

1. Permanent books of account such as journals and ledgers.
2. Permanent records such as receipts, invoices, check stubs and the like.
3. Permanent records and other documents which substantiate a particular type of transaction and which are required to be kept by [specific] Regulation or Ruling.[3]

None of the foregoing, however, suggests taxpayers must use paper documents or keep paper records.

Generally, the IRS may not command a taxpayer to make records retroactively. In *United States v. Mobil Corp.*[4] the Service sought to compel a corporate employer to create computer records setting forth payroll data in a particular format that was convenient to employment tax auditors. The employer refused, stating it would give the auditors the data only in the form in which it then existed: on paper forms.

[2]Treas. Reg. §1.446-1.

[3]R. Fishman, Intentional Destruction of Tax Workpapers: An Analysis of a Relatively Uncharted Area, J. Taxn. 214, 216 (Apr. 1983).

[4]499 F. Supp. 479 (N.D. Tx. 1980).

(It is unclear how much of this information was in the employer's computer system. Apparently, that which was computerized was not in the format the IRS requested.) Published IRS rules had required that this information be kept, but had not specified any particular form. The court held the employer "cannot be required to create new records or to alter the form of existing records to suit the government's convenience."[5] Yet the court explained, "There can be little doubt of the [IRS's] authority to require a taxpayer, on a prospective basis, to maintain annualized records, and perhaps even to maintain them in the form of magnetic tape, if [the IRS] deems such records necessary to show the extent of the taxpayer's liability."[6]

§12.3 FEDERAL PENALTIES FOR INADEQUATE RECORDS

Federal law can penalize taxpayers for maintaining inadequate records of electronic transactions. First, the IRS may disregard assertions made on the taxpayer's return and increase the taxpayer's liability accordingly. For example, the Service may disallow deductions for unsubstantiated business expenses, such as payments of invoices. The taxpayer bears the burden of proving the items asserted on the tax return.[1] In *Financial Principles Co. v. Commissioner*[2] the IRS successfully disallowed business expenses for which the taxpayer lacked receipts, invoices, and other documentation.

[5]*Id.* at 482.

[6]*Id. See also* United States v. Davey, 543 F.2d 996 (2d Cir. 1976) (IRS may demand access to taxpayer computer records and need not reimburse taxpayer expenses).

§12.3 [1]Financial Principles Co. v. Commissioner, 58 T.C.M. (CCH) 137 (1989).

[2]*Id.*

Although the taxpayer had a loose collection of some documents, it could not show what they related to or that the expenses shown thereon had in fact been paid.

In *Bard v. Commissioner*[3] the tax court sustained an IRS disallowance of deductions for the costs of certain goods sold. The taxpayer had bought and sold precious metals in cash transactions. Some purchase transactions were through the mail, and these were rather well documented with invoices or sales receipts and other records. Other purchase transactions were conducted in person, and these were supported by little more than a fragmentary telephone log kept in a looseleaf notebook, without numbered pages. It was as to the latter group of purchases that the IRS had disallowed deductions. The telephone log was simply unreliable evidence for substantiating the taxpayer's claims.

A taxpayer is liable for a penalty equal to 5 percent of the underpayment of tax resulting from her negligence (or disregard of rules or regulations) in recordkeeping.[4] In *Yee v. Commissioner*[5] the taxpayer's poor

> recordkeeping, reporting and bookkeeping methods, coupled with the substantial amount of unsubstantiated and inappropriately claimed deductions, clearly warrant[ed] the application of an additional tax for negligence or intentional disregard of the rules and regulations.[6]

Imposition of the negligence penalty depends on the circumstance. The court in *Bard,* above, upheld a negligence penalty for failure to substantiate recorded items, whereas in *Robinson v. Commissioner*[7] the court refused a negligence penalty

[3]60 T.C.M. (CCH) 485 (1990).

[4]I.R.C. §6653(a)(1). *See* §13.2.2 for a discussion of civil and criminal penalties for fraudulent tax recordkeeping.

[5]50 T.C.M. (CCH) 551 (1985).

[6]*Id.* at 555.

[7]51 T.C. 520 (1968).

where the taxpayer kept regular books of account but failed to keep bills and receipts to substantiate the books.

Regarding computer records, the Service has held that a taxpayer may incur a negligence penalty (and perhaps even criminal liability) if it fails to keep machine-sensible (i.e., computer-readable) records required by Revenue Ruling 71-20, which is discussed in the following Section.[8]

Another consequence of poor bookkeeping is that the IRS may disregard the taxpayer's method of accounting and recompute tax using a different method.

> If the taxpayer does not regularly employ a method of accounting which clearly reflects his income, the computation of taxable income shall be made in a manner which, in the opinion of the Commissioner, does clearly reflect income.[9]

This applies not to a mere failure to keep documents (for supporting data) that substantiate entries in accounting ledgers and journals, as was the case in *Bard* and *Robinson.* It applies instead to a failure to keep the accounting books themselves properly.[10]

§12.4 IRS GUIDELINES FOR COMPUTER RECORDS

§12.4.1 Revenue Ruling 71-20 and Revenue Procedure 86-19

To aid business taxpayers in their record making and to facilitate later IRS audit, the IRS has issued guidelines for

[8]Rev. Rul. 81-205, 1981-2 C.B. 225.

[9]Treas. Reg. §1.446-1(b)(1).

[10]Bard v. Commissioner, 60 T.C.M. (CCH) 485, at 497, n.16 (1990).

accounting records created by automated data processing (ADP) equipment. First, Revenue Ruling 71-20,[1] holds:

> [P]unched cards, magnetic tapes, disks, and other machine-sensible [i.e., computer-readable] data media used for recording, consolidating, and summarizing accounting transactions and records within a taxpayer's automatic data processing system are records within the meaning of section 6001 of the Code and section 1.6001-1 of the regulations and are required to be retained so long as the contents may become material in the administration of any internal revenue law.

This sweeping statement seems to mandate the keeping of all computer-readable media, without change, on which any tax-related data are ever stored for any length of time. Under a literal reading, if an accounting transaction is written to a hard disk embedded within a computer, the taxpayer must keep the hard disk and refrain from writing over the tax data on it. The taxpayer may not keep instead a copy on a tape. Still, the ruling seeks to avoid at least some redundant data storage. Speaking in terms of data processing technology prevalent in the late 1960s, the ruling provides:

> However, where punched cards are used merely as a means of input to the system and the information is duplicated on magnetic tapes, disks, or other [computer-readable] records, such punched cards need not be retained.

The reason the IRS desires the retention of computer-readable records is that they permit the IRS, using the taxpayer's computer, to conduct an automated audit.

In practice, Rev. Rul. 71-20's requirements are not always enforced literally. For example, one expert believes that a smaller corporate taxpayer that uses an independent computer service bureau to process its accounting records need

§12.4 [1]1971-1 C.B. 392.

not keep the bureau's computer media. The IRS would consider it satisfactory for the taxpayer to keep paper printouts of the records.[2]

In 1986, the Service issued Revenue Procedure 86-19,[3] which applies to taxpayers with assets of $10 million or more. It places substantial requirements on the design, documentation, and use of ADP accounting systems. Among the key provisions are:

1. "All machine-sensible [i.e., computer-readable] records must be retained by the taxpayer. The retained records must be in a retrievable format that provides the information necessary to determine the correct tax liability."
2. "Documentation that provides a complete description of the ADP portion of the accounting system and those files that feed into the accounting system must be retained. The statements and illustrations as to the scope of operations should be sufficiently detailed to indicate: (a) the application being performed, (b) the procedures employed in each application, and (c) the controls used to insure accurate and reliable processing. The following specific documentation for all files must also be retained:

   (1) record formats (including the meaning of all 'codes' used to represent information);
   (2) flowcharts (system and program);
   (3) label descriptions;
   (4) source program listings of programs that created the files retained; and
   (5) detailed charts of accounts (for specific periods)."

[2]Roberts, Working with the IRS, Tax Adviser 366, 368 (June 1971).
[3]1986-1 C.B. 558.

3. "Audit trails should be designed to insure that details underlying the summary accounting data, such as invoices and vouchers, may be easily identified and made available to the Service upon request."
4. "All retained records must be clearly labeled and stored in a secure environment."
5. "The taxpayer must have the capability to access the retained records at the time of a Service examination. When the data processing system that created the records is being replaced by a system in which the records would not be compatible, the taxpayer must convert them to a compatible system."
6. "The use of Data Base Management Systems . . . necessitates the implementation by the taxpayer of appropriate procedures to ensure that required records and other needed documentation are retained to comply with this revenue procedure. A taxpayer is in compliance if it creates, for Service use, a sequential file(s) that contains all detail transactions necessary to create an audit trail to trace back to the underlying source documents. . . . This process should be reviewed by the Service prior to creation."

Implicit here is probably a requirement that the taxpayer be able to print from its computer records.[4]

Together, the goals of Rev. Rul. 71-20 and Rev. Proc. 86-19 are to compel the preservation of all computer-readable records and to enable the IRS to audit ledgers and journals with automated techniques.[5]

[4]Roberts, Working with the IRS, Tax Adviser 366, 367 (June 1971).

[5]In an automated audit, an IRS agent might use the taxpayer's computer to run statistical and other analyses of the taxpayer's computer-readable records.

§12.4.2 Record Retention Reviews

To reduce its volume of stored data, and to confirm how best to keep records for its particular situation, the taxpayer may ask its local IRS District Director for a record retention review (RRR) of its data system.[6] An IRS computer audit specialist would then examine the taxpayer's system to pinpoint those data records most important to the Service. The Service and the taxpayer would negotiate and enter an agreement limiting, and tailoring the procedures for, data retention. Because RRRs can streamline later IRS audits, the Service often conducts reviews on its own initiative.

When it first issued Rev. Rul. 71-20, the Service gave its revenue agents administrative guidelines for conducting RRRs and negotiating retention agreements. Normally, two types of records are more important under the guidelines:

- Original transaction records of data essential to the maintenance and verification of the amounts shown in the general ledger accounts. In other words, the details of the transactions which are summarized into account totals for the year. The agent needs to be able to analyze the account total into its individual transactions and to be able to trace these transactions back to the source documents.
- Other data, including internal transactions, which affect federal tax liability and facilitate the substantiation of the figures on the tax return.

Magnetic tapes or other storage media containing data used to produce various management reports are normally of no interest to the tax auditor, even if accounting data are present. Tapes containing non-accounting data, such as those which are used for scheduling and control activities, would not be needed by the auditor. Also, there would be no need to retain

[6]Harper & Hoffman, EDP Records Retention—IRS Requirements, *in* Guide to Records Retention 561 (W. A. Hancock ed. 1988).

the intermediate processing tapes used to update and maintain files.[7]

One matter examined in an RRR is the taxpayer's internal control system. The Record Retention and Evaluation Guidelines in the IRS's Computer Audit Specialist Handbook advise the agent:

> The taxpayer's internal controls should be capable of ensuring that records are retained in spite of changes that may occur in tax department or data processing department personnel, to the computerized accounting system, or to the computer files management system. . . . Serious deficiencies detected in the taxpayer's system of internal controls must be discussed with the taxpayer. If the taxpayer fails to take corrective action within a reasonable period of time, consideration should be given to issuing a District Director's notification letter [which warns the taxpayer that the IRS may seek civil or criminal penalties if the taxpayer fails to keep required records].[8]

§12.4.3 Practical Assessment

These are some common taxpayer comments about Rev. Rul. 71-20 and Rev. Proc. 86-19 (apart from the special problems that paperless messages raise):

1. It is impractical for taxpayers to keep all computer-readable media on which relevant data may have been stored at one time or another. The only relief for the taxpayer is to undergo an RRR. But the proliferation of computers is making it impractical for

[7]Roberts, Working with the IRS, Tax Adviser 176, 179 (Mar. 1971).

[8]Internal Revenue Manual—Audit, Record Retention and Evaluation Guidelines *in* Computer Audit Specialist Handbook ¶522 (1988).

the Service to conduct an RRR of all computerized accounting systems.

2. Computer systems turn over rapidly, and taxpayers who have created data with old systems must either convert the data or store the old systems along with the data so the data can be retrieved. The retention of outdated hardware and software can be expensive.
3. Many taxpayers use off-the-shelf software from independent developers. These taxpayers seldom have source code listings for this software, even though Rev. Proc. 86-19 requires their retention.
4. Many software packages are in a constant state of revision. Making and keeping documentation for each version is expensive and burdensome.
5. It is unclear what rules apply to companies with less than $10 million in assets.

As for firm-to-firm electronic messages such as EDI, Rev. Rul. 71-20 and Rev. Proc. 86-19 were not drafted with them in mind. Instead, the drafters envisioned this: Companies transacting day-to-day business would create and exchange paper documents such as invoices and check stubs. Each company would keyboard the data therefrom into its computerized accounting books. It would also store each original or source document to substantiate those books.

Such source documents were the bedrock on which the calculation of tax liability stood. Although not impossible to forge, they were a control against fraud. Often, the source documents each taxpayer kept were created by other firms. The IRS guidelines aimed to ensure there were adequate records and audit trails tracing transactions from the taxpayer's return, back through the automated accounting system to the paper source documents.

Interfirm electronic messages eliminate the paper control. So it is uncertain whether, and if so how, Rev. Rul. 71-20 and Rev. Proc. 86-19 apply to the interenterprise portion of computer systems.[9] Recognizing the issue, the IRS is devising guidelines for the keeping of EDI (and perhaps other electronic message) records. As of this writing, the best guess as to when these will be issued is late 1991. The issues involved in formulating such guidelines are considered in Section 12.7 below.

Meanwhile, what does the taxpayer using EDI do? She must refer to the fundamental law. Treasury Regulation §1.6001-1(a) directs each taxpayer to "keep such . . . records . . . as are sufficient to establish the amount of gross income [or] deductions. . . ." Treasury Regulation §1.446-1 requires the taxpayer to keep "such accounting records as will enable [her] to file a correct [tax] return." Moreover, the taxpayer bears the burden of proof concerning matters she declares on her tax return.

If a taxpayer, such as the metal trader in *Bard* above,[10] cannot substantiate the claims she makes on her return, the IRS may disregard them. A simple, uncontrolled log of electronic messages may be incapable of satisfying the taxpayer's burden of proof. The log would be too easy to fabricate, even easier than a manual, paper log because it can easily be falsified at the time of creation and altered at any time thereafter.

The solution seems to be that the taxpayer should keep complete, controlled logs of electronic messages that have tax relevance. Chapters 5 and 6 and Appendix B suggest many control devices—independent recordkeepers, timestamps, logging routines, WORM media, and control audits by independent private auditors—for making credible records. Properly controlled logs can be credible and can substantiate the taxpayer's accounting books.

The tax law imposes no single regime for making records

[9]*See* B. Wright, EDI and American Law: A Practical Guide 65-66 (1989) for an analysis of the questions that would arise if Rev. Rul. 71-20 and Rev. Proc. 86-19 were applied literally to EDI.

[10]*See* §12.3.

reliable; it is the taxpayer's responsibility to devise and implement an effective scheme. A rational, documented, and consistently implemented scheme, however, will be easier for the taxpayer to defend.

A taxpayer designing recordkeeping methods will have questions that go beyond just control.[11] The local IRS District Director may be able to help.

§12.5 STATE TAX REGULATIONS

Many state income tax recordkeeping rules follow their federal counterparts. States may, however, be slow in issuing regulations that reflect the latest federal guidelines, such as Rev. Proc. 86-19.[1]

Recordkeeping laws for state sales and use taxes can be very general in describing electronic records. The Texas Sales and Use Tax Rules, for example, require the retention of accurate records "in such form as may readily be examined by" an auditor. Concerning computer records, the Rules simply add, "Records may be written, kept on microfilm or stored on data processing equipment."[2] There is no guidance on how they should be maintained or controlled. Logically, however, unsuitable system design and weak controls over electronic transaction records could disrupt a tax audit. Among the documents of interest to a sales tax auditor are invoices and certificates of sales tax exemption.[3] In addition,

[11]*See* §12.7.

§12.5 [1]D. Skupsky, Recordkeeping Requirements 173 (1988).

[2]Tex. Sales and Use Tax Rule 3.281, Tex. Tax Rep. (CCH) ¶66-000.

[3]Sales tax laws levy a tax on some sales transactions, but they exempt others, such as certain purchases for resale. For a transaction to be exempt, the laws often require the seller to obtain from the buyer a certificate of exemption. In Australia, Sales Tax Regulation 16 requires that the "certificate . . . be quoted in writing in accordance with" a specified form.

"[t]he typical [state tax] audit program includes verification of the [taxpayer's] accounting systems for accuracy, internal controls, and flow of documentation."[4]

The New York stock transfer tax regulations illustrate that state rules can be vague and confusing when they do refer to electronic messages. New York taxes the transfer of corporate stock shares. To permit audit of such transactions, New York Tax Regulation §446.1(c) requires stock brokers to "keep all memoranda including telegrams, teletypes and other communications relating to the transfer of shares or certificates. . . ." However, if a certificate is transferred via electronic or computer communication, the broker need not keep the relevant computer tape or disk, so long as he keeps a "paper" copy or record of the communication.[5]

The regulation implies that the broker may in the alternative elect to keep the computer tape or disk on which data from the communication were stored, but it does not say how. Presumably, the broker would also have to retain the hardware and software necessary to read the computer media. In addition, an electronic message is likely to be recorded on several tapes or disks in the course of its com-

---

The form contemplates the buyer signing the form when the certificate is quoted. Unsure whether coded electronic messages can satisfy Regulation 16, Australian firms asked the Commissioner of Taxation for guidance. By letter dated February 1, 1990, D. J. King, acting on behalf of the First Assistant Commissioner of Sales Tax, responded to Mr. L. Chan, Chairman of the EDI Council of Australia Authentication Working Party. The letter states that the law must be amended to clarify that certificates may be quoted electronically, and the Commissioner of Taxation is examining how the law should be amended. In the meantime, the letter states, a taxpayer using EDI may quote its certificate electronically, provided it is apparent in each electronic message that the certificate is being quoted. Problems similar to this are today arising under sales tax laws of the United States.

[4]K. Leong, Sales and Use Tax Audit Techniques and Procedures Employed for Retailers, 3 J. State Taxn. 129, 132 (Summer 1984).

[5]N.Y. Stock Transfer Tax Reg. §446.1(d), N.Y. Tax Rep. (CCH) ¶57-820.

munication. Logically, a broker would retain just one electronic record of each transaction, but the regulation does not say this is permissible. Rather, it suggests that if the broker elects to keep computer records, he must keep all tapes and disks on which a transaction ever resided. This motivates the broker just to print the transactions onto paper.

If a broker keeps paper memoranda and communications, he must keep the original documents and may not transfer these to microfilm until after the tax authorities have examined the relevant transactions and determined the original paper is no longer needed.[6] Apparently this curbs fraud. The same logic would say the regulations must require control over the process by which the broker creates paper or electronic records of computer transactions, but the regulations are silent on computer control.

§12.6 EUROPEAN EXPERIENCE WITH EDI RECORDS

The tax recordkeeping experience in other countries is instructive. Under its Trade Electronic Data Interchange Systems (TEDIS) program, the Commission of the European Communities sponsored a general study of legal obstacles to EDI in member states. The resulting report[1] revealed that in some countries accounting documents such as invoices must be on paper.

[6]N.Y. Stock Transfer Tax Reg. §446.3, N.Y. Tax Rep. (CCH) ¶57-822.

§12.6 [1]The report, originally published in French, is titled: TEDIS—Situation juridique des Estats membres au regard du transfert électronique de données (1989). Some of the report is summarized in United Nations Commission on International Trade Law, Electronic Data Interchange, U.N. GAOR, U.N. Doc. A/CN.9/333 (May 18, 1990), at 6-11, which is the source of the information in the text paragraph accompanying this footnote.

> For example, in Danish law, no general rule determines the form of an invoice. Therefore, an invoice can be validly transmitted by electronic means. However, the data that is supposed to be evidenced by the invoice can be taken into account, according to the rules on accounting and tax, only if a paper original or a certified copy of the paper original is kept.[2]

In other countries, such as Luxembourg and Belgium, special legislation or administrative actions now permit the acceptance of electronic invoices for tax and accounting purposes. In Italy, companies may use electronic tax and accounting documents in lieu of paper, provided appropriate government authorities specifically agree in advance.

In the United Kingdom (U.K.), the Computer and Audit Branch of HM Customs and Excise has promulgated, for EDI and similar electronic systems, special value-added-tax (VAT) regulations titled Computer Data Interchange, Electronic Mail and Direct Transmission Systems: The Requirements Regarding Computer Data Interchange of Invoice for Value Added Tax Purposes. To satisfy VAT law, products sellers in the U.K. must issue invoices, which buyers must retain for government audit.

If an invoice is electronic, the EDI VAT regulations require certain controls. First, before two firms use electronic invoices, they must notify the local VAT office. Then they must pilot test the system, allowing government observation. Thereafter, the firms must give the VAT office at least 30 days' advance notice before changing the system substantially.

For each invoice message, each firm must keep a *paper* audit log showing the sender and receiver, specified control data, and certain tax calculations. To confirm accuracy, the

[2]United Nations Commission on International Trade Law, Electronic Data Interchange, U.N. GAOR, U.N. Doc. A/CN.9/333 (May 18, 1990), at 11.

invoice recipient must repeat some of the tax calculations and print the results on the recipient's log. The firms must label each invoice with a unique serial number, and the recipient must check the number to guard against repeated messages.

Besides the audit log, each firm must store—on paper, computer media, or microfilm—the full contents of invoice messages. Normally, the messages must state each firm's full name and address and a complete description of the products covered. The firms may, however, communicate in codes (as is usually done with EDI) if the authorities consent in advance and the firms document the codes' meanings.

§12.7 ISSUES ON THE HORIZON

Authorities should explain to taxpayers how to record and control paperless transactions. In the U.K., HM Customs and Excise has done this (even though its paper log requirement seems cumbersome and rigid).

Authorities could simply declare the taxpayer has the burden of proving that its records are true and leave it to the taxpayer to devise its own controls. But that approach serves neither the taxpayer nor the government. Government guidance would introduce standardization in record control. That would save taxpayers time and effort and minimize their risk as they design systems, and would make audits quicker and less expensive for the government.

Rather than dictating a single control regime, however, the government may be wiser to recommend a series of different possibilities. For federal corporate income tax, the IRS might, for example, describe alternative "safe harbors." If a taxpayer implements the controls specified for a safe harbor, her records would be presumed credible. The taxpayer would remain responsible for record veracity, but satisfaction of a safe harbor would decrease the auditor's need to examine record credibility.

The government should take care not to stifle innovation, however. Multiple alternative safe harbors would be desirable, and no safe harbor should be mandatory.

Other questions that record-retention guideline drafters should consider include the following:

1. What system documentation and audit trails, if any, must the taxpayer keep for the communication system or network that links it and its trading partners? Much of this system is likely to be outside the taxpayer's control.
2. Must taxpayers adhere to message standards, such as public EDI standards (e.g., ANSI X12)? Auditing would be far easier if EDI users uniformly observed the same standards. But they do not. In practice, many (maybe most) EDI users modify EDI standards to suit their particular needs. Many others make their own standards.
3. Must taxpayers keep computer-readable logs of all electronic transactions? Computer-readable records could speed up the auditing process. Yet for systems with lower transaction volumes, the retention of paper-printout logs would be far less expensive than the retention of computer-readable logs.
4. At which stage in the communication process should logs be made? In EDI, the recipient might log a message (1) while in the possession of the recipient's network, (2) when the recipient takes possession of it, (3) after the recipient translates it out of EDI format, and into some other format, or (4) after the essence of the message is loaded into a large database.
5. How can uniform guidelines accommodate the rich diversity of electronic systems (EDI, e-mail, video-

tex, hybrids)? Many systems are already in place, and inventors are developing more.

Another observation is pertinent. The pace of economic activity is accelerating, and computer use is one cause.[1] Modern businesses are formed, bought, sold, reorganized, broken up, and dissolved more rapidly than their predecessors. Within companies, employees, managers, products, and computer systems turn over more swiftly. All this hampers tax audits conducted several years after transactions occur. If tax authorities would shorten audit cycles and otherwise enable taxpayers to discard records sooner, recordkeeping and audit costs would drop and audit quality would rise. Taxpayers may be willing to incur special costs upfront so they can destroy records earlier.

§12.7 [1]*See* A. Toffler, Powershift 233-238 (1990).

Chapter 13

Electronic Fraud

§13.1 INTRODUCTION

The border between liability for violations of laws covered in Chapters 11 and 12 and for fraud is indistinct. Fraud is a generic term embracing many types of deception or dishonesty for which civil or criminal liability may attach. It generally involves some intentional wrongdoing. A civil plaintiff realizes several advantages, such as the potential right to punitive damages, in an action for fraud compared with one for simple negligence, breach of contract, or breach of an agent's duty.

In many respects, the laws that will govern intentional defaults in recordkeeping and control in the electronic world are the same as those that have applied in the paper world. Thus, much of this chapter discusses cases involving manual recordkeeping and control systems. The lessons from those cases should apply by analogy to electronic systems. When companies shift from manual to automated systems, some controls can be lost, and new opportunities for fraud can open. These companies should pay special attention to controls. They must also ensure that systems are designed to properly and completely record electronic transactions, such as payments, in the companies' accounting books.

Data processing history is rich with legends of corporate insiders fraudulently falsifying computer records and circumventing controls. In one, an accountant for a fruit and vegetable shipping company took more than $1 million over six years. He fed into the company's computer system punch cards reflecting nonexistent purchase orders and receipts. These raised the expense and inventory accounts in the company's records. He then made the extra expenses payable to a dummy company he had formed.[1]

The infamous Equity Funding fraud involved the enormous overstatement of the net income and assets of a life insurance/financial services firm. Although the fraud derived in part from the preparation and recording of entries in accounting books that could have been done manually, computer processing made the scheme much easier. The company's books listed some 97,000 insurance policies in force, but of those, 56,000 existed only as phony data in the computer system. Special work by a programmer facilitated the fast and efficient recording and camouflaging of the false data in all the necessary journals, ledgers, and files. Whenever auditors reviewing computer printouts would ask for

§13.1 [1]Allen, Embezzler's Guide to the Computer, Harv. Bus. Rev. 79, 82 (July-Aug. 1975).

backup documentation (contracts and so forth) on a few selected policies, the company would simply forge it.[2]

Direct evidence of any particular fraud or theft may be difficult to obtain. The maintenance of good financial records and controls can deter fraud, and thus their absence can raise suspicions. As this chapter explains, civil or criminal actions for fraud can stand largely on the failure to maintain, or the destruction of, proper records or the thwarting of controls.

One practical lesson for the electronic message user is that rationally and consistently developed, documented, and implemented records management policies can quell potential suspicions. Electronic data can easily be altered and is often expected to be. Data can be recorded in any of many different forms with varying degrees of completeness. Without explicit policies, an observer could be confused whether the wrong intent motivated the omission, alteration, or destruction of any particular record.

Some EDI operations change messages after transmission, because, for example, a sender may have used the wrong product price or part number. To preclude an argument that this practice constitutes the unlawful alteration of documents, it should be subjected to control. Internal guidelines should prescribe when changes may be made, who may authorize them and which changes are permissible. Ideally, a record would show what a message originally stated and what it stated after modification. Such redundant recordkeeping could be prohibitively expensive, however.

[2]American Institute of Certified Public Accountants, Report of the Special Comm. on Equity Funding (1975); R. Soble & R. Dallos, The Impossible Dream: The Equity Funding Story: The Fraud of the Century 133-142 (1975).

§13.2 DIRECT LIABILITY

§13.2.1 Common Law

A false record, whether manual or electronic, is a misrepresentation. The most fundamental cause of action against the creator of a false electronic record would be the common law tort of deceit. Section 525 of the Restatement (Second) of Torts provides:

> One who fraudulently makes a misrepresentation of fact, opinion, intention or law for the purpose of inducing another to act or to refrain from action in reliance upon it, is subject to liability to the other in deceit for pecuniary loss caused to him by his justifiable reliance upon the misrepresentation.

Section 526 adds:

> A misrepresentation is fraudulent if the maker (a) knows or believes that the matter is not as he represents it to be, (b) does not have the confidence in the accuracy of his representation that he states or implies, or (c) knows that he does not have the basis for his representation that he states or implies.

An action in deceit might, for example, lie in favor of an investor or creditor who relies on false purchase order records in committing funds to a company. Consider *Warner Brothers Pictures Distribution Corp. v. Endicott Circuit, Inc.,*[1] in which a motion picture theater company had agreed to pay a distributor based on box-office receipts. The distributor alleged the theater company understated its receipts and falsified its books and records of receipts. The court held

§13.2 [1]55 N.Y.S.2d 300 (Sup. Ct.), *aff'd,* 269 A.D. 934, 58 N.Y.S.2d 344 (1945).

the distributor had stated a cause of action for fraud for which the theater company could be liable.

Another common law action would apply against agents who intentionally keep spurious electronic records of assets entrusted to them.[2] Deficient records, even though not obviously false, can themselves be sufficient evidence of fraud to assess an agent with liability. In *Backus v. Finkelstein,*[3] a suit by minority shareholders against controlling officers and shareholders of a corporation, the court remarked:

> The persistent failure to keep accurate books of account, and to preserve important records, alone places defendants in an almost hopeless position. In dealing with the property and rights of others, the necessity for keeping such accounts and of preserving such records is unqualified. . . . The almost necessary presumption is that the purpose of a failure in this respect has been to cover up or conceal what the records accurately kept would disclose.

In this case, the minority shareholders alleged that, through poor manual recordkeeping practices, the managing officers concealed the corporation's true financial status while they purchased the minority shares at a low price. The court rescinded the purchases.

The wrongful ruin of electronic records can also be a source of liability. In *Anheuser-Busch Brewing Association v. Green*[4] the court held officers personally liable to a corporate creditor for the willful destruction of manual corporate books and records. The creditor, possessing a judgment against the corporation, which was defunct, had tried to press a claim against the shareholders. The court found the officers had destroyed shareholder records with a view to hampering the creditor.

[2] *See* §11.2.1.
[3] 23 F.2d 357, 364 (D. Minn. 1927).
[4] 90 Cal. App. 453, 265 P. 1025 (1928).

§13.2.2 Tax Law

Tax authorities are forever vigilant for fraudulent[5] recordkeeping. The lack of clear guidelines for tax recordkeeping of electronic transactions, or even long-standing practices,[6] raises the possibility that a taxpayer's recordkeeping practices could be misconstrued. A taxpayer's manner of keeping books and his practices for the retention, alteration, or destruction of records can be relevant to an examination for fraud.[7] Tax fraud is a matter of wrongful intent—a deliberate purpose to conceal or cheat—and poor records can reveal such an intent.[8] Erroneous recordkeeping does not necessarily constitute fraud,[9] however, and books and recording practices are only one factor to be considered in evaluating an allegation of fraud.[10]

Korecky v. Commissioner[11] concerned a taxpayer who operated several small businesses, some wholesale and some retail. He kept two manual forms of income data: unnumbered wholesale sales invoices and monthly summaries of retail sales. He did not keep retail sales register tapes. Observing that poor recordkeeping practices are evidence of tax fraud, the Court of Appeals upheld a 50 percent civil fraud penalty against the taxpayer. Logically, however, the numbering of invoices and the retention of register tapes are not necessary for records to be correct. But based on its view of common sense under the circumstances, the court considered

[5]Federal tax fraud is a crime. I.R.C. §7206.

[6]*See* Chapter 12.

[7]*See* Halle v. Commissioner, 175 F.2d 500 (2d Cir. 1949); Blue Creek Coal, Inc. v. Commissioner, 48 T.C.M. (CCH) 579 (1984); Foundation Steel and Wire, Inc. v. Commissioner, 52 T.C.M (CCH) 429 (1986).

[8]*See* Harvey v. Early, 189 F.2d 169 (4th Cir. 1951); Ohio Fruit Prod. Co. v. Commissioner, 10 T.C.M. (CCH) 125 (1951).

[9]W. F. Shawver Co. v. Commissioner, 20 B.T.A. 723 (1930) (taxpayer's bookkeeping was a "comedy of errors").

[10]Factor v. Commissioner, 281 F.2d 100 (9th Cir. 1960).

[11]781 F.2d 1566 (11th Cir. 1986).

those practices important to this taxpayer's bookkeeping system.

The manipulation of records to conceal income can disclose fraudulent intent,[12] as can record destruction.[13] But the hint of fraud can be dispelled if the books contain an explanation of bookkeeping irregularities[14] or if the taxpayer can otherwise account for record changes or destruction.[15] In an electronic environment, where the changing of records is easy in principle, the presence of controls and policies that regulate and explain changes and create audit trails for transactions as they are processed can help allay any suspicions of wrongdoing.

§13.2.3 Securities Regulation

False electronic records can lead to false reporting under securities regulations or state corporate laws requiring the delivery of financial reports to shareholders or government entities. Among other provisions, §18 of the Securities Exchange Act of 1934[16] penalizes the making of false or misleading statements in corporate disclosure filings with the Securities and Exchange Commission (SEC) under that Act.

A private cause of action in favor of investors against management might arise under §10(b) of the 1934 Act (and perhaps other antifraud provisions) if corporate books are falsified with a view to affecting the price of securities trades.[17] The SEC can take civil action under the same law. In *SEC*

[12]Garden City Feeder Co. v. Commissioner, 27 B.T.A. 1132 (1933).

[13]*See* Anderson v. Commissioner, 250 F.2d 242 (5th Cir. 1957).

[14]W. F. Shawver v. Commissioner, 20 B.T.A. 723 (1930).

[15]Sharpsville Boiler Works Co., 3 B.T.A. 568 (1926); Frank J. Moore v. Commissioner, 37 B.T.A. 378 (1938).

[16]15 U.S.C. §78r (1988).

[17]*See* A. Jacobs, Litigation and Practice under Rule 10b-5, 6-40 (2d ed. 1990 revision).

v. World-Wide Coin Investments, Ltd,[18] the court held corporate executives liable under §10(b) and related Rule 10b-5 for, among other offenses, falsifying a manual corporate minute book so as to influence trading of the corporation's stock. Similarly, the SEC brought a civil suit against A. M. International, Inc. under both §10(b) and the Foreign Corrupt Practices Act (FCPA)[19] for, among other things, recording as sales products that had not been shipped; deliberate double-billing for products shipped; and recording substantial revenues without adequate supporting documentation. The company ultimately entered into a consent decree restraining it from future violations of the securities laws and agreed to take measures to prevent future violations.[20]

The Department of Justice prosecutes criminal actions under the federal securities laws, including the FCPA. In *United States v. Duquette*[21] the defendants pled guilty to criminal charges of filing false reports with the SEC and maintaining inaccurate books and records. The government alleged the defendants, officers of a publicly held company, maintained a corporate bank account not reflected on the company's books. They diverted to the secret account $2.7 million in funds that had been pledged to a lender. The defendants hid the scheme by recording false entries on company books and altering copies of invoices and customer checks.

In 1988 Congress amended the FCPA to make clear that a defendant must act knowingly to be subject to criminal prosecution under the FCPA's books and records provisions (§13(b)(2) of the Securities Exchange Act of 1934). Congress added §13(b)(4) and §13(b)(5) to the 1934 Act:[22]

[18]567 F. Supp. 724, 753-754 (N.D. Ga. 1983).

[19]*See* §11.3.

[20]SEC v. A.M. Intl., Inc., SEC Litig. Release No. 9980, May 2, 1983, 27 SEC Docket (CCH) 1077 (May 17, 1983).

[21]Reported in Dept. of Justice, Criminal Div., Fraud Section, Daily Report, *reprinted in* W. Hancock, ed., Foreign Corrupt Practices Reporter 696.74 (1985).

[22]15 U.S.C. §§78m(4), 78m(5) (1988).

(4) No criminal liability shall be imposed for failing to comply with the requirements of paragraph (2) of this subsection except as provided in paragraph (5) of this subsection.

(5) No person shall knowingly circumvent or knowingly fail to implement a system of internal accounting controls or knowingly falsify any book, record, or account described in paragraph (2).

These provisions preclude criminal prosecution for inadvertent or technical violations of the records and controls provisions (although they do not preclude civil actions by the SEC).

§13.2.4 Other Criminal and Evidence Law

The intentional falsification or destruction of electronic business messages or records thereof could implicate any number of other criminal statutes and invoke a negative inference in criminal or civil litigation.

The federal wire fraud statute[23] will cover many fraudulent electronic records, for their very creation will involve the interstate telephone system and thus interstate commerce. The Act penalizes anyone who,

> having devised or intending to devise any scheme or artifice to defraud, or for obtaining money or property by means of false or fraudulent pretenses, representations, or promises, transmits or causes to be transmitted by means of wire, radio, or television communication in interstate or foreign commerce, any writings, signs, signals, pictures, or sounds for the purpose of executing such scheme or artifice. . . .

United States v. Cowart[24] sustained a wire fraud conviction based on communications by telephone and fax that con-

[23] 18 U.S.C. §1343 (1988).
[24] 595 F.2d 1023, 1031 (5th Cir. 1979).

tributed to a fraudulent bank loan application scheme. In *United States v. Giovengo*[25] criminals were convicted for fraudulently using an interstate computer link to cause a terminal to print out airline tickets.

In a very sweeping criminal statute, federal law proscribes the making of misrepresentations in connection with federal government affairs:[26]

> Whoever, in any matter within the jurisdiction of any department or agency of the United States knowingly and willfully falsifies, conceals or covers up by any trick, scheme, or device a material fact, or makes any false, fictitious or fraudulent statements or representations, or makes or uses any false writing or document knowing the same to contain any false, fictitious or fraudulent statement or entry, shall be fined not more than $10,000 or imprisoned not more than five years, or both.

This law seems broadly worded enough to cover almost any electronic dealings with the government, including electronic filings and electronic contracting with government agencies. Convictions under it have obtained for such misdeeds as filing false statements with the government to acquire an export license[27] and submitting invoices with overcharges to a certain contractor for the Tennessee Valley Authority (a government entity).[28]

Another statute[29] criminalizes false and fraudulent entries in the books or records of federal banking institutions. The government employed a predecessor to this statute to convict a bank teller who fraudulently withheld receipts from a bank bookkeeper for the purpose of indirectly causing an

[25]637 F.2d 941, 945 (3d Cir. 1980).

[26]18 U.S.C. §1001 (1988).

[27]United States v. Pervez, 871 F.2d 310 (3d Cir.), *cert. denied,* 109 S. Ct. 3258 (1989).

[28]United States v. Gibson, 881 F.2d 318 (6th Cir. 1989).

[29]18 U.S.C. §1005 (1988).

inaccurate record to be made of the teller's receipts.[30] The same statute applied to a bank employee who wrongfully erased figures on a record and replaced them with different figures.[31]

Federal law[32] punishes the obstruction of justice during the pendency of a judicial proceeding. Although the statute does not explicitly cover the alteration and destruction of records, it has been so construed.[33] In addition, under general evidence law one destroying or altering a document can suffer special hardship in litigation (whether civil or criminal). The intentional destruction or alteration of evidence relevant to a pending proceeding or a reasonably foreseeable proceeding permits the trier of fact (typically the jury) to infer the evidence was unfavorable to the actor.[34] The inference does not apply, however, where records are destroyed under routine procedures, not in bad faith.[35] The clear message is that corporate electronic record destruction programs need to make exception for those records pertaining to or reasonably likely to pertain to particular litigation.

§13.2.5 Computer Crime Law

Another response to electronic business record falsification or destruction or the wrongful altering or disabling of elec-

[30]United States v. Giles, 300 U.S. 41 (1937).

[31]United States v. Crecilius, 34 F. 30 (E.D. Mo. 1888).

[32]18 U.S.C. §1503 (1988) provides:

> Whoever . . . corruptly . . . influences, obstructs, or impedes, or endeavors to influence, obstruct, or impede, the due administration of justice, shall be fined not more than $5000 or imprisoned not more than five years, or both.

[33]United States v. Faudman, 640 F.2d 20 (6th Cir. 1981) (defendant prosecuted under 18 U.S.C. §1503 for altering or destroying corporate records with knowledge that a grand jury sought them).

[34]*See* Bird Provision Co. v. Owens Country Sausage, Inc., 379 F. Supp. 744, 751 (N.D. Tex. 1974), *aff'd,* 568 F.2d 369 (5th Cir. 1978).

[35]Coates v. Johnson & Johnson, 756 F.2d 524, 551 (7th Cir. 1985).

tronic controls might be action under applicable computer crime statutes. The federal Computer Fraud and Abuse Act of 1986[36] generally proscribes unauthorized access into a "federal interest computer" (which embraces certain computers used by the federal government or financial institutions, or which are connected to interstate computer networks), when the access alters, damages, or destroys data. An employee may thus be criminally liable under this statute for gaining access to covered computers, without authority, and changing or destroying electronic transaction records. The statute applies only to "intentional" and not inadvertent actions. Another federal law, the Electronic Communications Privacy Act of 1986, prohibits the unauthorized access and damage to an electronic communication in storage.[37] This could apply to a message content record kept on a public network.[38]

Additionally, most states have some form of computer crime statute imposing criminal and/or civil penalties for designated infractions, which often include the unauthorized use of a computer or the unauthorized alteration or destruction of data.[39]

Key questions in the prosecution of an employee accused of altering or destroying electronic documents would be the scope of authority the employee had to use the computers and whether she exceeded it. Was she authorized to access the records but not change them? To change but not falsify them? Did her superiors approve her conduct? If so, are they responsible and not her? Maintenance of an explicit policy governing access and changes to important electronic records could prevent ambiguity here.

[36] 18 U.S.C. §1030 (1988).

[37] 18 U.S.C. §2701 (1988).

[38] *See* Chapter 19.

[39] *See, e.g.,* the New York computer crime law, N.Y. Penal Law art. 156 (McKinney 1988).

§13.3 VICARIOUS LIABILITY

For management or auditors, poor electronic records, or controls that allow insider fraud, can indirectly give rise to liability. Where company assets have been misappropriated, shoddy electronic records or controls can imply that the watchdogs in the company (managers and auditors) condoned the theft. Thus, in the presence of inadequate recordkeeping and controls for electronic transaction systems, liability can entangle even those who have no intent to steal.

The business judgment rule and the difficulty of reliably ascertaining damages usually bar corporate law actions by shareholders against executives for mismanagement.[1] But the business judgment rule defense collapses where an executive has been inattentive and uninformed or appears to have abetted a fraud. In addition, the determination of damages is simple in an embezzlement case—damages equal the amount taken.

The court in *Hollander v. Breeze Corporations,*[2] a derivative suit by corporate stockholders on behalf of their corporation, held both the president and the corporate directors liable for funds the president allegedly misappropriated. As the court explained, a key problem was inadequate records:

> Mascuch [the president] and the other individual defendants are liable for illegal withdrawals of funds of defendant corporation, a great many of which went into Mascuch's pocket. As directors of defendant corporation the individual defendants occupied a fiduciary position toward their stockholders and it was their duty to see that proper and clear records were kept of receipts and disbursements of corporate funds and to take and preserve vouchers for all payments made. The bur-

§13.3 [1]*See* §11.2.2.

[2]131 N.J. Eq. 585, 26 A.2d 507 (N.J. Ch. 1941), *aff'd,* 131 N.J. Eq. 613, 26 A.2d 522 (1942).

den of proof to support their claim of propriety for disbursements of corporate funds is on them.[3]

Francis v. United Jersey Bank[4] upheld a judgment against an inactive and uninformed director for negligently failing to ensure that internal controls were sufficient to thwart the theft of funds by other directors. The director did little to fulfill her duties of keeping informed about the corporation's business, reviewing financial statements, and, where appropriate, checking to see that the corporation adhered to accepted bookkeeping practices. In *Atherton v. Anderson*[5] bank directors who had disbanded a committee to audit the bank's business, and were otherwise remiss in establishing oversight controls, were held liable in negligence for the ensuing fraud by bank officers.

In *Tri-Bullion Smelting & Dev. Co. v. Curtis*[6] and *Boulicault v. Oriel Glass Co.*[7] corporate directors and officers were held responsible for embezzlement by other officers where in each case the defendants had ignored the corporations' businesses and neglected to see that adequate controls were in place. In the former case, the president and directors furnished an unscrupulous treasurer checks countersigned in blank to cover the corporation's expenses. The latter case involved a president who gave the company's bookkeeper signed blank checks, payable to the bookkeeper, but failed ever to compare the canceled checks with the checkbook stubs. An analogy in the electronic world would be for corporate officers and directors to allow a cash manager unfettered control over the corporation's electronic funds system.

Auditors could be similarly exposed to liability under several headings for assisting or failing to discover electronic

[3]26 A.2d at 519.
[4]87 N.J. 15, 432 A.2d 814 (1981).
[5]99 F.2d 883 (6th Cir. 1938).
[6]186 A.D. 613, 174 N.Y.S. 830 (1919).
[7]283 Mo. 237, 223 S.W. 423 (1920).

fraud. In *Tenants' Corp. v. Max Rothenberg & Co.*[8] a client recovered from an auditor that did not exercise due care in performing its work and thereby failed to recognize and warn the client about embezzlement by an employee. Missing invoices should have alerted the auditor to the fraud.

Auditors aiding securities fraud can incur civil liability to investors and even criminal liability. Liability usually derives from certifying false financial reports on which investors rely. The court in *SEC v. Seaboard Corp.*[9] stated that "an accountant may be liable as an aider or abettor if he knows, or is reckless in not knowing, that his client has committed a primary violation [of the securities antifraud rules], and he substantially aids the client in the overall enterprise." Recklessness in not knowing of fraud can be inferred from inadequate electronic records and controls. In *United States v. Weiner*[10] three auditors connected with the Equity Funding scandal[11] were convicted under the Securities Exchange Act of 1934 for furthering their client's fraud. It was Equity Funding's grossly defective records and internal controls that implicated the auditors. The court concluded that even though they may not have actively promoted the fraud, they must have condoned it because it would have been abundantly obvious if they had performed their job of reviewing records and controls.

[8] 36 A.D.2d 804, 319 N.Y.S.2d 1007 (1971).
[9] 677 F.2d 1301, 1312 (9th Cir. 1982).
[10] 578 F.2d 757 (9th Cir.), *cert. denied,* 439 U.S. 981 (1978).
[11] *See* §13.1.

PART V

ELECTRONIC CONTRACT ISSUES

Chapter 14

Industry Codes and Model Trading Agreements

§14.1 INTRODUCTION

The law applicable to electronic commerce is in some ways uncertain. In addition, the shift from paper to electronic trading changes the practical steps involved in negotiating a deal.

So electronic transaction users often need to clarify the rules governing their relationship. Many EDI users, for example, enter "trading partner agreements."[1] These are (usually) bilateral or multilateral paper contracts. In a more regulated environment, such as an electronic securities exchange, special electronic trading rules might be embodied in exchange or government regulations.

At bottom, the specifics of the new rules and the manner in which they are adopted are a matter of negotiation. The allocation of rights and responsibilities depends on wit, bargaining power, and the time and resources committed to negotiation. This is not to say trading partners should be hostile toward one another, but to acknowledge they do have adverse interests.

To aid the negotiation of EDI rules, organizations have issued a code of conduct and several model trading partner agreements.

§14.2 UNCID RULES OF CONDUCT

The first such product was the Uniform Rules of Conduct for Interchange of Trade Data by Teletransmission (UNCID), developed through the cooperation of many international organizations, and published by the International Chamber of Commerce (ICC).[1] According to the Foreword published with the rules, they are voluntary. Nevertheless, they may be considered to apply by default unless otherwise agreed when parties communicating EDI use the EDIFACT standard. These

§14.1 [1] "Trading Partner" seems to be a term of art in the EDI industry meaning a party with whom one trades. Companies may wish to avoid or qualify the term lest they cultivate the appearance that they have a legal "partnership" in which liabilities are shared among "partners."

§14.2 [1] A copy of the rules may be purchased from ICC Publishing Corp., 156 5th Avenue, New York, NY 10010, (212) 206-1150 (ICC Pub. No. 452).

succinct principles are the "Ten Commandments" of international EDI.

Generally speaking, UNCID requires that EDI users:

1. abide by their chosen EDI standard;
2. communicate with care;
3. instruct networks not to change messages without authority;
4. properly identify themselves in messages;
5. acknowledge or confirm good receipt when requested to do so;
6. take remedial action if a received message is not in good order or wrongly delivered;
7. maintain the security of protected data;
8. keep an unchanged log of exchanged data;
9. designate a person to certify the log; and
10. refer questions of UNCID interpretation to the ICC.

UNCID could be understood, at least within the EDIFACT world, as a usage of trade (or custom) that could aid the interpretation of an electronic contract.[2] The rules have not caught on among North American traders, however. The American Bar Association and Canadian model trading agreements (discussed below) are stronger candidates for being recognized someday as expressing any trade usages in North America.

§14.3 UNITED KINGDOM'S STANDARD AGREEMENT

The EDI Association of the United Kingdom[1] has published a Standard Electronic Data Interchange Agreement (2d edi-

[2]*See* Restatement (Second) of Contracts §202 (1981); U.C.C. §§1-205, 2-202, 2-208.

§14.3 [1]Venture House, 29 Glasshouse Street, London W1R 5RG, United Kingdom.

tion Aug. 1990). In many ways, it follows the UNCID rules, including the mutual obligation of the parties to keep an unmodified log of all exchanged data.

§14.4 AMERICAN BAR ASSOCIATION MODEL AGREEMENT

In *The Business Lawyer,* June 1990, the American Bar Association published a Model EDI Trading Partner Agreement and Commentary (ABA Model),[1] together with an explanatory report (ABA Report).[2] The Model and the Report culminate a study by the Electronic Messaging Services Task Force (ABA Task Force) on how EDI is implemented in practice and the use (or nonuse) of trading partner agreements. The ABA Model is a drafting tool to aid counsel in preparing an agreement between two parties using EDI to facilitate domestic sales of goods. Its provisions may be modified in practice.

The ABA Model's provisions break into three rough categories: (1) the enforceability of EDI contracts; (2) the manner in which EDI is conducted; and (3) the trade terms and conditions (TTCs) applicable to the underlying transactions (purchase and sale contracts) facilitated by EDI. The ABA Model is structured to strike a fair balance between the interests of both parties, whether sender or recipient, whether buyer or seller.

§14.4 [1]45 Bus. Law. 1717 (1990).

[2]Electronic Messaging Services Task Force, The Commercial Use of Electronic Data Interchange—A Report, 45 Bus. Law. 1647 (1990). The ABA Model (order number 507-0233-B9) and the ABA Report (507-0233-B10) may be purchased from ABA Order Fulfillment, 750 North Lake Shore Drive, Chicago, IL 60611, (312) 988-5555.

§14.4.1 Enforceability of Contracts

Of primary concern to the ABA Task Force was the Statute of Frauds in Article Two of the Uniform Commercial Code (U.C.C.), §2-201. The statute generally forbids the enforcement of a contract for the sale of goods for the price of $500 or more unless the contract is supported by a "signed" "writing."[3] In response, the ABA Model advances three overlapping strategies. It (1) defines certain EDI messages as "signed" and "written"; (2) provides that the conducting of EDI between the parties evidences a course of dealing and course of performance consistent with the enforceability of contracts formed via EDI; and (3) furnishes the basis for estopping each party from denying such enforceability.[4]

§14.4.2 EDI Conduct

The ABA Model sets preferences for the nature, timing, and sequence of messages between the parties. Its default provisions require a message recipient to return a functional acknowledgment to confirm receipt.[5] In addition, the parties can (and are encouraged to) require that the recipient of certain messages, such as purchase orders, return formal acceptances before the original messages can have legal effect.[6] This confines the formation of contracts to a classic offer-and-acceptance scheme. The ABA Model contemplates a *closed* communication system, in which only proper EDI messages have legal effect. Thus, acceptance of an EDI purchase order may not be by fax or telephone. Also, if the recipient receives a garbled message but fails to so notify the

[3]*See* Chapter 16.
[4]*See* §§16.4.4 & 16.5.
[5]ABA Model §2.2.
[6]ABA Model §2.3.

sender, the sender's record of the message's contents control over the recipient's.[7]

Like UNCID and the other model agreements, the ABA Model contemplates the parties having an affirmative duty to be prepared to conduct EDI competently.[8] Yet, a significant distinguishing feature of the ABA Model is that it does not explicitly require participants to keep EDI records.[9]

§14.4.3 Trade Terms and Conditions

TTCs are the terms of the underlying transactions, such as contracts for sales of goods, formed through EDI. TTCs might, for example, cover product warranties and the rules for returning nonconforming goods. In paper trading these are often either covered in a master agreement between the parties or negotiated through the exchange of standard forms setting forth TTCs on their backsides. EDI does not readily permit the communication of TTCs with messages.

So if there is no master agreement, the introduction of EDI will change the way TTCs are negotiated. The ABA Model provides three options for specifying which TTCs apply to EDI transactions in that case. The parties can (1) agree to specific TTCs incorporated into the trading agreement, (2) attach their form documents to the trading agreement and agree that TTCs will be handled just as if the form doc-

[7]ABA Model §2.4. The ABA Report suggests the invalidation of the recipient's record is the only penalty the recipient suffers for not responding. The language of §2.4 and the associated commentary, however, do not by their terms preclude the sender from winning damages for the recipient's breach of §2.4.

[8]For example, ABA Model §1.3 requires each party to procure the equipment and support services necessary to conduct EDI reliably, and §1.4 obligates the parties to use sufficient security procedures.

[9]However, ABA Model §1.3, which requires the parties to have appropriate equipment and services, might implicitly require record retention.

uments had been used in the usual way, or (3) permit application of the default terms the law would apply in the absence of an explicit agreement on TTCs.

The ABA Model was a primary source of the ideas incorporated into the Canadian Model EDI agreement introduced below. Chapters 15-17 consider the ABA Model and the ABA Report in more detail.

§14.5 CANADIAN MODEL AGREEMENT

In summer 1990 the Legal and Audit Issues Committee of the EDI Council of Canada published a Model Form of EDI Trading Partner Agreement and Commentary (Canadian Model).[1] The Canadian Model is similar to, but explicitly covers a broader range of issues than, the ABA Model. Some of its unique terms require each party to:

1. obtain an annual third-party review of the control procedures over its EDI system and deliver a copy of the review to the other party;[2]
2. keep a transaction log (i.e., a record of message contents) and designate a person to oversee and be able to certify it;[3] and
3. prepare and certify periodically a permanent, unalterable copy of the latest parts of the party's log.[4]

§14.5 [1]A copy can be acquired from the Council at 5401 Eglinton Avenue West, Suite 103, Etobicoke, Ontario, Canada M9C 5K6, (416) 621-7160.

[2]Canadian Model §5.07.

[3]*Id.* §7.01.

[4]*Id.* §7.02.

§14.6 STRATEGY AND THE ELECTRONIC TRADING LETTER

For general commercial electronic transactions, a formal trading partner agreement is desirable. Negotiation of such an agreement is relatively easy (although still an unwanted chore) if the parties already have between them a master purchase agreement, or something similar, into which the special electronic communication terms can be ingrafted. Otherwise, the negotiation of a trading agreement, particularly TTCs, can be time consuming and difficult.

A model agreement is just that, a model. It is intended to be used with care and can require considerable work by counsel. The Foreword to the ABA Model states:

> [I]t is not intended that the Model Agreement represent the only form in which [EDI legal] issues may be addressed by counsel considering the underlying business relationships. Those reviewing the Model Agreement and Commentary are strongly encouraged to consider and study their provisions and to use independent judgment as to the effectiveness of the provisions of the Model Agreement and the advisability of their use in particular transactions.

Some EDI users elect against formal trading agreements. They may not perceive the need, or may reasonably conclude the value at stake cannot justify the effort. A relevant fact may be that, even though EDI has been in use many years, there have been no commercial lawsuits reported that involved EDI transactions. Also, the need for a trading agreement is significantly reduced if the traders are not using EDI to form contracts, which is often the case.

Commonly, companies try to start EDI with many partners very quickly. A goal is to minimize one-on-one coordination between partners. For some users, a realistic way to address the legal issues is to send each trading partner an "electronic trading letter." It could be transmitted as a conventional paper letter, or as an e-mail message.

Appendix C sets forth a sample electronic trading letter (Electronic Trading Letter). It is drafted for EDI used for the sale of goods, but could be modified to cover other types of electronic transactions.

Inspired by UNCID, the ABA Model and the Canadian Model, the Electronic Trading Letter seeks brevity and readability. It deals primarily with three critical legal issues: electronic contract enforceability, rules for EDI communication, and the establishment of TTCs. As for the first issue, the Letter displays explicitly, and through the development of a course of dealing/performance, the parties' intent to attach legal significance to their electronic messages. The Letter also asserts that the messages are, under specified conditions, "written" and "signed."

Like its predecessors, the Electronic Trading Letter expresses neutral rules of communication, favoring neither buyer, seller, sender, or receiver. Neutral rules are more likely to be agreed to by the Letter recipient and more likely to be upheld in court.[1] The Letter displaces the mailbox rule and deems messages effective upon receipt rather than dispatch.[2] Unlike its predecessors, however, it obligates neither party to be capable of conducting EDI or to keep EDI records.

As for the third critical issue, the Letter imitates a conventional form document. Like a paper purchase order, it communicates the only TTCs the sender intends to adopt. It can incorporate, as Supplement B, the terms the sender usually includes with its paper forms. The Letter notifies the recipient that each electronic message will incorporate the

§14.6 [1]"Unconscionable" agreements may be unenforceable because they either were oppressive, unfair, or unreasonable (substantive unconscionability) or were presented in an unfair manner (procedural unconscionability). Procedural unconscionability might include forcing a much weaker party to contract electronically on unfavorable terms. *See generally,* Restatement (Second) of Contracts §208 (1981); U.C.C. §2-302.

[2]*See* §15.5.

Letter by reference and may contain a code to confirm that fact.

The Electronic Trading Letter aims to introduce terms to a relationship where it might otherwise be difficult to know what the terms are. It facilitates spontaneous trading. In part it is designed as an offer to be accepted by the recipient. If the recipient accepts, the parties should normally have a contract (or other enforceable understanding), mutually promising that the Letter's terms will control their transactions.

Ideally the recipient will sign and return, and thus explicitly adopt, the Letter. Yet it is drafted to function even if not returned. First, the Letter states the recipient will be deemed to have accepted it if she sends electronic messages to the Letter's originator. The argument for this effect would be that assent to a contract may be manifested by conduct, such as the sending of a message.[3] (There may nonetheless be a problem showing that the conduct was intended as assent.) Second, the recipient might respond with a separate communication that agrees to some of the Letter's terms, in which case there is a good chance at least those agreed terms will govern the relationship. Third, the Letter establishes the interpretation and intent the originator places on the trading relationship, which precludes the recipient from claiming it believed the originator understood or intended something different.[4] Finally, the Letter may help establish a course of dealing or performance[5] for interpreting the relationship and preclude the emergence of a contrary one.

A recipient might respond to the Electronic Trading Letter with an entirely contradictory communication. The parties then face risk, reward, and uncertainty similar to that in the battle of the forms in conventional paper trading.[6]

[3]Restatement (Second) of Contracts §19 (1981).

[4]*See* Restatement (Second) of Contracts §§201, 202 (1981).

[5]*See* Restatement (Second) of Contracts §202 (1981); U.C.C. §§1-205, 2-202, 2-208.

[6]*See* Chapter 17.

Their legal relationship is murky, but each party can take comfort in knowing it has asserted a position it desires to defend.

At any rate, users incur the least risk where, as contemplated by the ABA and Canadian Models, they enter bilateral trading agreements that specify all terms.

Chapter 15

The Trading Partner Relationship

§15.1 ELECTRONIC CONTRACTS AND AGENT AUTHORITY

The transmission of an electronic message can affect the sender's legal rights and obligations. It can, for example, bind him to a contract. Classically, a contract formed with messages comes into being when an offer message is met by an acceptance message. (*See* Figure 15-1.)

Corporations and government entities (principals) act through agents—officers and other representatives. A principal is generally not bound to a transaction unless its agent is authorized. Law and convention tell a party dealing with an agent how to ascertain her authority. How do these function in an electronic world?

FIGURE 15-1

Offer and Acceptance

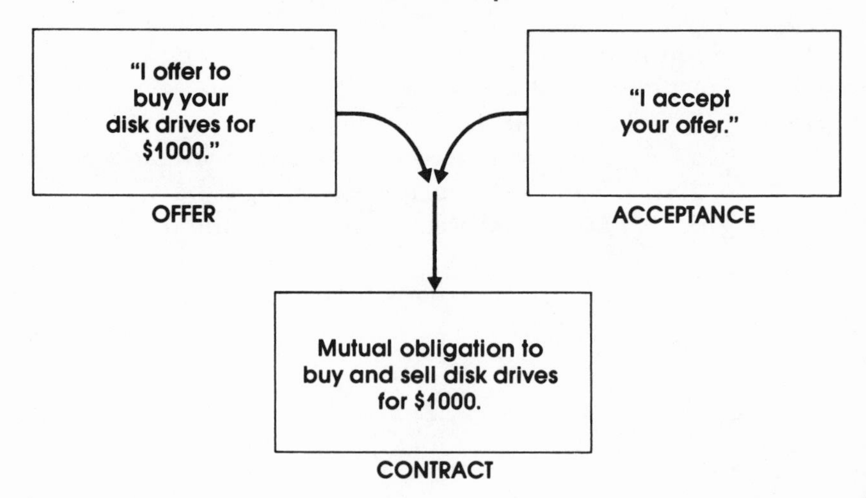

§15.1.1 Grant and Delegation of Authority

Modern businesses can legally use computer messages to transfer authority from principal to agent and from agent to subagent. A corporate president might, for example, send an e-mail message to a purchasing manager authorizing him to procure widgets. Absent special restraints (such as a bylaw requiring "written" authorization), agency law should recognize this new means of conveying authority. Although agency law requires the transfer of authority to be communicated,[1] communication can be oral, in writing, or in any other form that makes the agent believe he is authorized.[2] Unless otherwise specified by a particular law, even a statute demanding that a transaction be in writing does not require the authorization of an agent entering that transaction on a principal's behalf to be in writing.[3] Accordingly, an agent's authority to enter a contract need not under the statute of frauds[4] be in writing.[5]

From a practical perspective, one may be concerned about the provability of a particular act of delegation. In the paper environment, one addressed that concern by reducing the act to a paper and ink record. The same effect can be achieved in the electronic environment with a messaging system that incorporates adequate recordkeeping and control functions.[6]

§15.1 [1]Restatement (Second) of Agency §15 (1958).

[2]*Id.* §26.

[3]*Id.* §30. *But see* Cal. Civ. Code §2309 (West 1985). ("[A]uthority to enter into a contract required by law to be in writing can only be given by an instrument in writing."). *See* Chapter 16 for a discussion of when electronic messages are "written."

[4]*See* §16.1.

[5]Carrier v. Piggly Wiggly of San Francisco, 11 Cal. App. 2d 180, 53 P.2d 400 (1936).

[6]*See* Chapters 5 & 6.

§15.1.2 Exercise of Authority

An agent may possess "actual" authority, which the principal in fact expressly or impliedly grants. ("You are authorized to buy stock for me.") Or an agent may have "apparent" authority; that is, the principal's actions lead an observer to reasonably believe the agent has authority.[7] (The seller of stock understands *A* to have authority to buy for *P* if *P* gave *A* the funds to do it and has regularly permitted *A* to buy stock with the funds in the past.) An agent, such as a corporate president, may also have inherent authority by virtue of his status as an officer.[8]

By convention, in paper trading an agent (John Doe, President) acting on behalf of a corporation (Blue Co.) writes a legal message, such as a purchase order or an authorization for a warehouse to release goods, on paper and closes with this:

BLUE CO.

By: John Doe
John Doe, President

The convention makes clear that a natural person is acting as agent to bind the corporation. The signature is conventionally a handwritten autograph, although it legally could be any other type of symbol.[9] For formal legal documents, the convention also expects that ultimately an identified natural person (or persons in the case of coagents) acts as agent for a legal entity.

Electronic messaging interrupts these conventions in three respects. First, the signature cannot be a handwritten

[7]3 Am. Jur. 2d Agency §71 (1986).
[8]Restatement (Second) of Agency §8A (1958).
[9]*See* §16.3.2.

autograph. Second, the message could be generated by automatic action of a computer rather than by any natural person. An inventory management system, for example, might, without human intervention, issue an EDI purchase order when its records show inventory levels are too low.[10] Similarly, a cash management system might automatically issue an electronic funds transfer (EFT) order when the funds in a particular bank account exceed a predefined threshold. Third, an electronic message may identify the principal but not any particular agent.

The drafters of new Uniform Commercial Code (U.C.C.) Article 4A, which governs wholesale EFT, believed these differences dictate a new approach to the analysis of agency authority, at least for electronic messages from customers to banks ordering the transfer of funds.

> Common law concepts of authority of agent to bind principal are not helpful. There is no way of determining the identity or the authority of the person who caused the message to be sent. The receiving bank is not relying on the authority of any particular person to act for the purported sender.[11]

The drafters of Article 4A propounded a series of rules, set forth in §§4A-201, 202, and 203, to establish when a bank is and is not justified in executing a payment order. The rules rest, in large part, on the bank's use of "commercially reasonable security" procedures,[12] agreed to by the customer in advance, to test a message's genuineness.

The drafters' response is sound, although their reasoning overstates the problem. They (commendably) articulate procedures, specially designed for the EFT environment, that rather precisely define banks' and customers' responsibilities

[10] *See* §5.2.1.3.

[11] U.C.C. §4A-203 Official Comment 1.

[12] Security procedures might include passwords, cryptography, callback procedures, and other devices. U.C.C. §4A-201. See §1.3 & Chapter 5.

and risks. Yet the new rules are consistent with common law agency concepts; they just employ the law in a way different from traditional bank checking. Five reasons support this view.

First, human programmers and operators control computers. For any one computer, there might be a single agent operating it, or there could be an assembly of many coagents and subagents. This individual or group acts, by way of an EFT order message, for the principal. (Any argument that the computer itself is an "agent" seems strange.[13]) It is not unusual for a corporation to take an action attributable to it but not fully traceable to any individual agent. A corporation could, for example, publish an advertisement that stands on the authority of many different corporate officers but identifies none of them.

Second, an agent can bind a principal for future events. So nothing unusual occurs when an officer (possessing sufficient authority) agrees on a bank customer's behalf that it will in the future be bound to EFT order messages that pass specified security tests. In the Article 4A setting, the authority behind an EFT order message flows from that originally vested in the officer who agreed to security standards and the authority vested in the individual or group controlling the computer that issued the message. Neither source of authority is sufficient standing alone to move the principal's funds, but together they are.

Third, a bank ascertains authority for an EFT order message under Article 4A in two sensible steps. One, the bank determines the authority of the customer officer signing the agreement setting security standards. This is done in the way authority for contracts is routinely determined. Two, the bank tests the authority of the agent(s) behind the particular order with the security procedures agreed to by the first officer.

Fourth, the absence of a handwritten autograph on a

[13]*See* Restatement (Second) of Agency §21 comment a (1958), suggesting an agent must be capable of exercising "volition."

message does not change the agency law analysis. An autograph is just a popular, but not an exclusive, method for indicating approval of a message. There is no reason under agency law that an agent could not indicate approval with some other method, such as an agreed security procedure. One case shows that an agent's typewritten name on a telegram can be a satisfactory method of indicating approval, even though a telegraph operator, acting under the agent's oral direction, may have been the one who actually entered the name into the telegraph system.[14]

Finally, the generally accepted rule is that (absent a statute to the contrary) it does not invalidate a message for an agent to sign it in name of the principal only, with no disclosure of the agency relationship or the agent's name.[15] So the fact that an EFT order message merely states it is from Blue Co., but does not on its face indicate the agent(s) behind it, is immaterial under agency law.

A few courts have considered how agents act through computers. In *Kennison v. Daire,*[16] a case before the Australian High Court, the defendant had tricked an automatic teller machine into surrendering $200 cash after his account had been closed. The defendant argued the bank had consented—by virtue of the "authority" vested in the machine—to the payment. The court rejected the argument, suggesting that a machine may not possess authority to consent for a principal. *State Farm Mutual Automobile Insurance Co. v. Brockhorst*[17] involved a computer-generated notice of renewal of an insurance policy, which retroactively bound an insurance company to cover an automobile accident that had occurred earlier. Before the renewal's issuance, the insured had told a company representative about the accident; the

[14]Selma Sav. Bank v. Webster County Bank, 206 S.W. 870 (Ky. 1918).

[15]3 Am. Jur. 2d Agency §172 (1986); Kiekhoefer v. United States Natl. Bank of Los Angeles, 2 Cal. 2d 98, 39 P.2d 807 (1935).

[16]160 C.L.R. 129 (Austl. 1986).

[17]453 F.2d 533 (10th Cir. 1972).

company was therefore not required to issue the renewal, although the insured did not know that. The company argued in court that the renewal was ineffective because an "unimaginative" computer could not bind a company. Yet the court held the company to the renewal, reasoning that a "computer operates only in accordance with the information and directions supplied by its programmers."[18]

Kennison and *State Farm* could appear to contradict each other. They might be reconciled, however, with this reading of the law: A computer that effects legal transactions is not an agent of those who use it. Yet, through such a computer true agents may take an action that does bind their principal to an outside party, so long as the agents are acting within their authority. The outside party cannot claim the agents acted within their authority if the party knows the principal has not authorized the action.

§15.1.3 Government Agent Authority

Contracting in the government procurement arena is different from that in the private sector. Electronic transactions will raise special concerns in public purchasing. Agent authority to act for the government is strictly limited by statute, charter, ordinance, and regulation. In contrast to the role of agents in private contracting, government agents have no apparent authority.[19] Failure of an officer possessing the proper authority to execute a contract in the manner provided for by law invalidates the contract.[20] The outside contractor who does not inquire into the government agent's actual authority does so at her peril.[21]

[18] *Id.* at 537.

[19] *See* C. Sands & M. Libonati, 3 Local Government Law 22-14 (1982).

[20] Equitable doctrines such as quasi-contract may still provide remedy, however.

[21] O. Reynolds, Handbook of Local Government Law 653 (1982).

The law may provide rather rigid steps to be followed to authorize an officer to execute a contract.[22] For example, a recommended regulation, R2-205.4, for implementation with the American Bar Association's Model Procurement Code for State and Local Governments, provides: "The Chief Procurement Officer may delegate in writing such authority as may be deemed appropriate to the head of any department. . . . " This could be construed to require that delegation be reduced to paper. One could argue that an e-mail record on computer media is unsatisfactory; the government needs a reliable and easily accessible audit trail to ascertain its rights and obligations. Any given e-mail system may not incorporate sufficient controls. The opposite argument could be made where an electronic system is properly designed, controlled, and maintained to support audit.[23] Procurement laws should be reviewed carefully when governments implement electronic authorization and transaction systems.

§15.2 MANIFESTATION OF MUTUAL ASSENT

A contract is a binding promise or set of promises. A condition to the binding of a party to a typical contract (and many other types of duties) is that he must have manifested his voluntary assent to it.[1] Assent can be manifested electronically.

The common law of contracts sees the manifestation of assent in terms of offer by one party and acceptance by another. An offer message has to meet an acceptance, which

[22] *See* C. Rhyme, The Law of Local Government Operations 936-937 (1980).

[23] *See* Chapter 16.

§15.2 [1] Restatement (Second) of Contracts §17(1) (1981).

agrees to the offer entirely, for a contract to emerge.[2] The mutual assent has to be perfectly symmetrical, so that both parties have agreed to all terms.

U.C.C. Article Two,[3] shunning formalistic rules for ascertaining assent, permits its discovery wherever it may be and sometimes recognizes a contract even where it is unclear that the parties have assented to all terms. U.C.C. §2-204(1) states, "A contract for sale of goods may be made in any manner sufficient to show agreement, including conduct by both parties which recognizes the existence of such a contract." Conduct can suffice even if the parties' writings fail to establish a contract.[4] A contract may come into being even if some of its terms are indefinite, provided "the parties have intended to make a contract and there is a reasonably certain basis for giving an appropriate remedy."[5] So Article Two is more open to finding contracts, but it still demands assent to the basic terms by both parties.

Preston Farm & Ranch Supply, Inc. v. Bio-zyme Enterprises[6] gives a classic example of conduct manifesting assent. When a buyer accepted delivery of goods offered at a known price, he exhibited his assent to the obligation to pay the price. In *Apex Oil Co. v. Vanguard Oil & Service Co.*[7] a seller's conduct recognized that a deal it had with a buyer was a contract. The seller's conduct was (1) acknowledging to its banker that it would be paid on the deal and (2) requesting that the buyer permit the delivery date under the deal to be extended.

Users understand electronic messages to be manifestations of assent; therefore, the transmission of electronic messages can constitute either offer and acceptance under the

[2]*See* H. Hunter, Modern Law of Contracts ¶16.02[7] & [8] (1987).

[3]Article Two of the U.C.C. governs sales-of-goods contracts in all states but Louisiana.

[4]U.C.C. §2-207(3).

[5]U.C.C. §2-204(3).

[6]625 S.W.2d 295 (Tex. 1981).

[7]760 F.2d 417 (2d Cir. 1985).

common law or communication showing agreement under Article Two.[8] From the perspective of a messaging system designer, however, the more direct and unambiguous the manifestations the better. Debates over the interpretation of actions are disruptive.[9]

The ABA Model (to its credit) imposes a strict structure on the way in which assent is manifested through EDI.[10] Section 2.3 permits and encourages the parties to provide that some messages (such as purchase orders) will have no effect unless accepted with specific messages (such as purchase order acknowledgments). This common law offer-and-acceptance regime comports with the orderliness of EDI trading.

§15.3 MISUNDERSTANDING

A corollary to the proposition that a party must assent to a contract to be bound is that no contract arises if the parties fundamentally do not understand each other. Restatement (Second) of Contracts §20(1) provides:[1]

> There is no manifestation of mutual assent to an exchange if the parties attach materially different meanings to their manifestations and . . . neither party knows or has reason to know the meaning attached by the other. . . .

[8]The statute of frauds may nevertheless require that the contract, to be enforced, be supported by a signed writing. *See* Chapter 16.

[9]*See* §5.7.

[10]It also confirms the parties' messages signify their legal intent. ABA Model §3.3.1.

§15.3 [1]Note that under U.C.C. §1-103, the U.C.C. generally does not alter the common law of mistakes in contracting.

The famous *Raffles v. Wichelhaus*[2] case illustrates. The parties agreed to a sale of cotton and its transportation by the ship "Peerless" from Bombay. Unbeknown to the parties, two ships by that name, each equally capable, were to sail from Bombay, one in October and the other in December. Each party had in mind a different ship. The court held there was no mutual assent to fundamental terms and thus no contract for sale and transportation.

In electronic contracting, one can imagine a similar outcome where the complex and dynamic technical standards to which electronic messages conform are ambiguous. Suppose, for example, the data dictionary for an EDI standard indicates the code "NB" means either nuts or bolts. Blue Co. and Green Co. each purchase EDI translation-and-control software from different vendors, the first interpreting NB to mean nuts and the second, bolts. Blue sends an order, believing it is ordering nuts, and Green returns an acceptance, believing it is accepting an order for bolts. Under Restatement §20(1), there can be no mutual assent and thus no contract.

It is also conceivable in electronic contracting (although not frequent in competent, professionally maintained systems) that the message Blue Co. sends and the one Green Co. receives are materially different. An intermediary may inadvertently alter a message during transmission or format conversion (translation). Analogous problems have previously arisen where messages were communicated via telegraph companies or language translators.

Under §20(2) of the Second Restatement of Contracts, if at the time of the exchange one party knows of the interpretation the second places on the messages, and the second does not know of any different meaning, then the second's interpretation controls. In *Germain Fruit Co. v. Western Union Telegraph Co.*[3] a seller sent a telegram offering oranges at

[2] 2 Hurl. & C. 906, 159 Eng. Rep. 375 (Ex. 1864).
[3] 137 Cal. 598, 70 P. 658 (1902).

"two sixty" (i.e., $2.60) per box. The telegraph company dropped the "two." The buyer ordered oranges based on the telegram, and the seller delivered. The buyer, claiming it understood the telegram to offer $1.60, refused to pay more. The court found the buyer had reason to know the price was $2.60 (the well-known market value). The court said the seller could recover $2.60 per box from the buyer.[4]

Yet when neither party is aware of the intermediary's mistake, there is a split among the authorities. Under one line of reasoning, the offeror bears any resulting loss. The rationales are: (1) the offeror chose the medium of communication,[5] and (2) the intermediary is the offeror's agent.[6] An opposing line of reasoning says that because the intermediary is not really an agent and the parties achieved no mutual assent, no contract was formed.[7]

§15.4 NOTICE

Messages are useless if not successfully communicated. An acceptance, for example, is generally ineffective unless the offeror receives notice of the acceptance.[1]

[4]The court's reasoning can be read two ways: (1) a contract for $2.60 was formed, before the fruit was shipped, because the buyer had reason to know that was the intended price; or (2) no contract was formed until the fruit was sent and accepted, in which case the price was market value.

[5]Ayer v. Western Union Tel. Co., 79 Me. 493, 10 A. 495 (1887) The criticism: this rationale collapses where the offeree is the first to use the intermediary (e.g., by transmitting an inquiry to the offeror).

[6]Des Arc Oil Mill v. Western Union Tel. Co., 132 Ark. 335, 201 S.W. 273 (1918). The criticism: the intermediary is usually not a true agent but rather a public instrumentality.

[7]Strong v. Western Union Tel. Co., 18 Idaho 389, 109 P. 910 (1910); Western Union Tel. Co. v. Cowin & Co., 20 F.2d 103 (8th Cir. 1927).

§15.4 [1]H. Hunter, Modern Law of Contracts ¶16.02[6] (1987). Under the mailbox rule, however, some properly dispatched acceptances are effective even if not received. *See* §15.5.

Under contact law at least, one has legal notice of a fact when he actually knows or has good reason to know it.[2] Absent a special statute or agreement, notice need not necessarily be "written." Hence, electronic media are inherently just as capable of delivering legal notice as is paper. In Ontario, *Rolling v. Williann Investments Ltd.*[3] held that a notice required under a contract could in 1989 be sent by fax, rather than mail or courier, even though the contract was written in the 1970s, before fax was popular.

Paper notices delivered by courier or mail may nevertheless be required or advisable in many cases. First, it has long been the convention to deliver formal legal notices, such as subpoenas and other litigation documents, on paper. People recognize physically delivered paper as potentially important. Businesses establish procedures for handling it. The same may not be true of electronic messages. A person may not, for instance, have reason to know about information faxed to her if she has not seen the fax, did not expect it, had established no procedure to ensure it would be properly routed to her, and did not regularly use fax to receive important notices. Still, norms are rapidly changing, as the *Rolling* case shows. Telex has long been recognized as a medium for business, and telex has on at least one occasion been accepted as a means for serving litigation documents.[4] Fax is winning approval as a medium for some litigation documents in some jurisdictions.[5] Many businesses do consider fax and EDI to be proper channels for at least certain categories of important information.

Second, some statutes and regulations, using terms such

[2]*See generally* U.C.C. §1-201(25), (26) & (27); Restatement (Second) of Contracts §68 (1981).

[3]70 O.R. (2d) 578 (C.A. 1989).

[4]New England Merchants Natl. Bank v. Iran Power Generation and Transmission Co., 495 F. Supp. 73 (S.D.N.Y. 1980).

[5]*See, e.g.*, Matter of Changes to the Arkansas Rules of Civil Procedure, 780 S.W.2d 334 (1989).

as "written notice," may be construed to require notice by physically delivered paper.

Where electronic notice is desirable, the law may need to be clarified,[6] as is happening with fax in litigation.[7] Meanwhile, it is prudent to obtain recipient permission before electronically sending a notice such as an acceptance or a litigation document.[8]

Which electronic address is effective for giving notice? Assuming fax notice is satisfactory, is it just as effective to transmit to the machine used by workers on a firm's loading dock as the one in its legal department? It depends on the notice's purpose. The question is not unique to electronic communication. U.C.C. §1-201(27) provides that notice to an organization is effective

> for a particular transaction from the time when it is brought to the attention of the individual conducting that transaction, and in any event from the time when it would have been brought to his attention if the organization had exercised due diligence.[9]

When in doubt, the sender should ask the recipient how best to send the notice.

§15.5 TIME OF CONTRACT FORMATION (MAILBOX RULE)

U.C.C. Article Two, which covers sales of goods, furnishes no explicit framework for fixing the precise time that an offer

[6]*See* Chapter 16.

[7]*See* §4.4.2.

[8]Electronic notice may still be ill-advised if a statute or contract requires "written" notice or the like.

[9]The due diligence concept gives organizations incentive to have procedures for properly routing incoming business messages.

meets an acceptance or that a contract is otherwise formed. But it does not preclude parties from agreeing on their own framework. The ABA Model, which is designed for sales of goods through EDI, embraces the common law offer-and-acceptance structure in that its §2.3 encourages parties to provide that offer messages are ineffective until accepted with acceptance messages. Importantly, however, the Model departs from an element of the common law offer-and-acceptance scheme, the mailbox rule.

Morrison v. Thoelke[1] illustrates the mailbox rule. A buyer (the offeror) mailed to a seller (the offeree) a signed land purchase agreement (an offer), which the seller signed (as an acceptance) and mailed back. But before delivery to the buyer, the seller telephoned to repudiate the agreement. The question then was whether the repudiation was effective to cancel the seller's acceptance of the offer. The court held the acceptance was binding and a contract was formed when the seller deposited the agreement in the mail (i.e., in its mailbox). Restatement (Second) of Contracts §63 capsulizes the rule:

> Unless the offer provides otherwise, . . . an acceptance made in a manner and by a medium invited by an offer is operative and completes the manifestation of mutual assent as soon as put out of the offeree's possession, without regard to whether it ever reaches the offeror. . . .

The mailbox rule applies to acceptances by offerees, but not to revocations by offerors.[2] Suppose in *Morrison* the buyer, while the agreement was in transit to the seller, tried to revoke its offer with a mailed letter. The revocation would not be effective until its delivery to the seller. If the seller signed and dispatched the agreement before it received the revocation, the revocation would never be effective and the contract would still be born.

§15.5 [1]155 So. 2d 889 (Fla. Dist. Ct. App. 1963).
[2]Restatement (Second) of Contracts §42 (1981).

This scheme disfavors the offeror because if her message is lost in route or materially delayed, it is ineffective. Various rationales have been advanced. Professor Llewellyn argued the offeror was better able to bear the risk:

> As between hardship on the offeror which is really tough, and hardship on the offeree which would be even tougher, the vital reason for throwing the hardship of an odd delayed or lost letter upon the offeror remains this: the offeree is already relying, with the best reason in the world, on the deal being on; the offeror is only holding things open; and, in view of the efficiency of communication facilities, we can protect the offeree in *all* these deals at the price of hardship on offerors in very few of them. (emphasis supplied)[3]

Worms v. Burgess[4] also contends that it is fair to burden the offeror because she has the power to specify in her offer that the acceptance will be ineffective until receipt.[5] *E. Frederics, Inc. v. Felton Beauty Supply Co.*[6] argues that where the offeror has unilaterally chosen the postal service as its means for transmitting an offer the offeror makes the service its agent for communications regarding the offer. So when the offeree gives the acceptance to the postal service, the offeror is deemed immediately to have the notice.

Anyway, the critical point is that the mailbox rule marks a point of reference against which parties can assess the risks of lost or delayed communication.[7]

Does the mailbox rule cover messages transmitted via

[3]Llewellyn, Our Case Law of Contract: Offer and Acceptance (pt. 2), 48 Yale L.J. 779, 795 (1939).

[4]620 P.2d 455 (Okla. Ct. App. 1980).

[5]Some opinions reject the rule as unfair, reasoning that an offeree can (theoretically) mail an acceptance, then, before delivery, retrieve it from the postal service if he changes his mind. Rhode Island Tool Co. v. United States, 128 F. Supp. 417 (Ct. Cl. 1955); Dick v. United States, 82 F. Supp. 326 (Ct. Cl. 1949).

[6]58 Ga. App. 320, 198 S.E. 324 (1938).

[7]A. Corbin, 1 Corbin on Contracts §78 (1963).

any media other than the postal service? Yes, sometimes. Telegraph enjoys the rule's benefit.[8] Comment e to Restatement (Second) of Contracts §63 says the rule should also apply to messages in any public service instrumentality similar to mail or telegram. The rule does not activate, however, where the communication between parties is essentially instantaneous, as happens with telephone and conventional telex.[9] The rationales are that with instantaneous media (1) the offeree can accept with no risk that the offeror has already issued a revocation and (2) if communication fails, one or both parties will know immediately.[10]

Hence, absent an agreement between the parties, or a specification in the offer, it will be uncertain whether the mailbox rule applies to any particular electronic message system. The answer will depend on whether the particular system is deemed "public" in nature but yet not "instantaneous."[11]

One noteworthy British court applied a type of mailbox rule to e-mail in a noncontract case. *R. v. Pontypridd Juvenile Magistrates' Court*[12] involved the filing of a court document due by a certain date. It was entered into an e-mail system at a police station on Friday, before the deadline, but not printed out at the court until Monday, after the deadline. If the document had been printed on paper and dropped in the court's letter box on Friday, it would have met the deadline.

[8]Restatement (Second) of Contracts §63 comment a (1981).

[9]Restatement (Second) of Contracts §64 (1981).

[10]*Id.* comment a.

[11]From a practical perspective, this uncertainty will usually not have much consequence. The question whether the mailbox rule applies is more important when communication is slow and there is ample opportunity for a party to send a contradictory message while another is in transit. Electronic messages, however, are fast. (In litigation, however, the operation of the mailbox rule could affect choice-of-law issues. *See* Entores, Ltd. v. Miles Far East Corp., [1955] 2 Q.B. 327 (C.A.).)

[12]The London Times, July 28, 1988, at 27, col. 1; [1988] C.L.Y. 664.

The appellate court held the electronic version of the message met the deadline too. The court opined "that in 1988 it was unrealistic to suggest any distinction between feeding information into a computer which was printed after the time limit and posting a letter through the letter box which was opened after the time limit."[13] This case appears not to deal with transmission through an intermediary communication service, and it is unclear whether an intermediary's presence would have made a difference.

As indicated previously, American contract law is uncertain as to the mailbox rule's application to electronic messages. Section 2.1 of the ABA Model, commendably, settles the issue by displacing the rule for EDI users adopting the Model. The grounds are that the choice of medium in EDI is mutual, and EDI communication can be virtually instantaneous. Not only does EDI communication occur quickly, but EDI permits the prompt return of a functional acknowledgment, so the sender does not long stay ignorant whether its message arrived intact.[14]

Yet speed is relative. Usually EDI and e-mail are not perfectly instantaneous (in which case it would function in "real-time"). Messages, including acknowledgments, may take as much as a few hours to traverse store and forward systems. In a turbulent business climate, such as the international foreign exchange market, half an hour is a long duration. The mailbox rule may be needed there.

Note that application of the mailbox rule depends on the offeree exercising reasonable diligence to ensure successful transmission to the offeror.[15] Accordingly, an offeree denies himself the rule's advantage if he accepts by mail but uses the wrong address or by fax but dials the wrong fax number.

[13]*Id.*

[14]Electronic Messaging Services Task Force, The Commercial Use of Electronic Data Interchange—A Report, 45 Bus. Law. 1647, 1665-1673 (1990).

[15]Restatement (Second) of Contracts §66 (1981).

§15.6 MEDIUM OF ACCEPTANCE

Invocation of the mailbox rule depends on the offeree's use of an appropriate acceptance medium. The offeror, the offer's master, can dictate that acceptance be by a specified route—mail, fax, carrier pigeon. Acceptance by a medium contrary to the offeror's specification loses the rule's benefit.

There is an exception, however, if the acceptance arrives at least as soon as it would have if transmitted by the specified medium. For example, suppose an offer requires that acceptance be received by mail at Friday noon. If the offeree replies by "public and non-instantaneous" e-mail on Thursday, the mailbox rule would apply so long as the message arrives on or before Friday noon. So, if the offeree dispatches the acceptance at 8 a.m. Thursday, and it arrives at 10 a.m., a revocation by telephone call from the offeror at 9 a.m. Thursday is ineffective.[1]

Yet if the offer specifies no acceptance medium, the Second Restatement of Contracts and U.C.C. Article Two agree that acceptance may be "in any manner and by any medium reasonable in the circumstances."[2] Comments to both indicate the law is flexible and receptive to new media, which presumably could include electronic media.[3] They reject older cases suggesting, for example, that if an offer is by mail, an acceptance by telegram is denied the mailbox rule.[4]

§15.6 [1]Restatement (Second) of Contracts §67 illustration 1 (1981).

[2]Restatement (Second) of Contracts §30(2) (1981); U.C.C. §2-206(1).

[3]Restatement (Second) of Contracts §65 comment b (1981); U.C.C. §2-206 Official Comment 1.

[4]*See, e.g.*, Lucas v. Western Union Tel. Co., 131 Iowa 669, 109 N.W. 191 (1906).

§15.7 PRESUMPTION OF DELIVERY

Courtroom evidence law presumes that a message properly entrusted to the postal service or a telegraph company reaches its destination. Contrary evidence can overcome the presumption, but the presumption shifts the burden of proof to the party denying delivery. The presumption's purposes are to save time and enhance the likelihood of a just outcome at trial. So at trial, if Green Co. shows that it delivered its acceptance to a telegraph company for transmission to Blue Co., the court will presume Blue received it unless Blue introduces contradictory evidence (testimony or records).

The presumption's basis is the high probability that delivery did succeed and the difficulty of proving delivery in any other way.[1] Whether the presumption will extend to computer messages is unknown. Yet in a reliable electronic communication system, the same probability and difficulty rationales would seem to hold. So there is a good argument the presumption should apply.

The presumption vanishes, however, if a delivery receipt was requested, as with certified mail.[2] It follows, then, that no presumption can apply if an acknowledgment of receipt of an electronic message is requested. A sender would establish delivery not with the presumption, but with the acknowledgment.[3] ABA Model §2.2, which usually requires the return of functional acknowledgments, deems such an ac-

§15.7 [1]McCormick on Evidence §343 (Cleary ed., 3d ed. 1984). Perry v. German-American Bank, 53 Neb. 89, 73 N.W. 538 (1897) (presumption extends to telegraph companies because of their public nature).

[2]Mulder v. Commissioner, 855 F.2d 208 (5th Cir. 1988).

[3]*Compare* Evra Corp. v. Swiss Bank Corp., 522 F. Supp. 820 (N.D. Ill. 1981), *rev'd on other grounds,* 673 F.2d 951 (1982), *cert. denied,* 459 U.S. 1017 (1982) (trial court concluded that telex had been received because sender's transmission transcript showed communication of recipient's answerback).

knowledgment conclusive evidence of proper message receipt.

Even without the presumption, or an acknowledgment, a litigant can logically show a court that receipt of a proper electronic message was very likely. He may have to introduce evidence on the communication system's function and reliability. Consider *Gulf Coast Investment Corp. v. Secretary of Housing & Urban Development*,[4] where the issue was whether an insurance notice had been produced and mailed. The decision turned on the weight the court assigned to conflicting evidence. The defendant, trying to show the notice was produced and mailed, introduced testimony on the complex series of data processing procedures, and associated controls, it routinely employed to create and mail notices. To show the opposite, the plaintiff offered testimony that the notice was absent from the file in which it would have been placed if it had been received. The court believed the defendant's evidence and deemed the notice delivered.

§15.8 EDI OBLIGATIONS

§15.8.1 Capability and Competence Obligations

Some model EDI trading partner agreements obligate partners to conduct EDI competently. ABA Model §1.3 requires each party to buy sufficient equipment and services to conduct EDI "effectively and reliably." Section 2.2 obliges a message recipient to return a functional acknowledgment, and Section 2.4 requires her to notify the sender upon receiving a garbled message. The Canadian Model also binds

[4]509 F. Supp. 1321 (E.D. La. 1980).

each user, under §5.08, to use its best efforts to revive its EDI system if it fails.

These agreements incorporate critical and perhaps inapt assumptions about trading relationships. It is unusual for suppliers to agree formally that they will buy sufficient equipment and services to skillfully open and respond to correspondence. Whether one partner should be liable to the other for failing to conduct EDI (or related business techniques such as just-in-time (JIT) inventory) competently depends on the particular business bargain. Ideally, the attorney will raise this issue and let the business people resolve it for their particular situation.[1]

The parties are just as likely to reject liability as accept it. A supplier pushed by a customer may reluctantly agree to implement EDI, but refuse liability for any failure to do it in accordance with legal standards. From the supplier's perspective, EDI is a complex and maybe expensive technology. Some systems fail, and some users send and interpret messages incorrectly.[2]

The argument in favor of building liability into an agreement is that parties come to rely on EDI and JIT inventory. A customer may do business with a supplier as much for its efficient communications and logistics services as for its products. The customer may suffer greatly if the communications and logistics fail, in which case it may justifiably expect compensation.

ABA Model §4.6 limits the damages that may be recovered for mistakes in the transmission and receipt of messages to direct damages. It does not, however, necessarily limit the damages that may be recovered under the agreement for one party's failure to purchase sufficient equipment and services. One can imagine a customer complaining that

§15.8 [1]*See* §18.7 for a discussion of user liability for errors by service providers.

[2]*See generally* Eckerson, EDI Susceptible to Costly Order Errors, Network World, Sept. 17, 1990, at 23, col. 4.

it had to shut its plant down for several days (with considerable consequential damages) because its supplier failed to satisfy her obligation under ABA Model §1.3 to buy sufficient equipment and services to conduct EDI proficiently. Canadian Model §8.01 prohibits the recovery of any consequential damages under that agreement.

In contrast, the Electronic Trading Letter[3] contains no requirement to purchase equipment or services and disclaims any obligation of either party to conduct EDI. It merely fixes the interpretation, and states the terms that shall be a part, of EDI messages.

§15.8.2 Accurate Information Obligation

A separate source of liability for some EDI users could be the delivery of erroneous electronic information (as distinguished from the incompetent handling of messages). A railroad, for example, might transmit to a coal company weights of the contents of coal-laden railcars so that the coal company can bill its customers. Errors in the information could cost the coal company dearly. Restatement (Second) of Torts §552(1) provides:

> One who, in the course of his business, profession or employment, or in any other transaction in which he has a pecuniary interest, supplies false information for the guidance of others in their business transactions, is subject to liability for pecuniary loss caused to them by their justifiable reliance upon the information, if he fails to exercise reasonable care or competence in obtaining or communicating the information.[4]

[3]*See* §14.6 and Appendix C.

[4]*See* Independent School Dist. No. 454, Fairmont, Minn. v. Statistical Tabulating Corp., 359 F. Supp. 1095 (N.D. Ill. 1973) (liability for tabulation error caused by computer).

§15.8.3 Audit and Recordkeeping Obligations

Sometimes electronic data processing (EDP) auditors, to audit the electronic system of one trading partner, prefer to have independent assurance that the other partner's system is secure and competent. That is the basis for the Canadian Model's requirement that each partner obtain and report to the other an annual third-party review.[5] Third-party reviews of users have historically not been used widely in the EDI world, and they can be expensive. Whether they are necessary will vary from one situation to the next. Some users' auditors will be satisfied that no third-party review of trading partners is necessary (perhaps because the particular EDI implementation is supplemented by sufficient internal controls).

UNCID Article 10 and Canadian Model Article VII oblige each user to keep a log of EDI transactions and to designate an individual who can certify reproductions made from the log. Users are well advised to keep records, but the wisdom behind a legal duty to trading partners is very questionable. Partners in conventional trading do not undertake analogous legal obligations to one another. In addition, for a large user having many varied trading relationships, the presence of a separate recordkeeping duty to each of its partners could become an administrative nightmare. As systems and business needs change, the user may wish to delete or modify some records.[6] Records may have to be sold when related business assets are sold. Recordkeeping obligations to trading partners are an unwelcome straitjacket that limits the user's flexibility.

[5]Canadian Model §5.07 provides, "At least once in each calendar year . . . each party shall procure a control procedures review by a competent independent third party and shall provide the other party with the report of that reviewer."

[6]Some companies prefer as a policy—for cost, antitrust, and other liability reasons—to delete all but essential records as soon as possible.

The argument for one trading partner to require another to keep a log is that electronic messages and records can be changed inconspicuously. The retention of records by one's trading partner serves as a check against mistakes and fraud. The rebuttal argument is that one's own internal controls can be sufficient to protect message and record trustworthiness.[7] Furthermore, it is counterproductive to burden electronic messaging systems with procedures that are not clearly warranted.

[7] *See* Chapter 6.

Chapter 16

The Statute of Frauds and Other Enforceability Issues

§16.1 THE LAWS COMPELLING WRITINGS, SIGNINGS, AND THE LIKE

Lawmakers have long regulated transactions by insisting that they be "written" or "signed" to be fully effective. The paramount example, which originated in England in 1677 and now thrives throughout American law, is the statute of frauds that applies to contracts. Decrees requiring writings and signings are imperfect tools. Their meanings are sometimes debatable, and many courts have circumvented them even when they clearly apply.

Electronic messaging highlights the imperfection. Many EDI users, for example, form electronic contracts. A buyer may send an EDI purchase order to "offer" to purchase goods. If the seller responds with an EDI purchase order acknowledgment to "accept" the order, a contract is formed. The two EDI messages constitute the contract. But it is uncertain whether electronic messages are "written" or "signed." So there is some question whether the statute of frauds will allow enforcement of this electronic sales contract.

It is now necessary to repeal, change, or at least reinterpret some writing and signing requirements, but legal reform progresses slowly. Although users can often work around this problem,[1] it does retard electronic messaging use and thus causes economic inefficiency.

Requirements that transactions be "written," "signed," "executed," or memorialized in a "document" or "instrument" are stated (sometimes implicitly) in many statutes, regulations, contracts, and charters. Most states have a general statute of frauds, which requires that contracts in specified categories, to be enforced, be supported by written evidence signed by the parties against whom enforcement is sought. The usual categories are (1) contracts by executors and administrators, (2) suretyship agreements, (3) agreements in consideration of marriage, (4) contracts for the transfer of real property (land), and (5) contracts not to be performed within one year. Some states add brokerage agreements to the list.[2]

All states but Louisiana have adopted U.C.C. §2-201(1), which provides:

> [A] contract for the sale of goods for the price of $500 or more is not enforceable by way of action or defense unless there is some writing sufficient to indicate that a contract for sale has been made between the parties and signed by the party against whom enforcement is sought or by his authorized agent or broker. A writing is not insufficient because it omits or incorrectly states a term agreed upon but the contract is not enforceable under this paragraph beyond the quantity of goods shown in such writing.

The U.C.C. contains other statutes of frauds. U.C.C. §1-206 limits enforcement of unsigned and unwritten contracts for the sale of certain personal property for $5000 or more. Under U.C.C. §5-104(1), a letter of credit "must be in writing and signed by the issuer." U.C.C. §8-319 provides:

§16.1 [1]Private companies contracting between themselves electronically, for example, can usually work around it with a trading partner agreement.

[2]*See, e.g.*, N.Y. Gen. Oblig. Law §5-701.a.10 (McKinney 1989).

> A contract for the sale of securities is not enforceable by way of action or defense unless: [among other possibilities] (a) there is some writing signed by the party against whom enforcement is sought or by his authorized agent or broker, sufficient to indicate that a contract has been made for sale of a stated quantity of described securities at a defined or stated price. . . .

A portion of Federal Public Law 97-258, codified at 31 U.S.C. §1501, subjects federal government contracts to a type of statute of frauds. Subject to exceptions, it provides:

> An amount shall be recorded as an obligation of the United States Government only when supported by documentary evidence of—(1) a binding agreement between an agency and another person . . . that is—(A) in writing, in a way and form, and for a purpose authorized by law; and (B) executed before the end of the period of availability for obligation of the appropriation or fund. . . .

Section 2-110 of the Model Purchasing Ordinance, published for use by municipal governments by the National Institute of Municipal Law Officers, mandates that the purchase of supplies and services in excess of $5000 be "by formal, written contract."

Many statutes, contracts, bylaws and the like require legal notices or actions to be written or signed. U.C.C. §2-616(1), for example, provides that under certain circumstances a buyer of goods may "by written notification" terminate or modify a purchase contract. Section 401 of the Uniform Limited Partnership Act provides that new partners may be added to a partnership upon "written consent of all partners." Revised Model Business Corporation Act §7.22(b) permits a stockholder to appoint a proxy by "signing an appointment form." One example of a law requiring government filings to be written or signed is Federal Rule of Civil Procedure 11, which governs court filings: "Every pleading, motion, and other paper of a party represented by an attorney shall be signed. . . ."

§16.2 HISTORICAL PERSPECTIVE

The difficulty of applying writing and signing requirements to electronic transactions is only the latest manifestation of an eternal problem. It is impossible to draft practical legal rules that are absolutely unambiguous for all occasions. Mere words are too elastic, and the situations that can arise too varied. Hence, even long before EDI and e-mail it was not entirely certain how requirements such as writing and signing apply. Consider the interpretations of "writing," "signing," and similar terms in Exhibit 16.1.

EXHIBIT 16.1

Inconsistent Interpretations of Writing, Signing, and Similar Requirements

On a summons, a "written signature" means a handwritten autograph or, if the signer cannot write, a proper mark. *Ames v. Schurmeire,* 9 Minn. 221 (Gil. 206) (1864).

A typewritten name on a U.C.C. financing statement cannot qualify as a signature. *In re Carlstrom,* 3 U.C.C. Rep. Serv. 766 (Callaghan) (Bankr. D. Me. 1966).

A typewritten name on a U.C.C. financing statement is a signature. *Matter of Save-on-Carpets of Arizona, Inc.,* 545 F.2d 1239 (9th Cir. 1976).

A typewritten name on a declaration of candidacy for public office is not a satisfactory signature. *State ex rel.*

EXHIBIT 16.1, continued

Chatfield v. Board of Education of Hamilton County, 176 Ohio St. 93, 197 N.E.2d 797 (1964).

A fax signature is adequate for a declaration of candidacy, at least if it is soon followed by delivery of a conventional handwritten signature. *Madden v. Hegadorn,* 236 N.J. Super. 280, 565 A.2d 725 (Law Div.), *aff'd,* 239 N.J. Super. 268, 571 A.2d 296 (App. Div. 1989).

A typewritten name on a telegram is a signature under the statute of frauds. *Hillstrom v. Gosnay,* 188 Mont. 388, 614 P.2d 466 (1980).

A code ("1.2.8.") written in lead pencil as an endorsement on a bill of exchange is a binding endorsement. *Brown v. The Butchers and Drovers' Bank,* 6 Hill 443 (N.Y. 1844).

Signatures written with indelible pencil on an electoral petition qualify as "written in ink." *Thrailkill v. Smith,* 106 Ohio St. 1, 138 N.E. 532 (1922).

X-ray pictures constitute "written evidence." *Texas Employers' Insurance Association v. Crow,* 148 Tex. 113, 221 S.W.2d 235 (1949).

A state constitutional requirement that legislators vote by "written ballot" allows both handwritten and printed ballots. *Henshaw v. Foster,* 26 Mass. (9 Pick.) 312 (1830).

A will set forth on slate is not permanent enough to be "written." *Reed v. Woodward,* 11 Phila. 541 (Pa. 1875).

A will prepared and dated by the testator with a manual typewriter and signed in longhand does not qualify as "entirely written, dated and signed by the hand of the testator himself." *In re Dreyfus' Estate,* 175 Cal. 417, 165 P. 941 (1917).

A tape recording of an oral contract is not a "writing"

EXHIBIT 16.1, continued

under the statute of frauds. *Roos v. Aloi,* 127 Misc. 2d 864, 487 N.Y.S.2d 637 (Sup. Ct. 1985).

A tape recording of an oral contract is a "signed writing" under the statute of frauds. *Ellis Canning Co. v. Bernstein,* 348 F. Supp. 1212 (D. Colo. 1972).

A stenographer's typed report of courtroom testimony is not a "written instrument." *Patterson v. Churchman,* 122 Ind. 379, 23 N.E. 1082 (1890).

For purposes of a forgery statute, an automatic teller machine (ATM) card is not a "written instrument." *State v. White,* 47 Wash. App. 370, 735 P.2d 684 (1987).

Misuse of an ATM card constitutes forgery because the act of recording a personal identification number into the ATM is a form of writing. *Allstate Insurance Co. v. Renshaw,* 151 Ga. App. 80, 258 S.E.2d 744 (1979).

The typing of false identification into a computer network is not sufficient to create a false "instrument" so as to permit conviction under a British forgery statute. *R. v. Gold; R. v. Schifreen,* (1988) 87 Cr. App. 257.

A promissory note had been prepared on a printed form, with an interest rate of 7 percent being typed in, but a handwritten note on the document indicated the rate was 8 percent. Under the rule that "written" terms control over "printed" terms, the court held the typewritten 7 was "printed," but it suggested that if there were no handwritten 8 the typewritten 7 would be considered "written." *Acme Coal v. Northrup National Bank,* 23 Wyo. 66, 146 P. 593 (1915).

§16.3 THE STATUTE OF FRAUDS' FUNCTIONS AND JUSTIFICATIONS

The statute of frauds illustrates many of the functions of and justifications for writing and signing requirements. The statute generally denies enforcement to covered contracts that are unsupported by signed writings. Enforcement is withheld even though there might otherwise be enough evidence to prove the contracts. Over time, however, authorities have aggressively constrained the statute's effect by reading it narrowly and finding many loopholes in it.

§16.3.1 Writing Requirement

In contracting, writing is a ritual that makes a transaction psychologically binding and cautions the actors that they are entering a solemn matter.[1] Writing also "promotes deliberation, seriousness."[2] Thus, it fosters a carefully conceived and articulated contract. But the statute of frauds requires exceedingly little articulation. Under the U.C.C. Article Two version, the only term that must be stated in writing is the quantity of the goods to be sold. U.C.C. §2-201 Official Comment 1 explains: "All that is required is that the writing afford a basis for believing that [the assertion that a contract existed] rests on a real transaction." The general statute of frauds normally requires that the "essential terms" of the agreement be in writing.[3] Even this does not require the writing of "details and particulars," however.[4]

§16.3 [1]Perillo, The Statute of Frauds in the Light of the Functions and Dysfunctions of Form, 43 Fordham L. Rev. 39 (1974).

[2]Rabel, The Statute of Frauds and Comparative Legal History, 63 L.Q. Rev. 174, 178 (1947).

[3]*See* Restatement (Second) of Contracts §131 (1981).

[4]*Id.*, comment g.

The statute of fraud's foremost aim is to create evidence to help a court confirm a contract's existence.[5] This protects a defendant from spurious claims. However, the evidence created need not be great in either quantity or probative strength. Even a document that is lost or destroyed before it can be admitted as evidence in court can satisfy the writing requirement.[6]

A writing containing sufficient terms (and the requisite signature) may be an aggregate of several separate documents.[7] In the famous case *Crabtree v. Elizabeth Arden Sales Corp.*[8] a company president, Elizabeth Arden, made an *unsigned* memorandum on a telephone pad outlining a contract, including a two-year term, for an employee's services. In the ensuing months, other company officers made and initialed payroll cards consistent with the memorandum's terms. The company fired the employee before the two years were up; he sued, claiming he had a two-year contract. The company asserted a statute-of-frauds defense, contending no signed writing expressed the contract's essential terms, which would have to include the length of employment. Yet the court held the payroll cards were properly signed writings. Then it read the payroll cards and the unsigned memorandum as a unit because they logically interrelated. Together these constituted a signed writing that did state the essential terms.

Where the statute of frauds has been extended to require broker contracts to be signed and written, the purpose is to regulate a profession suspected of abuse.[9] Similarly, writing requirements for government contracts constrain govern-

[5]Perillo, above, at 68.

[6]Restatement (Second) of Contracts §137 (1981).

[7]2 A. Corbin, Corbin on Contracts §512 (1950) (hereinafter, 2 Corbin).

[8]305 N.Y. 48, 105 N.Y.S.2d 40, 110 N.E.2d 551 (1953).

[9]2 Corbin §416. The delivery of written information also gives the recipient a fair opportunity to notice it and easily keep a reliable record of it. The written record gives auditors an easy way to verify information.

ment agents, facilitate audit of their activities, and ensure their obligations can be ascertained after they leave office.[10]

§16.3.2 Signing Requirement

Like writing, signing is associated with seriousness and deliberation. In addition, conventional wisdom views a signature as proof (or forensic evidence) of a writing's authenticity and proof of the originator's assent to it. The proof is not strong, however, even with handwritten autographs.[11] Moreover, authorities have tended to disregard irregularities in form and to be very liberal in determining what constitutes a statute-of-frauds signature.[12] They have recognized initials, marks, typewritten names, and stamps.[13] Pen ink is not necessary. Pencil, carbon copy, or photographic signatures are acceptable.[14]

The essence of a signature is the intent to use it (whatever it happens to be) to adopt or approve a writing. Under U.C.C. §1-201(39), for example, " 'Signed' includes any symbol executed or adopted by a party with present intention to authenticate a writing." U.C.C. §1-201 Official Comment 39 explains:

> The inclusion of authentication in the definition of "signed" is to make clear that as the term is used in [the U.C.C.] a complete signature is not necessary. Authentication may be printed, stamped or written; it may be by initials or by thumbprint. It may be on any part of the document and in appropriate cases may be found in a billhead or letterhead. No catalog of possible authentications can be complete and the

[10]Perillo, above, at 58-59.
[11]*See* §5.4.
[12]Kohlmeyer & Co. v. Bowen, 126 Ga. App. 700, 192 S.E.2d 400 (1972).
[13]2 Corbin §522.
[14]Restatement (Second) of Contracts §134 comment a (1981).

court must use common sense and commercial experience in passing upon these matters.

Kohlmeyer & Co. v. Brown[15] involved a confirmation statement, for a sale of securities, written on a fill-in-the-blank form that contained the printed name and logo of the seller but no separate signature. The court held the printed name constituted the seller's signature because that was the intent evident from the form's use. *Interstate United Corp. v. White*[16] examined whether a seller had signed a contract for the sale of business assets. The seller had affixed no discrete symbol that might be construed as a signature. The court held, however, that the seller's conduct, rather than any written symbol, amounted to authentication. The conduct was the seller's preparation of a final draft of the contract and supporting papers, its requiring that the buyer obtain a certain consent to fulfill the contract, and its sending of certain letters to suppliers.

Still, the intent to sign or authenticate must be clear. A name in a recital on a document is not necessarily sufficient.[17]

Some renditions of the statute of frauds (and some interpretive statutes read with it) speak of the writing being "subscribed," and some courts have construed that to mean the signature must appear at the foot of the writing for all of it to be binding.[18] The dubious rationale is that a signature shows adoption of only the text preceding it.

At any rate, the signing requirement's purpose is to elicit some objective indication of assent.

[15]126 Ga. App. 700, 192 S.E.2d 400 (1972).

[16]388 F.2d 5 (10th Cir. 1967).

[17]Lee v. Vaughn Seed Store, 101 Ark. 68, 141 S.W. 496 (1911).

[18]R. C. Durr Co., Inc. v. Bennett Indus., Inc., 590 S.W.2d 338 (Ky. App. 1979).

§16.4 THE STATUTE OF FRAUDS' APPLICATION TO ELECTRONIC TRANSACTIONS

Conventionally, writing and signing mean reducing words to paper. Yet the terms are abstractly understood to embrace more than just ink on wood fibers. U.C.C. §1-201(46), for example, provides, " 'Written' or 'writing' includes printing, typewriting or any other intentional reduction to tangible form." In approving a pencil as a proper instrument for writing, the court in *Clason v. Bailey*[1] held a writing must be visible to the eye and suggested it must be durable.

§16.4.1 Telegraph, Telex, and Mailgram

Telegraph, telex, and mailgram deliver paper to the recipient. Courts have decidedly recognized these media as capable of satisfying the statute of frauds. In the early case *Howley v. Whipple,* the court remarked:

> [W]hen a contract is made by telegraph . . . that constitutes a contract in writing under the statute of frauds; . . . it makes no difference whether [the telegraph] operator writes the offer or the acceptance . . . with a steel pen an inch long attached to an ordinary penholder, or whether his pen be a copper wire a thousand miles long. In either case the thought is communicated to the paper by the use of the finger resting upon the pen; nor does it make any difference that in one case common record ink is used, while in the other case more subtle fluid, known as electricity, performs the same office.[2]

§16.4 [1]14 Johns. 484 (N.Y. 1817). *See also* U.C.C. §2-201 Official Comment 1, which recognizes pencil.

[2]48 N.H. 487, 488 (1869).

In *Selma Savings Bank v. Webster County Bank*[3] the court recognized a telegram bearing a typewritten name as a signed writing required under applicable law to accept a check. Issuance of the telegram was deemed the act of the officer under whose direction it was sent, even though the officer had telephoned the directions to an operator. Similarly, *Hillstrom v. Gosnay*[4] upheld under the statute of frauds a contract evidenced by a telegram that stated, "PLEASE CONSIDER THIS MY ACCEPTANCE . . ." and ended with a typewritten name. The court ruled the name was a signature because, judging from the telegram's words and other circumstantial evidence, that was the sender's intent. Again, the sender had dictated instructions by telephone to the telegraph operator. Neither *Selma Savings* nor *Hillstrom* inquired into the technical reliability of the multistep process by which the "signature" was initiated and finally affixed. The presence or absence of technical controls to ensure signature genuineness seemed irrelevant.

Joseph Denunzio Fruit Co. v. Crane,[5] a dispute over a contract for the sale of grapes, examined whether messages sent through the then new technology of telex (or teletype) satisfied the statute-of-frauds signing requirement. (That there was a "writing" was unquestioned.) The court determined certain codes in the messages did constitute signatures.

> [E]ach party was readily identifiable and known to the other by the symbols or code letters used, and there is no contention that the messages did not originate in the office of one and terminate in the office of the other.[6]

[3]182 Ky. 604, 206 S.W. 870 (Ct. App. 1918).

[4]188 Mont. 388, 614 P.2d 466 (1980).

[5]79 F. Supp. 117 (S.D. Cal. 1948), *vacated,* 89 F. Supp. 962 (1950), *reinstated,* 188 F.2d 569 (9th Cir.), *cert. denied,* 342 U.S. 820 (1951), *cert. denied,* 344 U.S. 829 (1952).

[6]79 F. Supp. at 128.

Noting the extensive use of telex in modern business, and the liberal definition of signature recognized in prior cases, the court ruled signatures were present.[7] The court made no inquiry, however, into whether a telex signature provided any particular degree of proof (or forensic evidence) that the sender had originated the message.

In *Hessenthaler v. Farzin*[8] the court held a mailgram satisfied the statute of frauds. The mailgram simply stated, "We, Dr. Mehdi and Marie Farzin, accept the offer of $520,000 for our property at 6175 and 6185 Hocker Drive Harrisburg, Pennsylvania." Nothing served as a separate signature; however, the court ruled the senders' names sufficed, explaining:

> [T]he focus [is] on whether there is some reliable indication that the person to be charged with performing under the writing intended to authenticate it. [T]he proper, realistic approach . . . is to look to the *reliability* of the memorandum [i.e., the mailgram], rather than to insist on a formal signature. (emphasis supplied)[9]

The court showed that reliability might be assessed from any of the facts and circumstances surrounding the message that show the sender's intent. Here, the necessary facts resided in the message's content.

> The detail contained in this mailgram is such that there can be little question of its reliability. [Sellers] were careful to begin the mailgram by identifying themselves. They then made certain that their intention would be properly understood by declaring their acceptance, and identifying both the property and the consideration involved. In light of the primary declaration of identity, combined with the inclusion of the precise

[7] *See also* Interocean Shipping Co. v. National Shipping and Trading Corp., 523 F.2d 527 (2d Cir. 1975), *cert. denied,* 423 U.S. 1054 (1976) (simple telex satisfies statute of frauds).

[8] 388 Pa. Super. 37, 564 A.2d 990 (1989).

[9] 564 A.2d at 993.

> terms of the agreement, we are satisfied that the mailgram sufficiently reveals [sellers'] intention to adopt the writing as their own, and thus is sufficient to constitute a "signed" writing for purposes of the Statute.[10]

Thus, reliability for this court does not necessarily refer to the integrity of the technical process by which the message is transmitted or the forensic strength of the "signature." The court strongly hinted this same analysis would apply to fax, telex, and e-mail.[11]

Two cases faintly signal a possible contrary view regarding telegram and telex. *Miller v. Wells Fargo Bank International Corp.*[12] raised the question, which went unanswered, whether a test key on a telex constitutes a signature on a security agreement under U.C.C. §9-203. The appeals court in the same case suggested "it is at least arguable" that the test key did constitute a signature under the U.C.C.[13] The court in *Houston Contracting Co. v. Chase Manhattan Bank, N.A.*,[14] opined that an "unsigned telex" was not a "demand item" under U.C.C. §4-302. However, the court did not analyze whether the telex was signed and discussed none of the precedent on the signing of telegrams and telexes. Moreover, this lower court's references to an "unsigned" telex seemed merely rhetorical because the court did not explicitly say §4-302 requires a signature.

§16.4.2 Fax

Several cases have examined faxes in commercial disputes, but none have directly ruled whether a fax can be a signed

[10] *Id.* at 994.

[11] *Id.* at 992, n.3.

[12] 406 F. Supp. 452, 483 n.36 (S.D.N.Y. 1975), *aff'd*, 540 F.2d 548 (1976).

[13] Miller v. Wells Fargo Bank Intl. Corp., 540 F.2d 548, 564 (1976).

[14] 539 F. Supp. 247 (S.D.N.Y. 1982).

writing under the statute of frauds. Given, however, the following cases and the telegram, telex, and mailgram cases in Section 16.4.1, it will be difficult to argue that a conventional fax bearing a facsimile signature is not a signed writing.

In *Bazak International Corp. v. Mast Industries, Inc.*,[15] it was assumed, without questioning, that printouts from a fax machine were writings under U.C.C. §2-201. The dispute revolved around the interpretation and effect, under a statute of frauds exception in §2-201, of the messages' contents. Similarly, in *American Multimedia, Inc. v. Dalton Packaging, Inc.*,[16] it was also assumed, without questioning, that a faxed purchase order was an agreement "in writing" for purposes of a federal arbitration requirement, 9 U.S.C. §2.

Beatty v. First Exploration Fund 1987 and Co., Limited Partnership,[17] is a notable British Columbian opinion on fax that, although not a statute-of-frauds dispute, deals squarely with writing and signing requirements. Limited partners signed and faxed proxy documents for delivery as printouts at a partnership meeting. The partnership agreement instructed that proxies be written and signed, and the question was whether the fax printouts so qualified. The court answered affirmatively. It did not examine the scientific reliability of fax technology, and it rejected arguments that the use of faxes over conventional documents increases the risk of fraud and creates uncertainty.

§16.4.3 Tape Recording

A few courts have addressed whether an audiotape recording satisfies the statute of frauds. A tape recording of an oral communication and a magnetic recording of a computer text message use similar technology. Their differences are that

[15] 73 N.Y.2d 113, 538 N.Y.S.2d 503, 535 N.E.2d 633 (1989).
[16] 143 Misc. 2d 295, 540 N.Y.S.2d 410 (Sup. Ct. 1989).
[17] 25 B.C.L.R.2d 377 (1988).

the oral communication does not use textual symbols (which removes it one more step from conventional writing) and a recorded oral communication is generally more difficult to fabricate than is a simple recording of a computer text message.

The tape recording courts are split. In *Ellis Canning v. Bernstein*[18] parties to a corporate stock sale, which was subject to the U.C.C. §8-319 statute of frauds, recorded their oral contract on magnetic tape. The court held the agreement was "written" because it had been "reduced to tangible form" within the meaning of U.C.C. §1-201(46). As for the signing issue, the court did not determine that any particular symbol constituted a signature, but it judged that the signing requirement's purpose—identification of the contracting parties—was fulfilled. Quoting from *Corpus Juris Secundum,* the court explained that the statute of frauds' mission had been accomplished—" 'to prevent fraud and perjury in the enforcement of obligations depending for their evidence on the unassisted memory of witnesses.' "[19]

In *Sonders v. Roosevelt,*[20] however, it was summarily ruled that a recorded telephone conversation is not a writing under the statute of frauds. One justice dissented.

§16.4.4 Purely Electronic Messages

No reported lawsuit has examined whether a purely electronic message satisfies the statute of frauds. The telegram, telex, mailgram, fax, and tape recording cases furnish compelling support for the proposition that a durably recorded electronic message, bearing a symbol or code intended as a signature, is written and signed. Commentators agree that at least some electronic messages can be deemed written and

[18]348 F. Supp. 1212 (D. Colo. 1972).
[19]348 F. Supp. at 1228.
[20]102 A.D.2d 701, 476 N.Y.S.2d 331 (1984).

signed, but there is debate over the criteria for judging which ones.

§16.4.4.1 Writing Requirement

The report (ABA Report) issued with the ABA Model EDI Trading Partner Agreement (ABA Model) seems to argue that, assuming use of reliable record retention procedures, EDI should be accepted as a statute-of-frauds writing.[21] An EDI

> message, however stored, constitutes objective, corroborating evidence, apart from the oral testimony of the parties, which demonstrates the possible existence of a contract. Thus, the evidentiary purpose of the writing requirement is met.[22]

The Report goes on to say that the paper printout that is or could be derived from an EDI record "should be sufficient to indicate a contract was made."[23]

The Report thus seems to argue (correctly) that a record is a condition to an EDI message satisfying the statute of frauds' writing requirement. So it is curious that §3.3.2 of the ABA Model[24] defines "writings" as EDI messages that have only been properly transmitted rather than transmitted *and* recorded. Under the Model, the writing and signing "requirements are intended to be satisfied by the transmitted [message] itself, regardless of the medium by which the record of the transmission is established and maintained . . . ," says the ABA Report.[25]

Suppose a sender created an EDI message, viewed it on

[21]Electronic Messaging Services Task Force, The Commercial Use of Electronic Data Interchange—A Report, 45 Bus. Law. 1647, 1686 (1990) (hereinafter, ABA Report).

[22]*Id.*

[23]*Id.* at 1688, n.177.

[24]*See* §14.4.

[25]ABA Report at 1691, n.189.

her computer screen, and then transmitted it. Suppose further that no one kept a record of the message. Later, when there was a dispute over the message, the sender could prove the message only by testifying that she saw it. Does it qualify as a "writing" under the statute of frauds? If the sender and receiver had an agreement based on the ABA Model, the strange answer would be yes, since the ABA Model does not by its terms require a record. The ABA Report does not recognize this inconsistency between the Model and the Report.

The better view, which is incorporated into the Electronic Trading Letter, is that data become "fixed in a tangible medium of expression" are "written."[26] Nevertheless, the question of whether the ABA Model should recognize as writings only messages fixed (or recorded) in a tangible medium is a fine point. Rarely will a user try to enforce an EDI transaction that was not fixed in a tangible medium.

Satisfaction of the statute of frauds does not require

[26]*See* Appendix C. The "fixed in a tangible medium of expression" language derives from the Copyright Act of 1976:

> Copyright protection subsists . . . in original works of authorship fixed in any tangible medium of expression, now known or later developed, from which they can be perceived, reproduced, or otherwise communicated, either directly or with the aid of a machine or device. [17 U.S.C. §102(a) (1988).]
>
> A work is "fixed" in a tangible medium of expression when its embodiment in a copy or phonorecord, by or under the authority of the author, is sufficiently permanent or stable to permit it to be perceived, reproduced, or otherwise communicated for a period of more than transitory duration. [17 U.S.C. §101 (1988).]

Fixation would exclude data captured momentarily in the memory of a computer but would include data captured on magnetic tape. H.R. (Judiciary Comm.) No. 94-1476, 94th Cong., 2d Sess., at 35 (Sept. 3, 1976), *reprinted in* 1976 U.S. Code Cong. & Admin. News 5659, 5666. The brilliant suggestion to borrow language from copyright law to deal with statute-of-frauds issues comes from a letter from Roy G. Saltman, computer scientist at the National Institute of Standards and Technology, to Peter Weiss, Deputy Associate Administrator, Office of Federal Procurement Policy (July 23, 1990).

delivery of the writing.[27] This suggests that if a record is a prerequisite for satisfying the statute (as it should be), the record could be kept by either sender or recipient.[28]

§16.4.4.2 Signing Requirement

Several members of the group that drafted the ABA Model (ABA Task Force) believe EDI could satisfy the signing requirement of the U.C.C. §2-201 statute of frauds. They seemingly subscribe to the idea that any symbol adopted to identify the sender can be adequate to authenticate a message.[29] This would include any electronic characters—the simple name "Blue Co." for instance. Apparently their conclusion is not conditioned on the symbol being subject to any degree of security or forensic reliability. This conclusion is wholly justified given the very plentiful array of symbols, such as names on mailgrams,[30] that courts have previously recognized. The author sides with this view.

An opposing argument is that the view of the Task Force's liberal members emasculates the statute of frauds and undercuts its prevention of deceit.[31] According to this argu-

[27]U.C.C. §2-201 Official Comment 6; S. Williston, 4 Williston on Contracts §579A (3d ed. 1961).

[28]For a conventional fax, either the original paper fed into the sending machine or the printout from the receiving machine should qualify as the writing.

[29]ABA Report at 1688, n.177.

[30]Hessenthaler v. Farzin, 388 Pa. Super. 37, 564 A.2d 990 (1989).

[31]Recognize, however, that the fraud at issue is quite limited. The statute of frauds does not set the security standards users should apply to protect themselves from impostors (Chapters 5, 11, and 13 discuss these standards), nor does it ensure they can prove in court who they were dealing with and what was agreed to (Chapters 5 and 6 and Part III address these issues). The statute merely sets the standard of evidence to be met before a court will enforce contracts that can otherwise be proved. The statute's value is questionable. *See* §16.7.2. Even if no statute of frauds exists, a court can still deny the enforcement of a bogus contract. It can simply determine from all the facts present that no contract exists.

ment, there is an important difference between purely electronic communications on the one hand and telegraph and telex on the other. The latter involve rigid technologies controlled by neutral communications carriers; the receiver cannot change the record to which a "signature" is attached. The EDI or e-mail receiver, however, can forge his record (absent controls).[32] Therefore, according to this argument, a record made by the recipient, which bears a simple code as the sender's signature, does not prevent fraud against the purported sender and should not satisfy the statute of frauds. (A different result might apply to a record kept by the sender himself.)

Part of this argument might also be that

> a signature's traceability to the signatory [is] very important. Paper-based signatures inherently include forensic traits such as a unique pen stroke, ink or paper which help identify the signatory. In the absence of paper documents, methods to authenticate EDI transactions (for example, introducing forensic traits to help identify the parties and message content) must be used to ensure trustworthiness and a degree of legally probative evidence comparable to that provided by conventional signatures.[33]

In support of this reasoning, one might cite *In re Carlstrom,*[34] which held that a typewritten name on a U.C.C. financing

[32]The rebuttal is that a sender could fabricate a telegram or telex by asking an imposter to send a false one. In practice, the strongest barrier to fabricated telegrams and telexes is the same one that hinders EDI and e-mail recipients from fabricating their records: the wealth of external facts and circumstances (the historical relationship between the parties, eyewitness observations, statements in other messages, and so forth) that surround the transactions.

[33]Baum, EDI and the Law, 2 EDI Forum 78 (1989).

[34]3 U.C.C. Rep. Serv. 766 (Callaghan) (D. Me., Bankr. 1966). *See also* Parshalle v. Roy, 567 A.2d 19 (Del. Ch. 1989) ("datagram" proxy created by shareholder telephoning proxy recording service, with no procedure to verify shareholder identity, does not create document with sufficient in-

statement was not a signature, for a signature must be "susceptible of evidentiary connection to the signatory."[35] One observer contends electronic contracts should be enforceable under the statute of frauds only if created with "commercially reasonable security" measures,[36] which presumably would ensure the gathering and preservation of forensic evidence sufficient to prevent fraud.

§16.5 PRACTICAL APPROACHES TO THE STATUTE OF FRAUDS

Considering the arguments, some uncertainty does exist today about when a purely electronic message satisfies the statute of frauds. There are, nevertheless, many paths around the statute's bar to enforcement. For a sale of goods, U.C.C. §2-201 provides exceptions for a contract between merchants

dicia of authenticity to be valid as evidence of agency relationship). *But see* Benedict v. Lebowitz, 346 F.2d 120 (2d Cir. 1965) (typewritten name on financing statement constitutes signature).

[35]3 U.C.C. Rep. Serv. at 773. The financing statement contained the typewritten name of the secured party and a printed block for the signature of an agent of the secured party. The printed block was blank. Although U.C.C. §1-201(39) contemplates that any symbol may constitute a signature, the court read U.C.C. §9-402 as requiring a symbol that can be forensically linked to the signatory. The case's result might be correct, but the rationale is wrong. The unfilled signature block on the document calls into question the secured party's *intent* for the typewritten name to be a signature. But by requiring that a legal signature be one that is traceable to the signer, the court sets a meaningless standard. Scientifically speaking, the typewritten symbols on the financing statement are "susceptible of evidentiary connection" to the secured party and its representative. To some appreciable degree, an expert document examiner could link the age, type style, and chemical makeup of the ink used to type the name back to the secured party's typewriter and thus to the secured party itself.

[36]Baum, Analysis of Legal Aspects, *in* EDI and the Law 129 (I. Walden ed. 1989).

confirmed in writing by one of them and not timely objected to by the other; a contract for specially manufactured goods; a contract to which the defendant admits during litigation; and certain partially performed contracts. Courts have additionally fashioned a host of other, nonuniform and less predictable exceptions, including constructive trusts, promissory estoppel, the main purpose rule, the joint obligor rule, the doctrine of part performance, and the fictions of quasi-contract.[1] These are equitable doctrines that soften the harshness of strict legal rules, but securing their application in any particular case may entail much litigation.

Under the doctrine of part performance, if a party takes some action to perform a contract, which convincingly confirms its existence, the party will not be heard to oppose enforceability under the statute of frauds.[2]

To prevent injustice, promissory estoppel can enforce promises (such as promises to sell things) that are unenforceable as contracts because of the statute of frauds. Restatement (Second) of Contracts §139(1) articulates the doctrine:

> A promise which the promisor should reasonably expect to induce action or forbearance on the part of the promisee or a third person and which does induce such action or forbearance is enforceable notwithstanding the Statute of Frauds if injustice can be avoided only by enforcement of the promise. The remedy for breach may be limited as justice requires.

The doctrine's application relies on subjective judgment. Among the factors a court considers are the presence of unconscionable injury, unjust enrichment, and conduct in re-

§16.5 [1]Perillo, above, at 72-74. Concerning the requirement at 31 U.S.C. §1501 that obligations of the federal government be in writing, *see* United States v. American Renaissance Lines, Inc., 494 F.2d 1059 (D.C. Cir.), *cert. denied,* 419 U.S. 1020 (1974), which recognized an unwritten obligation might be enforced under the doctrine of quantum meruit.

[2]*See* Burns v. McCormick, 233 N.Y. 230, 135 N.E. 273 (1922); Miller v. McCamish, 78 Wash. 2d 821, 479 P.2d 919 (1971).

liance on the promise that corroborates a contract's existence. Note there is some disagreement whether promissory estoppel can prevail over a statute-of-frauds defense under U.C.C. §2-201. Some argue §2-201's many explicit exceptions to the strict writing and signing decrees displace the estoppel doctrine in U.C.C. Article Two.[3]

A usage of trade (which is like an industry custom), a course of dealing (an understanding arising between parties from several similar transactions), and a course of performance (an understanding arising from actions during performance of a single contract) can each be relevant in applying estoppel. In *Northwest Potato Sales, Inc. v. Beck*[4] a seller backed out of an oral contract to sell seeds, citing the statute of frauds. Finding that it was common in the relevant industry for contracts not to be in writing, and that this seller had previously permitted the buyer to rely on the seller's oral promises, the court held the seller to his sales promise on an estoppel theory. Similarly, *H.B. Alexander & Son, Inc. v. Miracle Recreation Equip. Co.*[5] held a subcontractor to a bid it made by telephone to a general contractor in connection with the latter's preparation of a general bid on a construction project. The court determined that it was "custom" in the construction industry for general contractors to rely on such bids and that the parties had dealt with one another in this fashion previously. It held the subcontractor had "waived" a statute-of-frauds defense.[6]

As a practical matter, the statute of frauds' writing and signing clauses are almost illusory barriers to the enforcement of obligations. (This observation shows that the statute

[3]J. White & R. Summers, 1 Uniform Commercial Code, §2-7 (3d ed. 1988).

[4]678 P.2d 1138 (Mont. 1984).

[5]314 Pa. Super. 1, 460 A.2d 343 (1983).

[6]*See also* Gooch v. Farmers Mktg. Assn., 519 So. 2d 1214 (Miss. 1988) (oral contract for sale of soybeans is enforceable, but it is unclear whether the reason is that the course of dealing between the parties recognized oral contracts or that the defendant admitted the contract's existence).

of frauds is, at most, a minor problem for the participants in electronic trade.) Nonetheless, where an obligation is enforced under some court-initiated doctrines such as estoppel, it could be difficult to predict what the terms will be. Under estoppel, the court enforces, not a full contract under traditional and relatively predictable contract rules, but a promise, and only to the extent the court finds justice demands.

It is doubtful that an industry usage of trade, or an agreement between trading partners, that regarded the statute of frauds as inapplicable would be directly effective. U.C.C. §1-205 Official Comment 4 states:

> A distinction is to be drawn between mandatory rules of law such as the Statute of Frauds provisions of Article 2 on Sales whose very office is to control and restrict the actions of the parties, and which cannot be abrogated by agreement, or by a usage of trade, and [other] rules of law [which can be abrogated by agreement or usage of trade].

Still, where the statute of frauds is a perceived problem, trading partners can do much to proactively avoid its effect. The ABA Model advances three strategies for handling the statute's writing and signing requirements as they apply to agreements formed with EDI messages to sell goods.[7]

The first is definitional: By agreement under the ABA Model, a properly transmitted message is deemed "written,"

[7] The ABA Task Force was uncertain that a trading partner agreement to respond to the statute of frauds was necessary. *See* ABA Report at 1688. ABA Report footnote 177 argues that EDI does satisfy the statute's writing and signing requirements, but the Task Force felt compelled to prepare and recommend such an agreement to reassure risk-adverse user management.

A trading partner agreement based on the ABA Model could not itself satisfy the writing requirement because ABA Model §4.3 states that neither the agreement's execution nor its delivery implies an obligation to buy or sell goods.

and a designated symbol(s) or code(s) within the message is deemed a "signature."[8]

Second, the ABA Model deems conduct in agreement with its terms to be evidence of a course of dealing and course of performance in furtherance of the agreement and the transactions facilitated thereby.[9] This may be useful in confirming the intent to form enforceable contracts.

Third, the ABA Model establishes a foundation for estoppel. Section 3.3.4 obligates each party

> not to contest the validity or enforceability of [proper messages] under the provisions of any applicable law relating to whether certain agreements are to be in writing or signed by the party to be bound thereby.[10]

This is a mutual promise on which each party relies in using EDI rather than paper. In addition, the parties' mutual efforts to implement EDI (whether or not described in a trading partner agreement) could be the basis for estopping one partner from reneging on the buy/sell promises it makes through EDI.[11]

None of these strategies is guaranteed to succeed, but cumulatively they arm a party seeking enforcement with a fearsome arsenal of arguments.

Another strategy—one not suggested by the ABA Task Force—is available. Users can configure electronic systems to print all messages immediately and automatically upon

[8]ABA Model §3.3.2. *See* Section 16.4.4.1, which argues that messages should be considered written only if recorded. Note that under the ABA Model the identification and password a user discloses to gain access to a network may not constitute a "signature."

[9]ABA Model §3.3.3.

[10]As worded, could this be construed to prevent contesting a contract under any part of a statute of frauds? U.C.C. §2-201, for example, requires not only that a signed writing exist, but that it specify a quantity of goods. Does ABA Model §3.3.4 preclude an objection that the electronic signed writing contains no quantity term?

[11]*See* ABA Report at 1688.

transmission. The system would then function more like telegram and telex. The Globex system, for example, makes automatic printouts of commodity trade confirmations.

A final strategy, sometimes used in electronic purchasing systems, is this: In advance of trading, the buyer and seller enter a "blanket" purchase order written on paper. Later, the buyer sends the seller electronic "releases" against that order when the buyer needs goods. If the blanket purchase order is a requirements contract, where the buyer agrees to purchase from the seller all the buyer's requirements for the goods in question, then the blanket purchase order is a contract to buy goods. It is the "signed writing" that satisfies the statute of frauds. The releases are not offers or acceptances, and are not contracts that need to be written and signed. Rather, the releases are informational messages that implement the contract embodied in the blanket purchase order.

If the blanket purchase order is not a requirements contract, however, it is probably not a contract to buy goods. Neither party is obligated to buy or sell on the basis of the order. In effect, it says, if buyer sends a release, seller can fill it or decline to fill it at seller's discretion, but if seller chooses to fill it, the terms will be those in the blanket purchase order. In that case, any electronic releases are offers, which can be accepted to form electronic contracts.

§16.6 OTHER WRITING REQUIREMENTS

A writing requirement in a law can have purposes that go beyond those for the usual statute of frauds. A requirement for "written" notice of some matter may seek to ensure the notice is conspicuous to the recipient.[1] A "written" directive,

§16.6 [1]*See, e.g.*, U.C.C. §2-607(5)(a).

such as an order to a bailee to release goods,[2] may be a physical token that *A* gives to *B* so that *B* can show *C* what *A* directs to be done. A "written" document may be a negotiable document of title, which can be physically passed among a series of parties to effect and evidence transfer of ownership of property (such as cargo on a ship).

A writing requirement may be intended to force a stronger party, such as a lender, to carefully articulate all the terms of a transaction to a weaker party, such as a consumer borrower. That writing also produces a record that the weaker party can easily carry away and store.

The ability of an electronic message to serve any of these purposes depends on the circumstances. The more willing and sophisticated the parties involved, the more likely that these purposes will be served.

Practicing attorneys are forced to make judgment calls in advising clients on the risks of using electronic messages to satisfy writing requirements. These judgments should not be feared, for they are like so many other decisions business attorneys make. Seldom is the law crystal clear in its application to all aspects of a transaction.

In many dealings between two consenting businesses, the risk that an electronic message will not be considered a writing is clearly worth taking. First, the threat of a dispute, that makes it to court, over the writing issue is small. Second, the likelihood that a court would consider an electronic message a "writing" is high because the parties treat it as a writing and courts tend to be receptive to new means of communication.[3] Third, the amount of money or time to be made or saved by substituting electronic messages for paper can be great. Finally, the parties can take precautions, such as keeping reliable records of messages and entering agreements that confirm the messages are "writings."

[2] *See, e.g.,* U.C.C. §2-503(4)(b).

[3] Beatty v. First Exploration Fund 1987 and Co., 25 B.C.L.R.2d 377 (S.C. 1988).

§16.7 OPTIONS FOR THE LAW'S REVISION

The problems of properly drafting and construing rules on information communication and preservation will never disappear. New and unexpected situations will always emerge. Electronic communication technology ushers in only the latest puzzles.

Policymakers have several options in regard to the many laws that arguably conflict with electronic commercial practices. Varied responses will be appropriate.

§16.7.1 Maintenance of the Status Quo

Lawmakers could maintain the status quo. Some laws, such as those for the recording of real property deeds, may obviously not recognize electronic practices. Until there is a strong desire and feasible plan for electronic documents under these laws, the status quo seems in order.

§16.7.2 Elimination of Formal Requirements

Lawmakers could simplify particular laws to eliminate formal requirements such as "writings" and "signings." Some have called for repeal of the statute of frauds in U.C.C. §2-201.[1] Many versions of the statute, including §2-201, are long overdue for repeal. The statute is just as capable of

§16.7 [1]Cunningham, A Proposal to Repeal Section 2-201: The Statute of Frauds Section of Article 2, 85 Com. L.J. 361 (1980). *See also* H. Willis, The Statute of Frauds—A Legal Anachronism, 3 Ind. L.J. 427 pt. I, and 528 pt. II (1928). In 1990 a study committee under the Permanent Editorial Board for the U.C.C. issued a preliminary report strongly recommending that repeal of §2-201 be considered. ABA Report at 1689, n.182.

working an injustice, by denying enforcement of real contracts, as it is of preventing fraud. In an effort to circumvent this potential for inequity, courts have concocted a host of makeshift devices.[2] The proposition that courts need a specified type of physical evidence (i.e., a signed writing) to tell whether a contract exists is outdated and unworkable. Modern courts, unlike their predecessors when the statute was enacted, are adequately equipped to examine the full facts of a case to ascertain whether a contract truly exists. Moreover, the signed writing standard will be increasingly difficult to apply as technology spawns new forms of communication such as e-mail and teleconferencing.

One argument for retaining, and even strengthening, the statute of frauds is that it motivates parties to obtain reliable forensic evidence of a contract before acting on it. But evidence law itself furnishes parties substantial incentive to gather good evidence. The statute of frauds adds little to that.

A second argument for keeping the statute is that it shields a defendant from exposure to trial over an unsubstantiated claim. It permits a court to grant the defendant summary judgment and thus avoid a full trial on the facts to determine if a contract indeed existed.[3] Yet, essentially the same effect can be achieved under modern summary judgment rules, without resort to the statute of frauds. Under Federal Rule of Civil Procedure 56(c), for example, a defendant can win summary judgment if the evidence before the court prior to trial (pleadings, depositions, and so on) shows "that there is no genuine issue as to any material fact and that the [defendant] is entitled to a judgment as a matter of law." Where the plaintiff asserts a contract on the flimsiest of evidence (such as mere oral evidence where a written contract would, because of the transaction's magnitude, be ex-

[2]*See* §16.5.

[3]R. Givens, Practice Commentaries, *in* 23 N.Y. Gen. Oblig. Law 276, 283-284 (McKinney's 1989).

pected), the court will be reluctant to determine there is a genuine issue and will be justified in granting the defendant summary judgment. In *Matushita Electric Industrial Co. v. Zenith Radio Corp.*[4] it was held that under the Federal Rules of Civil Procedure an implausible claim must be supported by especially persuasive evidence to survive a summary judgment motion. The court in *Celotex Corp. v. Catrett*[5] held a party moving for summary judgment need not necessarily submit any factual information to prevail over a party with the burden of proof (such as a plaintiff asserting the existence of a contract).

Note that some different versions of the statutes of frauds may overlap. A contract for the sale of goods may satisfy U.C.C. §2-201 but still run afoul of a state's general statute of frauds because the contract will not be performed within one year.[6] So, to be fully effective, the repeal of one version of the statute must make clear that it affects the others as well.

§16.7.3 Explicit Recognition of Electronic Methods

Lawmakers could directly amend particular statutes and regulations to permit electronic transactions explicitly. If done in a fashion that is technically sensible, this approach would comfort users considerably. In 1989 the General Services Administration amended 41 C.F.R. part 101-41 to allow and set procedures for federal agencies to use EDI freight bills and other messages in connection with the procurement of transportation services. Now agencies can exchange elec-

[4] 475 U.S. 574 (1986).

[5] 477 U.S. 317 (1986).

[6] Seaman's Direct Buying Serv., Inc. v. Standard Oil Co. of Cal., 36 Cal. 3d 752, 206 Cal. Rptr. 354, 686 P.2d 1158 (1984). *But see* Roth Steel Prod. v. Sharon Steel Corp., 705 F.2d 134 (6th Cir. 1983).

tronic messages with private transportation carriers so long as the messages are authenticated with discrete codes, certified records are preserved, and proper controls prevent billing and payment abuses.[7]

Some legal schemes, such as those for negotiable bills of lading, may require substantial reworking. Simply to deem an electronic message a negotiable bill of lading may leave questions about how it will function. When it was decided that the U.C.C. should be specially updated to address wholesale electronic funds transfers, the drafters decided that, rather than simply amending the U.C.C. provisions covering paper checks, it was necessary to create an entirely new Article 4A.

§16.7.4 Amendment of Definitional Statutes

Lawmakers could address problematic laws indirectly with amendments to general statutory definitions. Some jurisdictions have statutes that define terms used generally within the jurisdictions' statutes. Title 1, §1 of the United States Code, for example, contains a definition of "writing."[8] A law such as this might, for example, be amended to say that "writing" includes "any expression (other than oral) of letters, numbers, or codes that is, or in connection with its communication from one party to another becomes, fixed in a tangible medium of expression."[9] This definition serves these purposes: (1) The "fixed in a tangible medium" language requires a record. (2) The "letters, numbers or codes" language requires more articulateness and deliberation than oral communication. (3) The "letters, numbers or codes" lan-

[7]54 Fed. Reg. 15940 (1989).

[8]It "includes printing and typewriting and reproductions of visual symbols by photographing, multigraphing, mimeographing, manifolding, or otherwise."

[9]Similar language might be used with any legal definition of "writing," whether the definition appears in a statute, regulation, or contract.

guage forces the communication to be conspicuous—at least conspicuous enough for business transactions. This definition may, however, be inappropriate for consumer transactions that must be in writing. The definition may not properly ensure that the consumer receives a message that he can easily recognize and use.

This approach's advantage is that it covers many laws at once. The hazard is that a handful of laws may be affected in unforeseen ways; this requires us to rely on courts to use common sense in interpreting the definition. The ideal course is to examine each particular law to determine whether electronic communication is appropriate, and under what conditions, and then to amend (or not amend) accordingly. The problem with the ideal is that it requires tremendous effort.

§16.7.5 Agency Reinterpretation of Law

A competent government agency could issue an interpretation of particular laws under its jurisdiction to permit electronic methods. The Securities and Exchange Commission, for example, adopted a temporary rule interpreting the writing requirement of the Securities Act of 1933.[10] The Commission construed "written" to include electronically formatted documents.[11] It also adopted a temporary rule interpreting the word "signed" to include the entry of electronic symbols "executed, adopted or authorized as a signature."[12]

§16.7.6 Court Interpretation

Policymakers could wait for the courts to act on a case-by-case basis to clarify how the law applies to electronic mes-

[10] 15 U.S.C. §77(b)(9) (1988).
[11] EDGAR Temporary Rule, 17 C.F.R. §230.499(b)(3) (1990).
[12] EDGAR Temporary Rule, 17 C.F.R. §230.499(b)(7) (1990).

sages. This leaves users at some risk. They may be uncertain how their transactions will be treated, and no one wants to argue a test case. Adoption of the technology may be impeded where users perceive substantial risks, which has to some extent already happened because of the statute of frauds. Still, given the myriad laws that contain writing and signing requirements, this must often be the de facto approach. Users can derive some comfort from historical judicial efforts to accommodate new technology,[13] and from knowledge that statutory ambiguity is just an inescapable fact. They can also take precautions, where appropriate, such as using trading partner agreements and keeping reliable records.

§16.7.7 Adoption of Customs

Industry groups could foster usages of trade (customs) within industry that recognize the legal efficacy of electronic messages. Trade usages can influence the legal interpretation of transactions.

§16.7.8 Setting a Trend

The best overall approach artfully combines all of the foregoing suggestions. Once a few statutes and regulations are changed or reinterpreted in favor of electronic transactions and once a few appellate court decisions rule that electronic messages are writings, a trend develops in the law. (In fact, such a trend is already under way.) It becomes generally understood, if not fully stated, that the law recognizes electronic messaging technology as a good thing and will not allow meaningless legal technicalities to impede its use. Of course, in some areas, such as consumer lending transac-

[13] *See* Beatty v. First Exploration Fund 1987 and Co., 25 B.C.L.R.2d 377 (1988).

tions, the law may rightfully choose to continue paper writing requirements.

As this trend becomes stronger, the risks for users will diminish and become better understood. Promoters of electronic commerce can nurture this trend by researching it, publicizing it, and lobbying for it.

Telex became generally accepted as a legally effective means of contracting as a result of a trend. Businesses began to rely on telex before courts or statutes had explicitly approved it. Then a few cases in a few jurisdictions enforced telex contracts. The legal community concluded from this handful of cases that telex is generally acceptable.

Where lawmakers wish to accommodate electronic communication but retain the rough equivalent of a writing requirement, it would seem that the law must contemplate that a record of electronic communication be made. Any requirement for a signature or its equivalent, however, should be critically scrutinized. Handwritten signatures protect message senders to a limited degree, but they do not protect recipients much at all.[14] To require merely that the actor have "adopted" a certain communication should often be adequate. With or without a signing requirement, the burden would still generally be on the recipient to show the sender's intent to adopt the message. Fulfillment of this burden usually must rely on the facts and circumstances surrounding the message.

§16.8 AGREEMENT ON PROOF

Under the heading of contract validity/enforceability, the ABA Model addresses the admissibility of EDI records as evidence in court. The drafters perceived uncertainty whether courts

[14]*See* §5.4.

will accept records of electronic messages. Although it is commendable that they tried to tackle the problem, their solution, a contract, is a clumsy and confusing approach. The ABA Model should not have dealt with evidence issues. Any concerns about the admissibility of electronic records as evidence are better addressed with good recordkeeping practices and controls.[1] Unnecessary provisions in a model trading agreement make the legal issues in EDI appear worse than they really are.

ABA Model §3.3.2 provides:

> Any [message] properly transmitted pursuant to this Agreement . . . [when properly signed] . . . shall be deemed for all purposes . . . to constitute an "original" when printed from electronic files or records established and maintained in the normal course of business.

This aims to clarify what is the "original" of a message for purposes of the best evidence rule.[2] It is doubtful this is strongly needed. The best evidence rule is unlikely to exclude from evidence all records of a message, although it may fix a preference if multiple records are available. The preference would at bottom be based on the trial judge's sense of justice under the circumstances (which is not a terrible thing). Section 3.3.2 does away with the preference by deeming all records to be equal. (All EDI records are likely to have been made in the ordinary course of business.)

ABA Model §3.3.4 further provides that printouts of proper messages will be admissible "to the same extent and under the same conditions as other business records originated and maintained in documentary form." Arguably this settles the highly academic debate whether a special foundation, based on expert testimony, is necessary for admitting

§16.8 [1]The ABA Task Force acknowledged the importance of sound recordkeeping and control practices. ABA Report at 1696.

[2]*See* Chapter 10.

electronic records under the hearsay rule's business records exception.[3] Paper records do not require expert testimony on how paper and ink function, and arguably this provision averts any requirement for similar testimony on the function of computers.

Each party additionally agrees under ABA Model §3.3.4 not to dispute the admissibility of proper messages "under either the business records exception to the hearsay rule or the best evidence rule on the basis that the [messages] were not originated or maintained in documentary form." This is a curious and unneeded provision, more likely to confuse than promote justice. Neither the hearsay rule nor the best evidence rule provides objections based on the medium in which information is communicated. The hearsay rule excludes from evidence out-of-court statements, of any nature, offered to prove their truth.[4] The best evidence rule (if it applies to electronic messages at all) establishes essentially a preference where more than one recording is available.[5] Under these rules, a statement is no more or less likely to be excluded on account of its medium of expression. The ABA Report cites no cases or arguments otherwise. Regarding the hearsay rule, the Report unpersuasively justifies this clause as a "belt and suspenders" approach that just makes sure the rule will not be an obstacle.[6]

Finally, ABA Model §1.5 states that an electronic signature is "sufficient to verify" the origin of a proper message. What does this mean? Does it mean that at trial the proponent of evidence of such a message need not offer any preliminary (foundational) evidence, other than a simple reference to the signature, to establish the message's origin? If so, the ABA Model accords more to electronic signatures than evidence law accords to conventional ink signatures. An ink

[3] *See* §9.3.2.
[4] *See* Chapter 9.
[5] *See* Chapter 10.
[6] ABA Report at 1696.

signature is not itself sufficient to establish the origin of a paper document in court.[7] Unless agreed otherwise between litigants at trial, the proponent must introduce extra evidence, such as the testimony of an expert document examiner, to show the paper's authenticity. Electronic messages should be treated the same as paper messages under evidence authentication rules, but §1.5 could be interpreted to require otherwise.

[7]*See* Chapter 8.

Chapter

17

The Battle of the Forms

§17.1 INTRODUCTION

To the extent they applied to electronic contracts, Chapters 15 and 16 addressed formation and enforceability. This chapter considers how it is ascertained what terms are and are not part of such contracts.

In initial EDI implementations, the negotiation of trade terms and conditions (TTCs) has proved the most nettlesome legal issue. TTCs refer to the detail terms that traditionally are printed on the backsides of form purchase orders, acknowledgments, and other documents. These are not the basic dickered terms, such as quantity, price, and delivery date, but rather the "standard" terms, such as products warranties, the time limits for filing any lawsuits, the policy for the return of defective goods, and so forth.

In paper trading, parties often handle TTCs through the so-called battle of the forms. Each party sends (or "fires") the other a form document that contains TTCs favoring the sender. Complex rules discussed later in this chapter determine which TTCs control after the smoke clears.

To understand the battle of the forms, consider this example, which shall serve the discussion in Sections 17.2 and 17.3: Blue Co., the buyer, sends Green Co., the seller, a message (such as a purchase order form) "offering" to buy computer chips from Green on certain terms. Green is not bound to sell chips just because it received an offer to buy. But Green "accepts" the offer, and presumably gives rise to a binding sales contract, by sending its own message (such as a purchase order acknowledgment form) to that effect. Blue's message stated that Green warrants the chips for four years. Green's message declared all warranties expire after one year. If, two years after the sale, there is a dispute over warranty, whose warranty terms control?[1]

§17.2 MIRROR IMAGE RULE

The traditional common law followed the "mirror image rule." An offer and acceptance must be mirror images of one

§17.1 [1]The discussion in §§17.1, 17.2 & 17.3 assume Blue and Green do not have a master purchase agreement between them.

another for a contract to be formed. So if Green accepts Blue's offer, without trying to vary any terms, a contract would be formed on Blue's terms. But if (as in the example) Green responds with an acceptance that does not match the offer exactly, no contract is formed. Green's message, in effect, rejects Blue's offer and is a counteroffer. Blue can accept Green's counteroffer by sending a new message, or taking other action, that accepts the counteroffer entirely.

Under the mirror image rule, if the messages do not match perfectly, he who fires the "last shot" usually wins. In practice, parties like Blue and Green do not read all the terms carefully to determine if they have a mirror image contract. They just inquire whether the basic terms (price, quantity, shipping date) match. If they do, the parties proceed with their transaction; that is, Green delivers chips and Blue pays. But the common law sees Green's counteroffer, the last message, as still outstanding as of the time of payment. When Blue pays, a contract is formed. Blue's payment effectively accepts that hanging counteroffer in toto, and thus Green's warranty terms control.[1]

The mirror image rule has shortcomings. First, it drives parties into an endless battle of messages, with each trying to be the last to send an offer/counteroffer before the transaction is consummated. Second, either party can walk away from a transaction until the last offer/counteroffer meets a mirror image acceptance.[2] So, for example, after Green sends its counteroffer, several weeks may transpire before Blue makes its payment. In the interim, neither party is bound to go forward with the deal, even though each acts in reliance on the belief that they are bound.

§17.2 [1]*See* H. Hunter, Modern Law of Contracts ¶16.02[7] & [8] (1987).

[2]*See* §17.3.3.

§17.3 U.C.C. §2-207

The drafters of Article Two of the Uniform Commercial Code (U.C.C.), which covers only sales of goods, tried a different approach to the battle of the forms, §2-207. The drafters inadvertently created immense confusion (which, ironically, may not have been all bad).

As explained in Chapter 15,[1] a conventional offer and acceptance is not necessary for a contract to be formed with messages under Article Two. Accordingly, under U.C.C. §2-207*(1)*, an acceptance need not be a mirror image of an offer.

> A definite and seasonable expression of acceptance . . . operates as an acceptance even though it states terms additional to or different from those offered . . . , unless acceptance is expressly made conditional on assent to the additional or different terms.[2]

Thus, going back to the example, if Green's message is an acceptance, a contract is formed unless Green expressly makes the acceptance conditional on Blue assenting to additional or different terms.

§17.3.1 Favoritism to Offerors

What if Green's acceptance has additional or different terms, but is not conditional on Blue's assent to them? U.C.C. §2-207*(2)* appears to kick in:

> The additional terms are to be construed as proposals for addition to the contract. Between merchants[3] such terms become part of the contract unless:

§17.3 [1]*See* §15.2.
[2]U.C.C. §2-207(1).
[3]U.C.C. §2-104 generally defines "merchant" as someone dealing in

(a) the offer expressly limits acceptance to the terms of the offer;

(b) they materially alter it; or

(c) notification of objection to them has already been given or is given within a reasonable time after notice of them is received.

Hence, the general rule is that the offeror's (Blue's) terms control. Any additional terms in the offeree's acceptance stand a good chance of being excluded.[4] Subsection (2) permits additional terms to be included only if the offer does not expressly exclude the additional terms, they are not material, and the offeror does not reject them.[5] Thus, §2-207(2) favors the offeror (Blue).[6]

The partiality §2-207(2) shows offerors often works against sellers such as Green, but not always. A seller can be an offeror. Suppose Blue sends a request for quotation, and Green replies with a quotation framed as an offer to sell. ("We quote our chips at $100 each, and we offer to sell them at that price.") An appropriate purchase order from Blue might then be an acceptance under §2-207(1). Sellers naturally try to choreograph transactions so their messages are offers, not acceptances.

---

the goods in question or otherwise expected to have special knowledge about them. This would cover many companies involved in commercial transactions. This discussion assumes Blue and Green are merchants.

[4]U.C.C. §2-207 Official Comment 3 suggests subsection (2) applies to both additional and different terms, but the topic is controversial.

[5]*See* Dorton v. Collins & Aikman Corp., 453 F.2d 1161 (6th Cir. 1972). There, the seller had sent an acceptance that included an arbitration clause. The seller invoked the clause when a dispute later arose, but the buyer said the arbitration clause was not part of the agreement. The court considered the arbitration clause an additional term governed by §2-207(2), ruling the clause would be part of the agreement only if it did not materially alter the buyer's offer (a question of fact to be determined at trial).

[6]*See* Lipman, On Winning the Battle of the Forms: An Analysis of Section 2-207 of the Uniform Commercial Code, 24 Bus. Law. 789, 802 (April 1969).

§17.3.2 Counteroffer by Offeree

Despite §2-207's favoritism toward offerors, offerees are not without options. Green (the offeree in the original example) might respond to an offer with an unambiguous counteroffer. Green's form could bluntly say, "We reject your offer and make this counteroffer." If Blue unequivocally accepted the counteroffer, Green's terms would control. The risk, however, is that Blue will anger and take its business elsewhere.

So Green might try a similar statement, which sounds less hostile, but may have the same effect. It could track the last part of §2-207(1): "We gladly accept your offer, but this acceptance is expressly made conditional on assent to our additional and different terms."[7] This too seems to be a counteroffer, but it is phrased like an acceptance.[8] Thus, even if Blue did not assent with words to Green's additional and different terms, Blue might proceed with the deal by accepting and paying for the chips. If there were a later dispute, Green would argue Blue had accepted Green's counteroffer.[9] Whether Green's argument would prevail is uncertain.[10]

One notorious case, *Roto-Lith, Ltd. v. F. P. Bartlett & Co.,*[11] followed logic similar to Green's. The buyer mailed a purchase order offering to buy certain material, with implied warranties. The seller responded with an acknowledgment that disclaimed express and implied warranties. The acknowledgment also stated:

[7]Murray, A Proposed Revision of Section 2-207 of the Uniform Commercial Code, 6 J. Law & Comm. 337, 346 (1986).

[8]*See* Koehring Co. v. Glowacki, 77 Wis. 2d 497, 253 N.W.2d 64 (1977). The buyer telegraphed an offer to buy machinery if the seller paid to load it. The seller responded with a telegram "accepting" the offer but stating the buyer must pay for loading. The court viewed the "acceptance" as a counteroffer. No contract was formed, and the buyer was not obligated.

[9]*See* Murray, The Chaos of the "Battle of the Forms": Solutions, 39 Vand. L. Rev. 1307, 1330-1343 (1986).

[10]Some would argue the transaction would be governed by Section 2-207(3). *See* §17.3.3.

[11]297 F.2d 497 (1st Cir. 1962).

> This acknowledgment contains all of the terms of this purchase and sale. . . . If these terms are not acceptable, Buyer must so notify Seller at once.[12]

Soon thereafter the seller shipped the material, and the buyer received and paid for it. The buyer later determined the material was unsuitable and sued for breach of warranty. The court, however, ruled the seller's warranty disclaimer controlled. It treated the seller's acknowledgment as an "expressly conditional" acceptance under U.C.C. §2-207(1). The seller's message was therefore a counteroffer that the buyer accepted when it received and paid for the goods. In effect, the court read the "expressly conditional" clause in §2-207(1) as perpetuating the old last-shot rule from the common law. Commentators have heaped a jumble of both praise[13] and criticism[14] on the decision.

§17.3.3 Contract by Conduct

The U.C.C. drafters sought to curtail welshing on sales transactions. Here is one scenario in which welshing would come up: Blue Co. sends an offer, and Green Co. returns an unambiguous counteroffer. The offer and counteroffer agree on buying and selling 100 chips for $100 each, but the two messages disagree on warranties. There is (probably) no contract

[12]*Id.* at 499.

[13]*See, e.g.,*Note, Uniform Commercial Code: Variation Between Offer and Acceptance under Section 2-207, 1962 Duke L.J. 613; Comment, A Look at a Strict Construction of Section 2-207 of the Uniform Commercial Code from the Seller's Point of View *or* What's So Bad about *Roto-Lith?,* 8 Akron L. Rev. 111 (1974).

[14]*See, e.g.,* Murray, Intention Over Terms: An Exploration of UCC 2-207 and New Section 60, Restatement of Contracts, 37 Fordam L. Rev. 317 (1969); J. White & R. Summers, 1 Uniform Commercial Code 33, 38, 44-45 (3d ed. 1988). Despite the criticism, the case remains precedent in the first circuit. *See* Alloy Computer Products v. Northern Telecom, Inc., 683 F. Supp. 12 (D. Mass. 1988).

at this point, but, as often happens in practice, Green and Blue act as though they have a contract. They conspicuously commit resources, make preparations, discuss the contract, and forgo other opportunities. But because they have no contract, either could, under common law, walk away before the deal is consummated.

U.C.C. §2-207*(3)* departs from the common law:

> Conduct by both parties which recognizes the existence of a contract is sufficient to establish a contract for sale although the writings of the parties do not otherwise establish a contract. In such case the terms of the particular contract consist of those terms on which the writings of the parties agree, together with any supplementary terms incorporated under any other provisions of [U.C.C. Article Two].

Thus, in this scenario Blue and Green would (arguably) have a contract because they acted as though they had one. Blue could successfully sue Green if it refused to deliver chips. The contract terms would be those on which the messages agree (quantity and price), together with supplementary or "gap-filler" terms supplied by Article Two.

Article Two contains many gap-filler provisions that supply terms for sale-of-goods contracts that do not provide otherwise. An example is the implied warranty by merchant sellers that all goods are fully "merchantable."[15]

The outcome of any given inquiry into (1) whether the parties' conduct recognizes a contract, (2) what terms of the parties' messages do and do not agree, and (3) precisely what gap-filler terms apply can be difficult to predict. Each issue is subject to considerable interpretation under any particular set of facts. Thus, the application of §2-207(3) to particular transactions is fraught with uncertainty.

[15] U.C.C. §2-314.

§17.3.4 The Merits of Uncertainty

So as the foregoing demonstrates, the battle of the forms is unpredictable.[16] No buyer or seller is guaranteed victory.

Unpredictability may not be all bad, however. On TTCs, buyer and seller are adversaries. Ideally, the two would negotiate definite terms, yet negotiation costs precious time and effort. Is business therefore stifled? No. The battle of the forms provides a viable option. Each side can declare its terms and then stand ready to fight for them. Seldom will a dispute occur, but if and when it does, she who has planned carefully will have a fair chance of winning. Hence, the law's uncertainty facilitates trade. It permits swift dealmaking, with neither side taking an unbalanced risk.

Sellers of goods, like Green Co., need to engage in the battle. If both buyer and seller are silent on TTCs, then Article Two's gap-filler terms apply. There is a view, widely held among sellers' counsel, that the gap-fillers favor buyers.[17] Among the gap-fillers sellers dislike are a full seller's warranty that goods are merchantable (U.C.C. §2-314), a possibility for buyer recovery of consequential damages (U.C.C. §2-714(3)), and a four-year statute of limitations on suits against the seller (U.C.C. §2-725(1)).

Accordingly, sellers like Green Co. feel compelled to declare limits on warranties and remedies. If a seller does so,

[16]Murray, The Chaos of the "Battle of the Forms": Solutions, 39 Vand. L. Rev. 1307 (1986).

The text does not discuss all battle-of-the-forms variations. A buyer and seller could, for example, reach an oral agreement and then exchange messages to confirm it. U.C.C. §2-207 contains language (omitted from the quotations in the text) making it apply to confirmations. Section 2-207's treatment of confirmations is just as confusing as its treatment of offer and acceptance messages.

[17]*See* Comment, A Look at a Strict Construction of Section 2-207 of the Uniform Commercial Code from the Seller's Point of View *or* What's So Bad about *Roto-Lith?*, 8 Akron L. Rev. 111 (1974). *See also* White & Summers, above, at 45-46.

then (1) the buyer might accept the limits, (2) the seller might otherwise prevail with them under U.C.C. §2-207, and (3) the buyer will, due to §2-207's confusion, at least have to endure protracted litigation to enforce either its own TTCs or the Article Two gap-fillers.

§17.4 BATTLE OF THE FORMS IN EDI

In theory, the battle of the forms works in electronic trading the same as in paper trading. The ammunition in any battle of forms is merely words. Words can be fired either on paper or electronically.

Yet in practice electronic communication dramatically changes the battle dynamics. It may not be easy or customary to communicate TTCs in a way that is analogous to writing them on the back of a standard form. Consider *American Multimedia, Inc. v. Dalton Packaging, Inc.*,[1] in which a buyer faxed a form purchase order to a seller. The buyer faxed only the form's frontside, apparently because, unlike mailing, faxing the backside would have meant extra time, effort, and expense. When a dispute arose later, the question at trial was whether the seller was bound to the terms on that backside. Thus, the use of the fax machine caused a question to arise that would not have come up if the form had been mailed.

This problem is more acute in EDI, in which highly structured and coded messages are communicated. EDI implementors prefer data to be machine readable, not written in human-readable free-text. EDI software is often designed to reject free-text or to flag it as an exception for special handling. EDI standard messages contain codes for basic terms (price, quantity, shipping date), but usually not for

§17.4 [1]143 Misc. 2d 295, 540 N.Y.S.2d 410 (Sup. Ct. 1989).

TTCs. Also, EDI transmission costs are based on volume, so lengthy free-text is expensive to send.

Accordingly, many EDI users are disinclined to communicate TTCs electronically. The battle-of-the-forms guns fall silent. Thus, for sales of goods, §2-207's delicate balance breaks. Sellers may particularly fear the application of Article Two's gap-filler provisions (a probability if neither party is communicating TTCs).[2] One logical alternative is to enter an EDI trading partner agreement to define the TTCs.[3]

Note that some EDI trading partners already have a master purchase agreement to cover TTCs. This is a general, long-term agreement that covers all purchases between the parties, whether effected through paper, fax, or EDI. This agreement is highly desirable because it avoids the battle of the forms entirely. Such an agreement can solve the TTC problem beautifully for EDI users. Some users, however, find that over time they expand EDI into transactions not covered by the master agreement.

§17.4.1 The ABA Model's Approaches

Section 3.1 of the ABA Model EDI Trading Partner Agreement (ABA Model)[4] provides three optional approaches to TTCs (where parties have no master purchase agreement):

[A] The TTCs will be those specified in the agreement's Appendix. This wins the most certainty.[5]

[B] The TTCs will be those printed on each party's respective standard form documents, copies of which are attached to the agreement. These terms control even though they may be inconsistent with each other. Option [B] pro-

[2]Depending on the situation, TTCs might also be influenced by statements communicated between the parties outside EDI (letters, oral conversations, prior dealings, marketing materials, and so on) and usages of trade (customs) within the relevant industry.

[3]*See* §§17.4.1 & 17.4.2.

[4]*See* §14.4.

[5]*See* §17.4.2.

vides that any dispute over the terms of a transaction "will be resolved as if such Transaction had been effected through the use of" the standard forms. The Report accompanying the ABA Model (ABA Report) cautions that option [B] furnishes less certainty. Nevertheless, business users urged the ABA Model drafters (ABA Task Force)[6] to include this provision because it reflects a common industry practice.[7] Comment 7 to ABA Model Section 3.1 indicates that Option [B] functions under U.C.C. §2-207. The Comment acknowledges that in a conventional exchange of paper forms §2-207's operation depends on the sequence in which forms are exchanged. (A purchase order, for example, can be either an offer or and acceptance depending on the circumstances.) But under Option [B] the standard forms are exchanged simultaneously. Comment 7 interprets Option [B] to mean that the standard forms will correspond to particular electronic messages. The forms, then, should be considered exchanged in the same sequence as the related electronic messages.

The advantage to option [B] is that it carries the neutral uncertainty of §2-207 into EDI. In addition, because option [B] is such an artificial device, it even compounds the uncertainty.

[C] The TTCs will be the default provisions provided by law, just as if there were no trading partner agreement or other understanding on the TTCs. For a sale of goods, the TTCs would therefore be U.C.C. Article Two's gap-fillers. Sellers will especially dislike Option [C]. They believe the gap-fillers disfavor sellers.

§17.4.2 Negotiation of Definitive Terms

Although desirable, the negotiation of definitive terms under Option [A] can be difficult and time consuming if the trading

[6] *See* §14.4.

[7] Electronic Messaging Services Task Force, The Commercial Use of Electronic Data Interchange—A Report, 45 Bus. Law. 1647, 1700 (1990).

partners battled with forms before EDI. They may start with starkly different negotiation positions. This problem particularly vexes those implementors having hundreds of trading partners to convert to EDI.

One practicing attorney, Ralph M. Savage, has developed a form, set forth as Appendix D, to speed negotiation. Mr. Savage observes that in most sales transactions there are, practically speaking, a few key issues that, if addressed, could provide both parties a reasonable degree of certainty and fairness on TTCs. His form ties the most important issues for his client's industry (electrical equipment manufacturing) into a unit that business managers can easily understand and use. Concentrated attention hastens negotiation.

The form is a sample. It does not necessarily cover all TTCs that might be critical in a given sales transaction. Counsel may need to modify the form for specific needs.

From a buyer's viewpoint, this form may have faults. It aims to limit the buyer's rights to warranties and remedies otherwise available under the U.C.C. The argument for a buyer to accept the form nevertheless is that its limitations of rights are consistent with what might be expected in many fully negotiated commercial transactions.

§17.4.3 Electronic Combat

Sometimes it may be practical to communicate TTCs electronically. The TTCs could be free-text included within operative electronic messages, or they could be incorporated by reference with electronic codes understood to refer to fully articulated TTCs. This would imitate the practice in paper trading, where TTCs are printed on the backside of form documents. Thus, the battle of the forms would advance to "electronic combat." Electronic combat should function similarly to battle with paper documents.

Incorporation of TTCs by reference in an electronic message, as opposed to free-text, would save transmission costs and otherwise ease communication. So long as the recipient has notice of the reference's meaning, there seems to be no reason this would not be just as effective as transmitting full text. *American Multimedia, Inc. v. Dalton Packaging, Inc.*[8] recognized the effectiveness of an incorporation of terms by reference in a fax. The fax stated it was subject to certain TTCs; the terms were not transmitted but were well known by both parties. The court held that those terms controlled.

Another issue affecting terms in electronic negotiation is the rules for the sequence and timing of messages. This is particularly important in EDI, where it is preferable for communication to follow structured patterns. These are the types of questions the rules must address: To be effective, must a purchase order be accepted by a purchase order acknowledgment? Will this be true even when the purchase order follows a quotation from the seller? Is a shipping notice satisfactory to accept a purchase order? Does silence after receipt of an order constitute a binding acceptance? How soon must messages, such as change orders, be transmitted to be effective?[9] Which messages are offers and which are acceptances under U.C.C. §2-207?[10]

The rules should be set forth in industry standards or in a trading partner agreement or its equivalent. The ABA Model generally leaves this issue for parties to work out in the Model's Appendix.

§17.4.4 Declaration of Terms

The Electronic Trading Letter[11] offers another option, which combines both the trading-partner-agreement and the elec-

[8]143 Misc. 2d 295, 540 N.Y.S.2d 410 (Sup. Ct. 1989).

[9]Particular industry groups may have guidelines for these issues in EDI. *See, e.g.,* Industry Standard Practice for Purchasing Transactions, developed under the Automotive Industry Action Group in Nov. 1988.

[10]*See* §17.3.1.

[11]*See* §14.6 and Appendix C.

tronic-combat approaches. First, it aims to form a trading partner agreement that fixes terms. Whether the Letter will succeed in forming a mutual trading partner agreement will not always be certain.[12] Second, the Letter states that the terms the sender declares are incorporated by reference into its messages, and notifies the recipient that messages may contain a code to signify the incorporation by reference.

Some terms must be "conspicuous" to be effective. U.C.C. §2-316(2), for instance, generally requires a written exclusion of a warranty of merchantability to be conspicuous. A customary way to ensure conspicuousness on paper is to print words in bold or capitalized letters. Placement of a free-text disclaimer in an EDI message, when the recipient is not expecting the disclaimer, may not be conspicuous.[13] The same might be true if a disclaimer is merely incorporated by reference and not otherwise impressed on the recipient. The Electronic Trading Letter addresses this concern by stating in all capital letters that all terms are conspicuous. To enhance the Letter's effect in this regard, it might be advisable periodically to send reminders.

§17.5 PAROL EVIDENCE RULE

Under common law, the parol evidence rule provides that when parties reduce their contract to an "integrated writing," a court will not consider "extrinsic" evidence to determine what the agreed-upon terms were. Extrinsic evidence is any prior oral or written agreement showing that the terms were different from those in the integrated writing.

[12]*See* §14.6.

[13]However, U.C.C. §1-201(10) provides that any term stated in a "telegram" is conspicuous. Section 1-201(41) defines "telegram" to include "a message transmitted by radio, teletype, cable, any mechanical method of transmission, or the like."

Suppose Blue Co. and Green Co. negotiate face-to-face over the terms of a construction project. They conclude with a formal written contract, which they intend to be the final expression of terms.[1] In effect, the parties say, "This is it." If there is later a dispute, the parol evidence rule forbids either from introducing evidence at trial to show that during negotiation the parties agreed to terms different from those in the written contract.[2] Thus, if the written contract says the fee will be $50,000, neither party may introduce evidence showing they orally agreed on $60,000.

The parol evidence rule narrows the scope of evidence a court will consider to ascertain contract terms. It cuts off evidence of prior negotiations and agreements on the theory that when the parties adopted the integrated writing, they intended to supersede all prior understandings.[3]

A writing may be only a "partial integration." The parties may reduce only some of the terms of their deal, such as fee and completion date, to writing and leave others, such as warranties, to be understood informally. If that is the case, extrinsic evidence is admissible to show the warranty terms but not the fee or completion date terms.

Determining what is a "written integration" is a question of fact about what the parties intended to be a final, integrated statement.[4] An integrated writing need not be a single, formal document. It can be a series of letters and telegrams.[5] Yet depending on the facts, a series of writings may indeed not be integrated. In *Continental Illinois National*

§17.5 [1]A formal contract may state that it is the final expression of terms and supersedes all previous agreements. This helps a court conclude the agreement is an integrated writing.

[2]The parol evidence rule is subject to exceptions for fraud, mutual mistake, duress, and the like. S. Williston, 4 Williston on Contracts §631 (1961).

[3]*See* A. Corbin, 3 Corbin on Contracts §674 (1950).

[4]4 Williston, above, §633.

[5]J. Wigmore, 9 Wigmore on Evidence §2425 (Chadborne rev. 1981).

Bank & Trust Co. v. National Casket Co.,[6] for example, a property owner negotiated orally with a contractor for the placement of a marquee on a building. The parties may have then agreed orally on how the marquee would be installed. The contractor sent a written estimate describing the installation, and the property owner returned a letter further describing it. When a dispute later arose over the contractor's performance, the court found the writings did not constitute an integration. It allowed testimony to determine whether the parties had agreed orally on the installation method.

An integrated writing does not necessarily require a signature.[7] Moreover, in principle, the "writing" need not be an expression in any particular form—even an unrecorded oral statement could be a "writing" for parol evidence rule purposes.[8] Hence, an electronically communicated message is inherently just as capable of being an integrated writing as a paper document. (It is immaterial whether the message is recorded).

For example, suppose Blue Co. sends an electronic order for nine modems, at $50 each, to Green Co. Green Co. follows with an electronic acceptance of the order's terms. Together, the electronic order and the electronic acceptance constitute the integrated writing. If there were later a dispute and a trial, Green Co. could not introduce evidence that before Blue Co. sent its electronic order a Blue Co. employee agreed the order would be twelve modems at $75 each. The order and acceptance are the final expression of the covered terms agreed upon by the parties.[9]

[6]27 Ill. App. 2d 447, 169 N.E.2d 853 (1960).

[7]Tow v. Miners Memorial Hosp. Assn., Inc., 305 F.2d 73 (4th Cir. 1921); Braude & McDonnell v. Isadore Cohen Co., 87 W. Va. 763, 106 S.E. 52 (1921).

[8]9 Wigmore, above, §2425; Restatement (Second) of Contracts §209 comment b (1981).

[9]An EDI message could be a "unilateral" contract, where the offeror does not expect to receive a message accepting its offer. A buyer, for example, might transmit a purchase order for immediate delivery of wid-

One technique for linking different messages into an integrated writing is incorporation by reference. Paragraph 5 of the Electronic Trading Letter provides that each electronic message is deemed to incorporate the Letter by reference and may contain a code to confirm that intent.

An integrated writing is one adopted by both parties, not a mere note or memorandum of an agreement kept by one party.[10] Accordingly, if Blue Co. kept a record of an oral agreement with Green Co., the record itself could not be an integrated writing. In electronic contracting, one must distinguish messages and records of messages. In the example two paragraphs above, the order and acceptance messages are the integrated writing. To prove what the writing said, either party might introduce its record of the messages as evidence. Yet neither record is the integrated writing itself. If there were differences in records, the court might examine extrinsic evidence (even oral testimony) to discern what the messages said. But under the parol evidence rule, the court would not look to extrinsic evidence to determine what the terms of agreement were.

The parol evidence rule prohibits the admission of extrinsic evidence that contradicts the terms of an integrated writing, but it does not prohibit extrinsic evidence that merely aids interpretation of those terms.[11] Thus, for example, if an EDI message were deemed an integrated writing, the rule would not bar evidence concerning the communication standard (such as ANSI X12) to which the message conformed. This evidence would shed light on the message's meaning. It would not directly say what the terms of agreement were.

U.C.C. §2-202 sets forth a parol evidence rule for sales

---

gets. It would not desire a purchase order acknowledgment, just immediate delivery. The purchase order message could still be considered "integrated" because the buyer intended it to be the final expression of terms. *See* 3 Corbin, above, §588, n.60.

[10] 3 Corbin, above, §588.

[11] 3 Corbin, above, §579.

of goods that differs somewhat from the common law rule. It provides:

> Terms with respect to which the confirmatory memoranda of the parties agree or which are otherwise set forth in a writing intended by the parties as a final expression of their agreement with respect to such terms as are included therein may not be contradicted by evidence of any prior agreement or of a contemporaneous oral agreement but may be explained or supplemented
>
> (a) by course of dealing or usage of trade . . . or by course or performance . . . ; and
>
> (b) by evidence of consistent additional terms unless the court finds the writing to have been intended also as a complete and exclusive statement of the terms of the agreement.

Section 2-202 emphasizes the search for partial integration, where some but perhaps not all contract terms have become integrated. For those terms that have become integrated, no contradictory extrinsic evidence is admissible at trial.

One problem under §2-202 is that the rule is based on a specific definition of "writing," U.C.C. §1-201(46), which defines writing as including "reduction to tangible form." The arguments whether an electronic message constitutes a writing under U.C.C. §2-201 (statute of frauds)[12] also apply here. Therefore, it is not absolutely certain whether a purely electronic message may be an integrated writing under §2-202. So while the common law parol evidence rule contemplates that any statements, even oral ones, may be integrated, the U.C.C. rule may be less flexible. A trading partner agreement that defines which messages are deemed "written" can avoid any uncertainty here.

[12]*See* Chapter 16.

PART VI

NETWORK SERVICE PROVIDERS AND CUSTOMERS

Chapter 18

Liability for Deficient Service

§18.1 THE THREATS

Computer networks are fallible. Even the most sophisticated and dependable systems can skid to a halt. On January 15,

1990, a computer malfunction locked up a major portion of the AT&T telephone network.[1] Then on February 9 AT&T suffered a second accident, this one interrupting service to tens of thousands of WATS service callers. A technician had forgotten to program necessary information into a network computer.[2]

Financial trading markets enjoy no immunity from electronic failure. A hardware snag in 1986 shut down the London Stock Exchange for a day.[3] In New York, five major futures and options exchanges fell silent for three hours in April 1990 because of a computer communications jam. Technicians believed the culprit was an electrical short in damaged wires.[4]

Even functioning systems can make costly mistakes. *ComputerWorld* reports that a computer system operated by Control Data Corp. mistakenly permitted the printing of too many winning tickets in the Delaware state lottery. As much as $55,000 in unintended tickets were distributed and redeemed.[5]

Failures can stem from both sabotage and inadvertence. For example, employees of computer service bureaus that process payroll for client firms have been known to use their access to confidential information to forge client checks.[6] I (the author) have suffered the loss of in-coming public e-mail messages. In an effort to upgrade its system, my service pro-

§18.1 [1]Sims, Disruption of Phone Service Is Laid to Computer Program, N.Y. Times, Jan. 17, 1990, at A1, col. 1 (natl. ed.).

[2]Keller, AT&T's 800 Service Disrupted Friday, In Another Embarrassing Breakdown, Wall St. J., Feb. 13, 1990, at B4, col. 3 (eastern ed.).

[3]System Failure Halts London Stock Exchange, EDPACS 10 (June 1986).

[4]Cowan, A Glitch in the System Halts Five New York Exchanges, N.Y. Times, Apr. 28, 1990, at 17, col. 1 (natl. ed.).

[5]Pastore, Lottery Agents Hit Jackpot, Courtesy of Systems Glitch, ComputerWorld, Jan. 8, 1990, col. 3, p.1.

[6]Wilkinson, Auditing Clients Who Use Service Bureaus, J. Accounting & EDP 8 (Spring 1986).

vider had changed the mailbox addressing scheme but, because of an earlier special arrangement with me, failed to activate my new address properly. The messages were irretrievably lost.

§18.2 POLICY ISSUES

To what extent should service providers be liable to users for the damages caused by network blunders? The question elicits a battle royal of competing theories favoring or disfavoring liability. Predicting which theory will prevail in any particular lawsuit may be difficult. Much depends on the suit's particular facts and the court's interpretation of them. Little legislation or case law precedent directly applies to computer message networks. This chapter introduces the competing theories, the reasoning behind them, and their application. The upshot here is that the subject suffers considerable uncertainty.

At the core of many disputes here will be a war between two forces espousing different ideals: freedom of commercial parties to govern their own affairs through contract and the demarcation of minimum and maximum boundaries of accountability for service providers. The tension is between autonomy and social responsibility. As a practical matter, then, an explicit contract between a provider and its customer can considerably influence, but not necessarily dictate, an outcome. Most computer service providers seek insulation from liability through contracts.[1]

Ironically, however, even the companies most adamant and successful in limiting their liability sometimes recognize a moral duty to offer compensation for their fumbles. AT&T,

§18.2 [1]*See* B. Wright, EDI and American Law: A Practical Guide 37-51 (1989), for a clause-by-clause discussion of EDI network agreements.

while not legally required to do so, gave customers a day of discounted service as atonement for its January 15, 1990, disaster. And Control Data Corp. apparently owed nothing under its contract to Delaware for the lottery ticket snafu, but the company declared it would reimburse the $55,000 anyway. Moral duty does not necessarily imply legal duty, however.

Legal liability rules derive from (1) the contract between user and provider; (2) common law decisions; or (3) government regulations.[2] A rulemaker might weigh the following arguments in setting the rules.

Those favoring less provider liability:

1. Computer reliability cannot be guaranteed. "Bugs" can spring to life after years of dormancy.
2. Risks of loss are best allocated to those benefiting from the system, the users.
3. Users are best positioned to take precautions and buy insurance.[3]
4. System administration is simplified if all messages travel under a uniform price structure, regardless of the consequences if they fail. In EFT, U.C.C. §4A-305 generally bars recovery of "consequential" damages from a receiving bank for failure properly to execute a payment order. The policy reason is that it is difficult and time consuming for a bank to evaluate the risks for each transaction based on what might happen if it fails. A rule making risks to the bank smaller and more uniform promotes lower transmission fees and greater execution speed.[4]

[2]An advantage of regulation is that it fixes uniform rules so individual participants need not negotiate contracts.

[3]*See* Mosteshar, Liability Issues of EDI, *in* EDI and the Law 51 (I. Walden ed. 1989).

[4]U.C.C. §4A-305 Official Comment 2. With the exception of the text accompanying this footnote, this chapter does not cover a bank's liability for failure of an EFT transaction. *See* U.C.C. art. 4A.

5. The fee a provider charges for sending any given message is low.

Those favoring more provider liability:

1. While computers may be complex and prone to hidden "bugs," professional service providers should be expected to control, though not necessarily eliminate, the number and magnitude of problems.
2. Customers buy more than access to systems. They buy service and support from the provider's expert technical staff. Like other employers, the provider should be accountable for employee lapses.
3. Providers need incentive to maintain quality service.
4. Holding a provider to standards does not necessarily mean making it an insurer. A provider who, for example, must exercise "due care" is not liable for failures that occur despite its fulfillment of that duty.
5. Customers usually do not contract for service on a message-by-message basis. Rather, they contract for continuous service over a long period of time, and the cumulative fees over this contract period can be substantial.

§18.3 CONTRACT THEORIES

Contract is the first category of legal theory dividing risks between service provider and customer. Often the parties will have negotiated and signed a formal, written contract.[1] The service contract could, however, be implicit.

§18.3 [1]A data processing agreement is a contract for services rather than goods, even though reels of tape containing data may be exchanged between the customer and provider. Liberty Fin. Mgmt. Corp. v. Beneficial Data Processing Corp., 670 S.W.2d 40 (Mo. Ct. App. 1984).

A provider is liable for the explicit and implicit warranties it undertakes in a service contract. An example of an explicit warranty would be that the network will be fully operational 98 percent of the time in any given month. As for implicit warranties, one who contracts to accomplish a result, such as the movement of data, impliedly agrees to do what is necessary to succeed.[2] And, unless otherwise agreed, a service contract carries an implied warranty that the contractor will exercise proper skill and use proper equipment.[3]

A lost, delayed, or garbled message, a cessation of service or a pattern of poor performance could evidence a provider's breach of contract. What are the customer's rights if a provider breaches? The customer has the right to recover money damages from the provider. If necessary, the customer can enforce that right with a lawsuit. Under classic contract damages doctrine, the provider (defendant) could be required to pay its customer (plaintiff) sufficient (but not more) money to put her in the place she would be if the breach had not occurred.[4] To establish that amount at trial requires careful examination of the facts and maybe considerable speculation about what would have happened.

A contract damages award seeks to protect one or more of the plaintiff's "expectation," "reliance," or "restitution" interests.[5] Expectation damages, the most common form of damages, aim to put the plaintiff "in as good a position as he would have been in had the contract been performed."[6] For example, WhiteNet agrees to deliver messages for Blue

[2]17 Am. Jur. 2d Contracts §289 (1964).

[3]17A C.J.S. Contracts §329 (1963). *See* Data Processing Serv. v. L. H. Smith Oil Corp., 492 N.E.2d 314 (Ind. App. 1986) (computer programmer impliedly promises to have reasonable skill and to exercise ordinary diligence).

[4]Other remedies, such as a specific requirement that the service be performed as agreed, may also be awarded. *See* Trans Union Credit Info. Co. v. Associated Credit Services, Inc., 805 F.2d 188 (6th Cir. 1986).

[5]Restatement (Second) of Contracts §344 (1981).

[6]*Id.*

Co. during June for $100. WhiteNet then reneges, and Blue Co. must use YellowNet, who charges $150 for the same service. Blue is entitled to $50 damages from WhiteNet. If WhiteNet had performed the contract, Blue could have transmitted for $50 less than the amount it had to pay.

To recover, a plaintiff must show a sufficient causal connection between breach and damage. Any damages must be proved to a reasonable certainty and reflect more than mere speculation. *Newsome v. Western Union Telegraph Co.*[7] humorously illustrates. The plaintiff telegraphed an order for four gallons of corn whiskey for his crew, which was about to embark on a timber raft. The telegraph company botched the transmission, so no beverage came. The thirsty crew mutinied and refused to shove off. Meanwhile, the river dropped, making navigation impossible. By the time the plaintiff finally got his timber downstream, the price for timber had fallen. The plaintiff sued the telegraph company for the difference in the timber's market value. The court disallowed recovery because it saw a weak causal link between the bungled telegram and the plaintiff's loss. It reasoned that even if the telegram was properly delivered, the whisky might not have arrived, the crew might still not have shoved off, and the raft might still not have made it to market in time.

Damages may be recovered only if they were foreseeable by the defendant as a probable consequence of the breach. Damages might be foreseeable because they would be expected to occur from the breach either in the ordinary course of events or as a result of special circumstances known to the defendant.[8] Distinguishing the ordinary from the special involves much judgment on the part of a court.[9]

When can a plaintiff recover for lost profits? Must the

[7]153 N.C. 153, 69 S.E. 10 (1910).

[8]Restatement (Second) of Contracts §351 (1981).

[9]Some contract authorities refer to "consequential" damages, a concept similar to damages resulting from "special" circumstances. *See* U.C.C. §2-715.

defendant have known of special circumstances? The courts vary on such questions. Under one line of reasoning, loss of profit is always expected as an ordinary result of breach of any commercial contract.[10]

But consider *Evra Corp. v. Swiss Bank Corp.*,[11] a leading case on the damages recoverable for a failure to process a business message. The plaintiff needed to make a payment in Europe to keep a ship charter, so the plaintiff's bank telexed a wire funds transfer to a Swiss bank. The latter, which was ignorant of the message's purpose, lost it. The plaintiff consequently forfeited the charter and had to secure another at a higher price. The plaintiff sued the Swiss bank, seeking as damages the difference in charter prices. The court denied an award, on the grounds (in part) that the defendant could not have foreseen that its error would inflict such injury. The court implied, however, that the defendant could have been liable if it had known the plaintiff's special circumstances.[12]

If a service provider works closely with its customers, as is often the case in EDI, it is likely to know much about the likely lost profits and other special injuries its customers will suffer from a network failure.

A plaintiff may not recover for injuries it could, after the contract breach, have avoided without undue effort. Thus the plaintiff has incentive to mitigate damages.[13] When it sees a message has not succeeded, it cannot watch idly as the injury runs its course.

[10]H. Hunter, Modern Law of Contracts ¶7.03[3][d] (1986).

[11]673 F.2d 951 (7th Cir.), *cert. denied,* 459 U.S. 1017 (1982).

[12]Although the plaintiff had no contract with the Swiss bank, the court for policy reasons applied the foreseeability test of contract theory to determine what damages were recoverable.

[13]*See* Chatlos Sys., Inc. v. National Cash Register Corp., 479 F. Supp. 738, (D.N.J. 1979), *aff'd in part, rev'd in part on other grounds,* 635 F.2d 1081 (3d Cir. 1980), *cert. denied,* 457 U.S. 1112 (1982).

§18.3.1 Warranty Disclaimers and Contract Liability Releases

Using exculpatory clauses in standard form service agreements, network providers commonly seek strict limits on contract warranties and remedies. A warranty disclaimer might say, for example, that the provider does not warrant that its service will check for syntax errors in EDI messages. This reduces the number of grounds on which a provider might be liable for breach of contract. A limitation on remedies, on the other hand, might say, for example, that the provider will in no event be liable for damages over $5000. This caps the recovery if a breach is established. Many providers prefer to limit their liability to the amount of the service fee.

Under contract law, the parol evidence rule blocks the reading of additional or different warranties and terms into an agreement that the parties have adopted as their contract's "final written expression."[14] A service agreement may contain an "integration" clause to clarify that the agreement is the final and exclusive writing. This can invalidate any oral terms and warranties that might have come up during a sales pitch. (Hence, customers are motivated to write all important terms into their agreements.)

Warranty and contract remedy disclaimers in contracts are usually upheld.[15] Yet legal doctrines do constrain them. First, standard form contracts are construed against the drafter; so equivocal language can vitiate a provider's exculpatory clause.[16] Second, "unconscionable" contract clauses are

[14]*See* §17.5.

[15]*See* S. Williston, Williston on Contracts §781A (Jaeger rev. 3d ed. 1961). *See also* Liberty Fin. Mgmt. Corp. v. Beneficial Data Processing Corp., 670 S.W.2d 40 (Mo. Ct. App. 1984) (sustaining disclaimer of liability in data processing services contract for any damages except out-of-pocket expenses incurred as a result of gross negligence or willful wrongdoing).

[16]*See* Western Union Tel. Co. v. Moore, 12 Ind. App. 136, 39 N.E. 874 (1895) (telegraph case).

unenforceable.[17] Courts hesitate to find unconscionability between commercial parties of roughly equal ability. The courts prefer that the parties enjoy the freedom to write their contract as they see fit. But some commercial contract clauses have been found unconscionable. To assess conscionability, a court considers the totality of the facts and circumstances: Was a standard form contract offered on a take-it-or-leave-it basis? Did one party take advantage of the other's inexperience or bargaining weakness?[18] Were the terms patently unfair?[19]

A clause eliminating liability for willful or reckless misconduct by a provider, such as the condoning of forgery of transactions by employees, would be a strong candidate for unconscionability.

Also, if a service agreement indicates the service provider is not liable for any failure of service whatsoever, then it is not a mutually binding contract. Accordingly, the provider will be unable to enforce any obligation against the customer, even an obligation to pay fees for service.[20]

§18.3.2 Force Majeure Clauses

A special contract provision to limit liability, the so-called force majeure clause, is common in commercial agreements. Generally it excuses a party, such as a service provider, from performance failures caused by extraordinary events, such as wars and other conditions beyond the party's reasonable control. However, if a provider is not liable for interrupted service, the customer bears the loss. The logic is that the customer should anticipate that extraordinary events will sometimes occur and therefore take precautions.

[17] Restatement (Second) of Contracts §208 (1981).

[18] Weaver v. American Oil Co., 276 N.E.2d 144 (Ind. 1971).

[19] H. Hunter, Modern Law of Contracts ¶12.06 (1986).

[20] Sterling Computer Sys. of Tex., Inc. v. Texas Pipe Bending Co., 507 S.W.2d 282 (Tex. Civ. App. 1974).

Critical question: What is beyond a provider's reasonable control? U.C.C. §4-108 sheds some light. U.C.C. Article Four usually obligates a bank to return a dishonored check by midnight of the next banking day following the check's receipt. Section 4-108(2) pardons a bank if a war or certain other circumstances beyond the bank's control cause delay. But the bank is excused only if it "exercises such diligence as the circumstances require."

Courts have considered whether equipment malfunctions qualify as circumstances sufficiently beyond a bank's control. In *Blake v. Woodford Bank and Trust Co.*[21] the combination of equipment breakdown, employee absence, and a heavy holiday workload prevented a check's return. Yet the court ruled the holdup was not beyond the bank's control because the bank could have foreseen the extra workload, and the equipment had stalled before. The court in *Congress Factors Corp. v. Extebank*[22] rejected a bank's excuse for delay after a computer failure and power outage. The court held the bank lacked the necessary diligence because it had no backup system and it relied on a computer that took several hours to revive after a brief power interruption. *North Carolina National Bank v. South Carolina National Bank*[23] ruled that a 24-hour computer breakdown did not justify a four-day delay.

Nevertheless, one court has concluded that a computer malfunction will pardon delay if the bank has a reasonable disaster recovery plan. In *Port City State Bank v. American National Bank, Lawton, Oklahoma,*[24] the bank had arranged for a backup computer system. When the primary system quit, the bank attempted, unsuccessfully, to fix it. It also temporarily switched to the backup system, but time was

[21]555 S.W.2d 589 (Ky. Ct. App. 1977).

[22]32 U.C.C. Rep. Serv. (Callaghan) 1559 (N.Y. Civ. Ct. 1982).

[23]449 F. Supp. 616 (D.S.C. 1976), *aff'd,* 573 F.2d 1305 (4th Cir.), *cert. denied,* 439 U.S. 985 (1978).

[24]486 F.2d 196 (10th Cir. 1973).

lost and two checks were delayed. The court exonerated the bank, finding that it had been duly diligent with a disaster plan and repair effort.

These cases suggest that for a business such as a network provider many equipment failures will be considered within control under a contract's force majeure clause. Yet if the business takes reasonable preventive measures and still suffers a computer disaster, it may be deemed beyond control.[25]

Some catastrophes may relieve a service provider from its obligations even without a force majeure clause. Under the "impracticality" doctrine, an unexpected event that drastically changes the situation between the parties discharges a contract.[26]

§18.4 TORT THEORIES

The second category of provider liability theory is tort. Generally, torts are a class of wrongs, other than breach of contract, for which the law provides the victim a remedy in damages. Contract obligations relate to the enforcement of bargained-for promises between consenting parties. Tort obligations on the other hand are imposed on parties by law; they generally arise independent of any contract. A general tort rule (negligence) is that one who acts must do so with reasonable care to avoid danger to persons and property. Put differently, one who operates a computer network must use reasonable care to protect network traffic. If she does not, she can be required to pay for any ensuing damages.

Tort and contract law overlap in that a single action, such as a lawyer's rendering of inadequate service to a client,

[25]*See generally* Burk & Winer, Failure to Prepare: Who's Liable in a Data Processing Disaster?, 5 S.C. Computer & High Tech. L.J. 19 (1989).

[26]*See* Restatement (Second) of Contracts §261 (1981).

can give rise to an action for both breach of contract and tort for failure to use reasonable care (misfeasance). But a failure to act at all (nonfeasance) tends not to support a claim in tort,[1] while it may constitute breach of contract.

For a plaintiff, tort can be a path around contractual disclaimers of warranties and remedies, parol evidence rule exclusions of contract terms, and other technical impediments to promise enforcement.[2] Although many courts sustain tort claims between contract parties,[3] some hesitate.[4]

One committee under the Association of the Bar of the City of New York opines (against dissent) that tort is generally an undesirable theory for governing commercial sales of computer hardware and software. Where the purchaser's loss is economic, "the contract terms between the parties should control and traditional contract law apply."[5] The committee disparages the application of negligence and related tort theories in these cases (although it believes classic, intentional fraud theory should apply where appropriate). The committee argues that because the relationship between the parties is consensual, autonomy and freedom of contract should prevail. Some might apply similar reasoning to commercial sales of computer services.

Tort liability is limited to injuries "proximately caused" by the defendant's wrongdoing. Proximate cause, an elastic concept, is potentially more inclusive than the cause and

§18.4 [1]An exception sometimes applies for public service companies, such as common carriers and utilities.

[2]W. Prosser & W. Keeton, The Law of Torts §92 (5th ed. 1984).

[3]*See, e.g.,* Berwind Corp. v. Litton Indus., 532 F.2d 1 (7th Cir. 1976) (recovery awarded for negligence in design and manufacture of equipment where contract barred recovery under warranty).

[4]*See, e.g.,* Better Food Markets, Inc. v. American Dist. Tel. Co., 40 Cal. 2d 179, 253 P.2d 10 (1953).

[5]The Special Comm. on Computers and Law, Comm. Reports: Tort Theories in Computer Litigation, 38 Record of Assn. of Bar of City of N.Y. 426, 427 (1983).

foreseeability concepts in contract law.[6] Still, as under contract law, a plaintiff cannot recover for damages he could have avoided after the fact with reasonable effort.[7]

The greatest harm a service provider customer is likely to suffer is economic loss, such as lost profits. Traditionally, courts limited the scope of tort, particularly negligence, liability to harm to persons or property, and excluded economic interests. The rationales were that economic losses are better handled through contract law,[8] and the protection of economic interests is not so socially important. More recently, some (although not all) courts have extended recovery for negligence to economic injury.[9] Also, the recovery of punitive damages is more likely in successful tort, particularly fraud, cases as compared with contract cases.[10]

§18.4.1 Negligence

Under classic tort law, a plaintiff may recover money damages for negligence if the defendant owed a duty of care to him, breached it, and thereby hurt him. An employer is generally liable for the harm caused by the negligence of employees acting within the scope of their employment.[11] So, a service provider could be held accountable under negligence law for its own shoddy service or that of its staff.

[6]*See* §18.3. Note, however, in Evra Corp. v. Swiss Bank Corp., which is discussed in §18.3, the plaintiff sued in tort, but the court applied the contract foreseeability standard for determining the scope of liability. The court reasoned that in this situation the tort proximate cause standard should parallel the contract foreseeability standard.

[7]Restatement (Second) of Torts §918 (1979).

[8]Prosser & Keeton, above, §92.

[9]*See, e.g.*, People's Express Airlines, Inc. v. Consolidated Rail Corp., 100 N.J. 246, 495 A.2d 107 (1985).

[10]*See* The Glovatorium, Inc. v. NCR Corp., 684 F.2d 658 (9th Cir. 1982) (punitive damages for vendor's intentional misrepresentation of computer system's capabilities).

[11]Restatement (Second) of Agency §219 (1958).

No computers work flawlessly, and negligence law does not make defendants insurers against all problems. In a negligence action, a service provider will be liable only if it breached the standard of care society expects of it. If it did not, it bears no liability—even though injury may have occurred.

What standard of care does society expect? Most defendants must do what the "reasonable man of ordinary prudence" would do "under the same or similar circumstances" to guard against unreasonable risk of harm (the "ordinary care" standard).[12] The defendant's standard of care increases as her skill increases, however. One with talent must use it.

A topic in the computer law field is whether a computer specialist should be held to a professional's standard of care. For negligence purposes, a professional is deemed to possess special skills, even if he does not. *Diversified Graphics, Ltd. v. Groves*[13] is a leading opinion holding that at least some computer specialists can be held to a professional's standard. Previous leading courts[14] had rejected this theory. In *Groves,* a company that was unsophisticated in computers went to Ernst & Whinney (E&W), an accounting and consulting firm with which it had a long relationship, for help in acquiring an in-house computer system. The customer claimed E&W promised to locate a "turnkey" system that required little employee training. The delivered system fell short of that description. The court held E&W liable to the customer for failure to exercise professional care.

The attachment of professional standards to computer specialists (including service providers) means: (1) It may be

[12]Prosser & Keeton, above, §32. *See* Ford Motor Credit Co. v. Swarens, 447 S.W.2d 53 (Ky. 1969) (obligation of computer user to exercise reasonable prudence).

[13]868 F.2d 293 (8th Cir. 1989).

[14]*See, e.g.,* Triangle Underwriters, Inc. v. Honeywell, Inc., 604 F.2d 737 (2d Cir. 1979).

slightly easier to show negligence because a professional is presumed to be highly skilled.[15] (2) The recovery of economic losses may be easier.[16] (3) The circle of potential plaintiffs who can recover from the defendant may expand.[17] (4) Liability may be more difficult to limit by contract.

§18.4.2 Misrepresentation

If a salesman misdescribes a service, the customer may have a tort action against the salesman's company for misrepresentation (fraud).[18] The computer vendor in *The Glovatorium v. NCR Corp.*[19] was liable for (1) knowingly making false claims about a system's function and (2) showing the buyer a demonstration product that, unknown to the buyer, was specially modified to out-perform the actual system for sale.

Misrepresentation should, in principle, be distinguished from a vendor's puffery or exaggerations about a service's value or quality.[20]

Conceptually, the distinction between a misrepresentation tort claim and a breach of contract warranty claim is

[15]A defendant is normally expected to use the skills she possesses to avoid unreasonable danger to others. Restatement (Second) of Torts §299 comment f (1965). If she is a professional, she is expected to use the skills normally possessed by members of the profession, even if she herself does not possess them. *Id.* §299A.

[16]R. Nimmer, The Law of Computer Technology, 7—20 (1985).

[17]Historically, professionals were liable only to those with whom they had a direct contract. *See* Ultramares Corp. v. Touche, 255 N.Y. 170, 174 N.E. 441 (1931). Now some courts are assigning liability to a broader range of plaintiffs. *See, e.g.,* Rosenblum v. Adler, 93 N.J. 324, 461 A.2d 138 (1983) (accountant liable to corporation's public stockholders).

[18]There may also be an action under state deceptive trade practices laws. *See* Sun Power, Inc. v. Adams, 751 S.W.2d 689 (Tx. Ct. App. 1988).

[19]684 F.2d 658 (9th Cir. 1982).

[20]Shivers v. Sweda Intl., Inc., 146 Ga. App. 758, 247 S.E.2d 576 (1978). *See also* 37 Am. Jur. 2d Fraud and Deceit §54 (1968).

obscure.[21] Misrepresentation can cover any false statement, regardless of whether a contract existed. Breach of warranty claims must grow from explicit or implicit statements in a contract. Contract integration clauses and the parol evidence rule[22] aim to prevent plaintiffs from relying on promises and warranties not included in a final written contract. The more an alleged false statement involves something contemplated within the contract, the stronger the argument that contract rather than tort law should control.

The misrepresentation tort involves a false statement on which the plaintiff justifiably relied to his detriment. Recovery may be made under this cause of action for economic loss (i.e., lost profits).

Controversy encircles the degree of defendant culpability needed to sustain a misrepresentation action. The classic and accepted fraud cause of action requires intentional misrepresentation—which may be inferred from a misstatement that is conscious or made with reckless disregard for whether it is true.[23] Intentional wrongdoing can be difficult to prove in court, however.

One line of reasoning recognizes actions for negligent misrepresentation in the course of a sale. Proponents of this reasoning cite §552(1) of the Second Restatement of Torts:

> One who, in the course of his business, profession or employment, or in any other transaction in which he has a pecuniary interest, supplies false information for the guidance of others

[21] *Compare* Invacare Corp. v. Sperry Corp., 612 F. Supp. 448 (N.D. Ohio 1984) (fraud allegations not barred by integration clause) *with* Investors Premium Corp. v. Burroughs Corp., 389 F. Supp. 39, 44 ("That plaintiff cannot have recourse to supposed representations or warranties claimed to have been made by representatives of defendant prior to the said written contract is elemental; the terms of such a contract cannot be varied by parol evidence.").

[22] *See* §18.3.1.

[23] Prosser & Keeton, above, §107. *See* Dunn Appraisal Co. v. Honeywell Info. Sys., Inc., 687 F.2d 877 (6th Cir. 1982).

> in their business transactions, is subject to liability for pecuniary loss caused to them by their justifiable reliance upon the information, if he fails to exercise reasonable care or competence in obtaining or communicating the information.

The justification for applying this to sales is that it promotes honesty.

A second line of cases goes so far as to impose strict liability on a vendor for false statements upon which a customer justifiably and detrimentally relies. The essence of the claim is not that the defendant intentionally or negligently misspoke, but that she asserted she knew facts as true when she simply did not. *Clements Auto Co. v. Service Bureau Corp.*[24] upheld a misrepresentation claim in the sale of electronic data processing services to an automotive parts wholesaler. The central misstatement the salesmen made was that the services were capable of effectively and efficiently controlling the customer's inventory. (Not a strange statement for salesmen to make!) The computer salesmen also made ancillary false statements: (1) the only way to achieve the results desired was to computerize; and (2) the system had rigorous controls. The service turned out to be dismal.

Another line of reasoning rejects the foregoing negligence or strict liability misrepresentation theories where the defendant's alleged misstatement occurred in a sales pitch. This reasoning considers Restatement §552 as policing the business of selling information, such as from a database, not the general business of marketing.[25] It prefers contract as the law for allocating liability between a vendor and a customer, except where intentional wrongdoing exists.[26]

At any rate, the law does motivate service providers to be truthful in their sales presentations.

[24]444 F.2d 169 (8th Cir. 1971).

[25]*See* Black, Jackson and Simmons Ins. Brokerage, Inc. v. International Business Machines Corp., 109 Ill. App. 3d 132, 440 N.E.2d 282 (1982).

[26]*See* Rio Grande Jewelers Supply Co. v. Data General Corp., 101 N.M. 798, 689 P.2d 1269 (1984).

§18.4.3 Contractual Limitations

Although disfavored, contractual disclaimers and limitations of some tort liability are valid. To be effective, they must be unambiguous.

> A plaintiff who by contract or otherwise expressly agrees to accept a risk of harm arising from the defendant's negligence or reckless conduct cannot recover for such harm, unless the agreement is invalid as contrary to public policy.[27]

An example of an agreed disclaimer of negligence that might contradict public policy is one between a public utility and a weaker customer, who has no choice but to accept. Disclaimers of liability for intentional misrepresentation (fraud) are also contrary to public policy.

Tort liability disclaimers have succeeded in data processing service contracts. In *Liberty Finance Management Corp. v. Beneficial Data Processing Corp.*[28] a service provider made serious errors in the conversion of customer data from one format to another, suffered excessive computer breakdowns, and failed to make necessary progress reports. But the contract between the parties disclaimed the provider's liability for negligence, and the court honored it when the customer sued for damages. The customer, a large corporation, argued unsuccessfully that the disclaimer was unconscionable and caused the contract to fail of its essential purpose.[29]

§18.5 PUBLIC SERVICE COMPANIES

The law recognizes special contract and tort rules for some classes of businesses, such as warehouses, common carriers,

[27]Restatement (Second) of Torts §496B (1965).
[28]670 S.W.2d 40 (Mo. Ct. App. 1984).
[29]*Compare,* U.C.C. §2-719(2).

telegraph companies, and utilities, that provide public services. Whether a computer message service provider fits this class is debatable.[1]

Under the U.C.C., a "warehouseman" is one who takes certain bailments as a business.[2] A bailment is the holding of personal property for another. Strictly speaking, a "common carrier" is a business, such as a railroad, that transports persons or property for the public.

Warehousemen must exercise reasonable care to protect goods entrusted with them.[3] They may not disclaim their duty of care,[4] although they may agree with customers to cap (but not eliminate) the damages owing if they breach that duty.[5] Under common law, common carriers are insurers of the goods they carry.[6] They may contract with customers to limit liability, but, like warehousemen, they generally may not relieve themselves of a duty to exercise reasonable care.[7] One reason for this extra burden on warehousemen and carriers is that the public lacks equal bargaining power with them.[8]

Under common law, telegraph companies are neither bailees, warehousemen, nor common carriers. Nor are they

§18.5 [1]Sections 18.5 and 18.7 generalize about the common law of warehousemen and transportation and telegraph carriers. Conclusions here are tentative because there are many, often conflicting, cases.

[2]U.C.C. §7-102(1)(h).

[3]U.C.C. §7-204(1). Bailees who are given property for the purpose of performing service on it are expected to exercise skill commensurate with the task. 8 Am. Jur. 2d Bailments §234 (1980).

[4]Restatement (Second) of Torts §496B comment g (1965). *See also* U.C.C. §7-202(3).

[5]U.C.C. §7-204(2). *See* Restatement (Second) of Torts §496B comments h & i (1965) (carrier, warehouseman, and telegraph company may contract to cap liability if customer is given option of full protection in exchange for higher rate).

[6]14 Am. Jur. 2d Carriers §508 (1964).

[7]*Id.* §§537 & 554.

[8]8 Am. Jur. 2d Bailments §145 (1980).

insurers of the messages they handle.[9] The reasoning is that, unlike a bailee or common carrier, a telegraph company has no special opportunity to steal the value of the thing it holds for the customer. A message has no intrinsic worth, as a physical object does. Loss of a message bears no relationship to the injury that might flow from the failure to deliver the message.[10]

Courts disagree on the extent to which a telegraph company may under common law relieve itself from liability for errors.[11] It is generally agreed that a telegraph company cannot entirely eliminate its liability for negligence. This appears to stem from the view that a telegraph company is a quasi-public entity resembling a warehouseman and common carrier. But courts split over whether the company may limit its contract and tort liability to a specific amount. Under one line of cases, a contractual limit of liability to some amount, such as the transmission price, is valid.[12] This advances the freedom of contract policy. These decisions tend to be conditioned on (1) not relieving the company for its "gross" negligence or willful misconduct and (2) the company having offered, for an additional fee and no liability limit, to repeat the message to catch errors.

Under a second line of cases, limitations for telegraph company negligence are void as against public policy, even if the sender had been given the option to repeat.[13]

Network service providers are like telegraph companies in that they tend to be large companies that move written messages. The argument, however, that they should not be treated like warehousemen, common carriers, or telegraph

[9]Primrose v. Western Union Tel. Co., 154 U.S. 1 (1894); Western Union Tel. Co. v. Neill, 57 Tex. 283 (1882).

[10]Primrose v. Western Union Tel. Co., 154 U.S. 1 (1894).

[11]175 A.L.R. 8 §§26-35 (1948).

[12]*See, e.g.*, Primrose v. Western Union Tel. Co., 154 U.S. 1 (1894).

[13]*See, e.g.*, Western Union Tel. Co. v. Chamblee, 122 Ala. 428, 25 So. 232 (1899).

companies—and should thus be allowed to contract freely for disclaimers and limits on liability—is that network providers usually operate in a very competitive, nationwide market. Customers usually have a choice of providers. The service provider contracts tend to be negotiable (within limits). If a customer dislikes one provider's terms, he can go, with modest effort, elsewhere.[14] Service provider customers have more bargaining leverage than telegraph customers because network contracts typically cover many messages over a time period, rather than a single message.

The equities can shift, however. In a particular market, such as a securities exchange, a network provider may attain a monopoly. Or, all the providers in a market may demand the same onerous terms, and all customers may be smaller businesses.[15]

In sum, a persuasive argument can be made that, absent monopolistic overtones, network service providers should not be subject to the special rules for public service companies.

§18.6 REGULATED ENVIRONMENTS

Federal and state legislation regulates many common carriers and other public businesses. Agencies administering the legislation influence service rates, the manner of service, and the degrees of provider liability. Regulated carriers file tariffs, which the agencies review and, if appropriate, approve.

Tariffs impose absolute terms.[1] Usually, tariffs substan-

[14]One argument advanced for allowing warehousemen more freedom to disclaim liability than common carriers is that warehousemen operate in a more competitive market. 78 Am. Jur. 2d Warehouses §233 (1975).

[15]*See* Restatement (Second) of Torts §496B comment j (1965).

§18.6 [1]*See* Western Union Tel. Co. v. Esteve Bros. & Co., 256 U.S. 566 (1921).

tially restrict the carriers' contract and tort liability. In *Lebowitz Jewelers, Ltd. v. New England Telephone and Telegraph Co.*,[2] for example, a jewelry store's security alarm relied on a telephone link to the police station. Burglars bypassed the alarm at the telephone company's nearby junction box and looted the store. The telephone company was not liable to the store, however, because its tariff excluded liability.

The theory for curbing liability is that the potential exposure would otherwise be overwhelming, and economic damages from service interruptions or errors are better allocated to customers. Those most likely to suffer sizable losses are large businesses. It is better to make them buy insurance and install safeguards than to burden the carriers' ratepayers.[3] In return for their liability shield, the common carriers are subjected to public scrutiny under regulatory agencies.

Interstate telecommunications "common carriers" are specially defined for purposes of the federal Communications Act of 1934,[4] under which they must file tariffs with the Federal Communications Commission (FCC).[5] Historically under the Act the FCC considered telephone service providers "common carriers," while excluding pure data processing service providers from that category. Over time, telephone and data processing technology became virtually indistinguishable. In its 1980 Computer Inquiry II decision, the FCC defined two terms, "basic service" and "enhanced service," to separate common carriers from other communications service providers.

> [B]asic service is limited to the common carrier offering of transmission capacity for the movement of information, whereas enhanced service combines basic service with com-

[2] 24 Mass. App. Ct. 268, 508 N.E.2d 125 (1987).

[3] Prosser & Keeton, above, §92.

[4] 47 U.S.C. §§151-613 (1988). "Common carrier" under this Act is not necessarily the same as "common carrier" under common law.

[5] 47 U.S.C. §203 (1988). Intrastate communications may be regulated by state agencies. 47 U.S.C. §152(b) (1988).

> puter processing applications that act on the format, content, code, protocol or similar aspects of the subscriber's transmitted information, or provide the subscriber additional, different, or restructured information, or involve subscriber interaction with stored information.[6]

The FCC has further described basic service as a "transmission pipeline."[7]

Essentially, the FCC regulates basic service, requiring tariff filing, and does not regulate enhanced service.[8] A provider of value-added-network service, which processes and stores computer messages, is generally considered an enhanced service provider and exempt from filing. (Thus, the FCC does not regulate the typical service provider discussed in this book.) Contract and tort law govern this provider's liability to customers. Nonetheless, regulated basic service providers, such as local telephone companies, do move electronic messages to, from, and among network providers.

§18.7 INTERNETWORKING AND REMOTE PLAINTIFFS

The foregoing sections in this chapter concentrate on liability between a provider and its immediate customer, but network errors can affect other parties. For example, suppose the customer (Blue Co.) contracts and deals with one provider (White

[6] Amendment of §64.702 of the Commission's Rules and Regulations (Second Computer Inquiry), 77 F.C.C.2d 384, 387 (1980) (Final Decision).

[7] Amendment of §64.702 of the Commission's Rules and Regulations (Second Computer Inquiry), 84 F.C.C.2d 50, 54 (1980) (Memorandum Opinion and Order).

[8] *See generally* Wyde, Telecommunications Law and Electronic Fund Transfer Services, 44 Bus. Law. 1101 (1989); J. Soma, Computer Technology and the Law 164-175 (1983).

Net), but to serve the customer, the provider must exchange messages through a second provider (Yellow Net), one lacking a direct contract with the customer.[1] (*See* Figure 18-1.) It could be cumbersome for a customer and a remote provider to negotiate a contract.

To ascertain the law here, it is enlightening to analogize to telegraph law, which in turn is influenced by the rules on transportation common carriers.

FIGURE 18-1
Internetworking

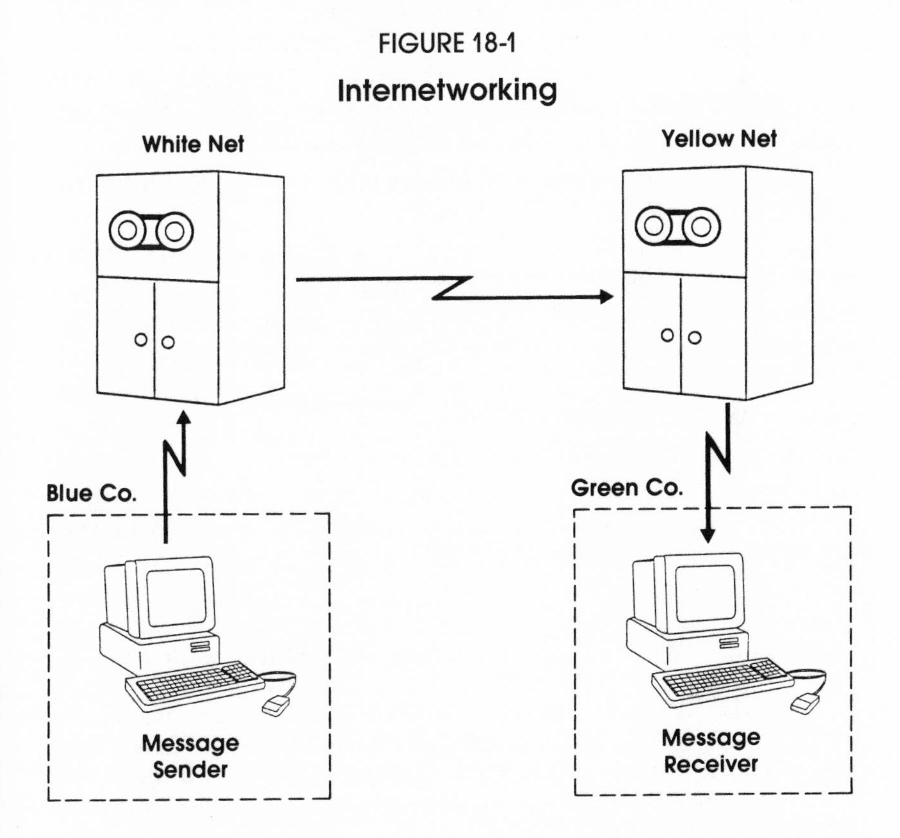

§18.7 [1]This network interconnection can be the focal point for errors. EDI veterans tell stories of messages lost in poor internetwork connections. *See* §5.3.

Can a network service provider (Yellow Net) be liable for mistakes that affect a remote customer (Blue)? Analogy says probably so. First, a remote customer can recover from a telegraph carrier that loses the message it handles.[2]

Second, authorities seem to agree that the telegram addressee, who, like the remote network customer, did not pay for transmission, has a cause of action against the telegraph company that botches the transmission. The authorities disagree on the legal theory, however. Some say the telegraph company is directly liable in contract because the addressee as principal contracted with the company through the addressee's agent, the sender; others say the addressee is a beneficiary of the contract between the sender and the company; and still others contend the company is liable in tort.[3]

Can an initial service provider (White Net) be liable for a connecting provider's (Yellow Net) failures? In telegraph, as in transportation, the general rule is that the first company's liability ends when it passes the message to the connecting company.[4] Still, there could be some question if the contract between the sender and the first company is construed to mean that the carrier is responsible for getting the message to its destination.

Can an initial service provider contract with a customer to lower the liability of a connecting provider? If the initial provider acts as the connecting provider's agent, and the intent to limit the latter's liability is clear, probably so.[5] The

[2]Smith v. Western Union Tel. Co., 84 Tex. 359, 19 S.W. 441 (1892).

[3]74 Am. Jur. 2d Telecommunications §127 (1974).

[4]Basila v. Western Union Tel. Co., 24 F.2d 569 (D.C.S.D. Fla. 1928). W. Elliot, A Treatise on the Law of Bailments and Carriers §247 (W. Hemingway rev., 2d ed. 1929). The outcome might be different if the initial and connecting carriers were legal "partners" in a business for the movement of messages.

[5]What if the initial network is not an agent? If the intent to limit liability is clear, the connecting network might be a beneficiary of the customer's contract to restrict liability. Alternatively, the customer might be barred under "promissory estoppel" from suing for more than the agreed liability.

weight of authority seems to be that terms applicable to the telegram sender also bind the sendee.[6] But a connecting telegraph company cannot avail itself of terms that purport only to limit the liability of the initial company.[7]

In light of these uncertainties and potential liabilities, some network providers may insist that their customers indemnify them from any liability to remote customers. The argument from the provider's perspective is that it can afford to undertake only known obligations to its customer, not unknown obligations to the world at large.[8] The opposing view is that providers should be liable for their own errors. Customers have no control over network service. The potential liability, according to this view, will not dissuade providers from offering service. The law will not make providers insurers; it will hold them only to exercise an appropriate level of care.

ABA Model Trading Partner Agreement[9] §1.2.3, an optional clause, provides that users will be liable to one another for network service provider errors. If they contract with different providers, then each party is responsible for its own provider's lapses.[10] If they use the same one, then the sender takes the liability. This paradoxically motivates the customer to demand indemnification from the provider, while the provider wishes indemnification from the customer.

An interesting device—the "through" transportation contract—exists in the common carriage industry.[11] If the shipper and the initial carrier agree to a through contract,

[6]20 A.L.R.2d 761 §2 (1951).

[7]Squire v. Western Union Tel. Co., 98 Mass. 232 (1867).

[8]*See* Bank Admin. Inst., Wire Transfer Customer Agreements 24 (1985).

[9]*See* §14.4.

[10]The wording of Section 1.2.3 is unfortunate, in that it says each party "shall be liable for" provider errors. This might be read to relieve providers, as beneficiaries of the contract, from liability. The clause could be improved if it were changed to provide that the users will indemnify one another for losses caused by provider errors.

[11]Elliot, above, §247.

the initial carrier is liable to the shipper for damage occurring at any point on the trip, even after the cargo has left the initial carrier's hands. Each connecting carrier must indemnify the initial carrier for damages caused by that connecting carrier.[12] The initial carrier can, within limits, contract with the customer to reduce the liability of all the carriers.[13] The advantages of the device are that the sender need negotiate with only one carrier, and no carrier need negotiate with a remote customer. The future development of a similar concept in the electronic messaging industry may have merit. It would efficiently and fairly allocate liability among customers and service providers.

[12] *See* U.C.C. §7-302(3).

[13] Elliot, above, §250; 14 Am. Jur. 2d Carriers 718 (1964).

Chapter

19

Confidentiality and Control of Data

§19.1 INTRODUCTION

Like a depositor of money in a bank, a service provider customer expects its data to be safe. So it wishes to know whether its provider may, either voluntarily or not, compromise data confidentiality, or may assert a lien on data in the event of a payment dispute with the customer.[1]

Electronic message records are a tempting target of discovery in legal actions. Controversy over such records erupted in the investigation of the 1989 oil spill by Exxon Co. U.S.A. in Alaska's Prince William Sound. A federal court had ordered Exxon to preserve all records relating to the spill, but a computer operator, apparently acting inadvertently, erased records of some relevant e-mail messages. The incident became a public issue in the investigation.[2] In *United States v. Horowitz*[3] data transmitted by computer and modem and then stored on computer tapes became critical evidence in a prosecution involving an alleged theft of government contract price information.

For the service provider customer, an obvious approach to confidentiality and lien issues is an explicit contract with the provider that confirms the customer's rights to data confidentiality and possession. The contract could also require the provider to notify the customer if anyone presents a warrant or other order for the data's release.

Contract law cannot answer all concerns. In 1986, the U.S. Congress adopted the Electronic Communications Pri-

§19.1 [1]Unless stated otherwise, the data at issue in this chapter are assumed to belong to the customer who claims it. This chapter generally does not deal with the situation in which a service provider might claim it owns data in whole or in part. Nor does it cover the division of data ownership between two or more users. These subjects must await later work.

[2]Eckerson, E-mail Nets Pose Hidden Legal Issues, Network World, July 31, 1989, at 1, col. 5.

[3]806 F.2d 1222 (4th Cir. 1986). *See* §19.3.2.

vacy Act of 1986 (ECPA)[4] to update federal wiretapping laws relative to electronic messaging technology such as e-mail and EDI. The 1986 Act amended Title III of the Omnibus Crime Control and Safe Streets Act of 1968 (as amended, Title III or the Act).[5] Title III forbids the intentional and unauthorized interception of an electronic communication in transmission, and the knowing disclosure or use of a communication so intercepted.[6] It also prohibits a "public" communications service provider from intentionally and illegitimately disclosing an electronic message in transmission.[7]

Title III regulates access by the government (federal or state) to stored electronic messages and service provider transactional (e.g., billing) records.[8] Further, it outlaws the intentional, unauthorized access of an electronic communication service, which access leads to the obtaining of or tampering with a stored message.[9] Thus, it inhibits a "hacker" or other unauthorized person from retrieving messages "in electronic storage."

Title III also prohibits a "public" provider of electronic communication or remote computing service from knowingly and illicitly disclosing a communication's contents

[4]For a detailed discussion of the ECPA, from a service provider's perspective, *see* J. Podesta & M. Sher, Protecting Electronic Messaging: A Guide to the Electronic Communications Privacy Act of 1986 (1990).

[5]18 U.S.C. §2510 et seq. (1988).

[6]18 U.S.C. §2511(1) (1988). The prohibition is subject to statutory exceptions, including interception by one of the parties to the communication. 18 U.S.C. §2511(2)(c) (1988). *See* United States v. Seidlitz, 589 F.2d 152 (4th Cir. 1978), *cert. denied,* 441 U.S. 922 (1979) (no violation of Title III (before its amendment by the ECPA) where computer operator intercepted unauthorized communication between its computer and outside intruder).

[7]18 U.S.C. §2511(3) (1988). The federal Communications Act of 1934 may also impair the freedom of a provider to divulge messages. *See* 47 U.S.C. §605 (1988).

[8]18 U.S.C. §§2701-2710 (1988).

[9]18 U.S.C. §2701(a) (1988).

while in electronic storage.[10] The law sets out several circumstances under which disclosure is allowed, however, including when the message sender or receiver consents.[11]

The government can generally penalize Title III violators under criminal law.[12] In addition, injured parties may generally recover civil damages (including attorney fees) from violators.[13] Overall, Title III is very complex. The Act suffers some ambiguity, and many of its general rules have multiple exceptions.

§19.2 GOVERNMENT POWERS TO COMPEL DISCLOSURE

Law enforcement thrives on information. A raft of statutory powers enables government agencies to compel private parties to disclose information in connection with civil or criminal investigations.

Government criminal prosecutors employ law enforcement agencies, such as the Federal Bureau of Investigation, and criminal grand juries to investigate crime. A prosecutor or law enforcement agency may, under applicable criminal procedure rules,[1] apply to court for a warrant authorizing the search of specified premises or objects. Alternatively, a

[10]18 U.S.C. §2702(a) (1988). The ban on remote computing service disclosure does not apply if the service is authorized to access record contents for some purpose other than rendering storage or computer processing service. Suppose, for instance, that a remote computing service is a securities trading clearinghouse, which processes and stores data and examines it for regulatory surveillance purposes. Title III would not block the clearinghouse from disclosing the data (although other laws might).

[11]18 U.S.C. §2702(b) (1988).

[12]18 U.S.C. §§2511(4), 2701(b) (1988).

[13]18 U.S.C. §§2520, 2707 (1988).

§19.2 [1]*See, e.g.*, Fed. R. Crim. Proc. 41.

grand jury may issue a subpoena commanding a witness to testify before, or present documents or other evidence to, the jury.[2]

Federal administrative agencies may issue subpoenas and conduct other discovery in implementing and enforcing the laws under their jurisdiction. If subjects disregard subpoenas, agencies usually may enforce them by court order. Unless required by statute, agencies need not notify investigation "targets" when subpoenas are issued to third parties such as independent recordkeepers.[3]

An example of a federal statute authorizing a subpoena is the Inspector General Act of 1978.[4] Under it, the inspectors general within various federal agencies investigate, among other things, fraud and abuse in federal procurement. It authorizes the inspectors to issue subpoenas for "all [relevant] information, documents, reports, answers, records, accounts, papers, and other data and documentary evidence . . ."[5] Similarly, to ascertain whether a taxpayer has complied with the Internal Revenue Code, the Internal Revenue Service (IRS) may, through a summons, compel any third parties holding taxpayer records to disclose them.[6]

If a government agency demands disclosure of sensitive corporate data, the corporation may wish to: (1) challenge the demand as illegal or unnecessary;[7] (2) act to restrict the demand's scope; (3) insist on safeguards to prevent abuse of the information by the government or its employees; (4) press for limits on the information's uses; (5) demand notice before

[2]*See, e.g.,* Fed. R. Crim. Proc. 17.

[3]SEC v. Jerry T. O'Brien Inc., 467 U.S. 735 (1984).

[4]5 U.S.C. Appendix—Inspector General Act of 1978 (1988).

[5]*Id.* §6(a)(4).

[6]I.R.C. §7602(a)(2). *See* United States v. Davey, 543 F.2d 996 (2d Cir. 1976) (IRS summons can compel production of relevant computer tapes in taxpayer's possession). *See* §19.5.3.

[7]Constitutional grounds for challenging a disclosure of records might arise under the first, fourth, fifth, or fourteenth amendments. H.R. Rep. No. 647, 99th Cong., 2d Sess., at 69 (1986).

the information is aired in public or other proceedings; or (6) request that in legal proceedings the information be viewed by a court in camera rather than in public.[8] To take these actions, the corporation needs early notice that its data are being inspected. Notice is usually timely and unavoidable if the corporation keeps the data under its own roof, but the same may not be true if a third party holds the data.

Moreover, the corporation's right to challenge a government search through records depends greatly on whether the U.S. Constitution protects them. If they are in third-party hands, the outlook for such protection is bleak.

§19.3 FOURTH AMENDMENT PROTECTIONS FROM GOVERNMENT

The U.S. Constitution, particularly the fourth amendment, checks the government's power to obtain private information.[1] The use of forced disclosure laws, such as criminal procedure rules and administrative subpoena statutes, is conditioned on the constitution's satisfaction. The fourth amendment provides:

> The right of the people to be secure in their persons, houses, papers, and effects, against unreasonable searches and seizures, shall not be violated, and no Warrants shall issue, but upon probable cause, supported by Oath or affirmation, and particularly describing the place to be searched, and the persons or things to be seized.

[8] *See* C. Duffney, Response to Government Information Requests, Corporate Practice Series Portfolio No. 29 (BNA 1982) A-22.

§19.3 [1] Other constitutional provisions, such as the fifth amendment right of due process, also restrain government power.

§19.3.1 Reasonable Expectations of Privacy

Neither the fourth amendment, nor the U.S. Supreme Court cases interpreting it, plainly define a "search." The classic example of a search occurs when police forcibly burst into a home and look for evidence of crime. The target has little if any legal opportunity to challenge the action in advance.

The Supreme Court interprets the fourth amendment to regulate government invasions of a person's "justifiable," "reasonable," or "legitimate expectation of privacy."[2] Government agents usually must secure a warrant before making such an invasion or search.[3] A warrant is an order issued by a "neutral and detached magistrate" or judge who has determined, based on evidence government agents present her, that probable cause justifies the search.[4] This is a high standard for law enforcement agents to satisfy.

A subpoena (or a summons) to deliver documents is generally a written demand that the party controlling the documents make them available by a certain date to an administrative agency or a party acting under court authority. The document holder has time to challenge the matter legally. Like a search, a subpoena must pass fourth amendment scrutiny, but the standard is lower than for a search. A subpoena issued by an administrative agency must be "sufficiently limited in scope, relevant in purpose, and specific in directive so that compliance will not be unreasonably burdensome."[5] Such a subpoena may be enforced only by court

[2]Smith v. Maryland, 442 U.S. 735, 740 (1979).

[3]Camara v. Municipal Court of the City and County of San Francisco, 387 U.S. 523, 528-529 (1967).

[4]Johnson v. United States, 333 U.S. 10, 14 (1948) ("Probable cause" means that, based on all the circumstances, "there is a fair probability that . . . evidence of a crime will be found in a particular place."). *See* Illinois v. Gates, 462 U.S. 213, 238 (1983) (The showing of probable cause to an independent judge is generally more difficult for the government than the obtaining of a subpoena.).

[5]See v. City of Seattle, 387 U.S. 541, 544 (1967).

sanctions; law enforcement agents may not execute it with physical force (i.e., a classic search).[6] A subpoena for documents, issued by a criminal grand jury, may not be overly sweeping.[7]

Fourth amendment rights extend only to that which a person takes steps to keep private. "What a person knowingly exposes to the public, even in his own home or office, is not a subject of Fourth Amendment protection. . . . But what he seeks to preserve as private, even in an area accessible to the public, may be constitutionally protected."[8] Thus the fourth amendment requires the police to obtain a search warrant before tapping a private telephone conversation coming from a public booth.[9]

Under the fourth amendment, people usually have reasonable expectations of privacy in their places of business.[10] Moreover, the fourth amendment protects corporations and other businesses much as it protects individuals.[11]

Although the courts have not spoken definitely, the proposition that computer records maintained by a corporation in its own facilities enjoy fourth amendment protection seems to ring true.[12] The Third Circuit Court of Appeals has held that the owner of an audiotape recording can have a reasonable expectation of privacy in the recording's contents.[13]

§19.3.2 Privacy of Third-Party Records

Yet how does the fourth amendment apply to information possessed by a third party such as a computer service pro-

[6] *Id.* at 544-545.

[7] United States v. Dionisio, 410 U.S. 1, 11 (1973).

[8] Katz v. United States, 389 U.S. 347, 351-352 (1967).

[9] *Id.* at 354-359.

[10] Marshall v. Barlow's, Inc., 436 U.S. 307, 311-313 (1978).

[11] G.M. Leasing Corp. v. United States, 429 U.S. 338, 353-354 (1977).

[12] Note, Search Warrants and Computer Records, 67 B.U.L. Rev. 179, 196-199 (1987).

[13] United States v. Feldon, 753 F.2d 256, 262 (3d Cir. 1985).

vider?[14] If that information is intended and configured as a private communication in transmission, the argument that the user reasonably expects privacy and therefore should enjoy fourth amendment protection seems strong.[15] The information is like a private letter or telephone conversation.[16] Yet if the information is held by a third party as a record, the argument for protection withers. The current trend in cases is to accord parties little right to challenge searches of records or property controlled by others.

In reviewing two allegedly defective subpoenas for documents, the court in *United States v. Miller*[17] held that a bank customer has no legitimate expectation of privacy in bank records concerning transactions in the customer's account. The records were the property, and in the possession, of the two banks involved. "All of the documents obtained, including financial statements and deposit slips, contain only information voluntarily conveyed to the banks and exposed to their employees in the ordinary course of business."[18] The court reasoned that "[t]he depositor takes the risk, in revealing his affairs to another, that the information will be conveyed by that person to the Government."[19] So the court held the subpoenas intruded on no constitutionally protected interests of the customer.[20] The court further explained that under the fourth amendment the customer would have no legitimate expectation of privacy even if he had actually expected the bank to keep the information in confidence.[21]

[14]*See generally* Note, Search Warrants and Computer Records, 67 B.U.L. Rev. 179 (1987).

[15]H.R. Rep. No. 647, 99th Cong., 2d Sess., at 22 (1986).

[16]*See* §19.5.3.

[17]425 U.S. 435 (1976).

[18]*Id.* at 442.

[19]*Id.* at 443.

[20]This result motivates the customer to obtain its bank's agreement that it will resist unjustified demands for records. Service provider customers may desire the same from their providers.

[21]425 U.S. at 443.

Smith v. Maryland[22] held that the fourth amendment does not shield records of the numbers a caller dials with a telephone. The caller cannot legitimately expect privacy because he should know the telephone company records the numbers and uses the records in its business. *Rawlings v. Kentucky*[23] declared that a defendant has no reasonable expectation of privacy relative to his property (drugs) that he keeps in another's purse. *Couch v. United States*[24] held that a taxpayer may not under the fourth amendment challenge an IRS summons to her accountant for the taxpayer's records. *United States v. Matlock*[25] taught that no legitimate privacy expectation by a defendant is compromised if an appropriate third party grants government access to a place or object to be searched. The third party must have "common authority over or other sufficient relationship to the premises or effects sought to be inspected."[26] In *Matlock,* the defendant's co-occupant had granted the police permission to search the defendant's residence.

One case, *United States v. Horowitz,*[27] is particularly relevant to companies exchanging commercial data electronically. The defendant was convicted for lying to a board investigating alleged fraud by a federal government contractor. He allegedly had stolen contract bid data from his employer, Pratt & Whitney Aircraft, and sold it to a third party, Electro-Methods, Inc. (EMI). The defendant transmitted the data to EMI by modem from a computer in his home. The data then resided on magnetic tapes in EMI's computer, although the defendant apparently could still access the data on the tapes through the modem link between his computer and EMI's. Under a valid warrant for the search of EMI's

[22]442 U.S. 735 (1979).
[23]448 U.S. 98 (1980).
[24]409 U.S. 322 (1973).
[25]415 U.S. 164 (1974).
[26]*Id.* at 171.
[27]806 F.2d 1222 (4th Cir. 1986).

premises, government investigators confiscated EMI's tapes, then inspected them to discover the data, which incriminated the defendant. The defendant asserted that by reading the tapes, without obtaining a separate warrant specifically pertaining to the tapes' contents, the government invaded his fourth amendment reasonable expectation of privacy. He argued the records were his " 'electronic file cabinet,' an extension of his private home office."[28] The court, however, held the defendant had no reasonable expectation of privacy in EMI's records and therefore had no standing to complain about the lack of a special warrant. He had sold the bid data to EMI, and had neither control over, nor any ability to prevent others from using, EMI's tapes. In contrast, EMI could have excluded the defendant from the tapes by simply removing them from its computer.

§19.4 CONSTITUTIONAL PROTECTIONS FROM STATE GOVERNMENT

By virtue of the fourteenth amendment to the U.S. Constitution, the fourth amendment applies to state governments.[1] So it sets a minimum standard that all states must observe when conducting searches. In addition, many state constitutions limit government power to search private places or objects,[2] and some constitutions have been interpreted to fix standards higher than the fourth amendment. Disagreeing with *Miller,* some state courts have ruled on state constitutional grounds that the government must obtain a warrant before searching bank customer records.[3]

[28]*Id.* at 1225.

§19.4 [1]Mapp v. Ohio, 367 U.S. 643 (1961).

[2]E.g., Cal. Const. art. 1, §13.

[3]E.g., Burrows v. Superior Court of San Bernadino County, 13 Cal. 3d 238, 118 Cal. Rptr. 166, 529 P.2d 590 (1974).

§19.5 TITLE III PROTECTIONS FROM GOVERNMENT

Some have feared that modern communication modes, such as computer messaging, are constitutionally less confidential than older ones, such as telephone or postal mail. One commentator[1] posits three fourth amendment arguments that might be advanced to justify warrantless searches of computer messages, or records thereof, under the control of a third-party computer service provider:

1. The user disclosed her messages to the third party, as the customer in *Miller*[2] disclosed his financial information to the bank, and thereby assumed the risk that the third party would disclose them to the government.[3]
2. The third party's ability to access the user's messages deprives the user of any legitimate expectation of privacy, as happened in *Smith* and *Rawlings*.[4]
3. The third party has power to consent to a search because it has "concurrent authority" over the records, as happened in *Matlock*.[5]

§19.5 [1]Note, Search Warrants and Computer Records, 67 B.U.L. Rev. 179, 199-200 (1987). The commentator argues in favor of extending fourth amendment protection to records kept by service providers.

[2]*See* §19.3.2.

[3]A possible distinction exists between the records in *Miller* and customer archives that might be kept for safekeeping by a third-party recordkeeper. The *Miller* records belonged to the banks. They were not customer property that the banks were holding for safekeeping. Arguably, customer property held for safe recordkeeping is protected by the fourth amendment. However, considering the trend of cases opposing fourth amendment rights in third-party possessions, it is doubtful courts will definitively recognize such a distinction in the near term. Thus, user companies cannot rely on the distinction today.

[4]*See* §19.3.2.

[5]*See* §19.3.2.

Congress amended Title III to clarify the existence of and limits to the confidentiality rights of electronic message users.[6] It mooted arguments number (1) and (2) (insofar as they pertain to private messages in transit and short-term records thereof), but left number (3) largely intact.

Title III does not displace the fourth amendment. It sets statutory search standards that are (presumably) at least equal to or higher than fourth amendment standards. If in any situation Title III's standards are lower than the fourth amendment's, then the latter's standards control.

Congress started by making it a criminal offense for anyone (private person or government agent) wrongfully to intercept or disclose an electronic message in transit or to uncover or disclose a stored message. Thus Title III, as a specific criminal statute, appears to supplement more general statutes, such as the Inspectors General Act and the Internal Revenue Code,[7] that authorize the compulsion of third parties to disclose information to the government. It seems that the government must now comply with the procedures of both Title III and the more general statutes (if any are applicable) in order to monitor messages and obtain their disclosure.

§19.5.1 Messages in Transit

Generally, Title III permits law enforcement officials to obtain a court order for the interception of messages in transit if the officials show (1) probable cause exists to believe that a listed crime has been, is being, or will be committed; (2) probable cause exists that relevant messages will be intercepted; (3) ordinary investigative methods are ineffective; and (4) probable cause exists that the communication facil-

[6]Some states have statutes similar to Title III. *See, e.g.,* Tex. Code Crim. Proc. art. 18.21 (Vernon Supp. 1991).

[7]*See* §19.2.

ities in question are being used for crime or are normally used by the person under investigation.[8] This order would be similar to a search warrant. Title III and other federal law generally bar outside parties (service providers) from informing others that messages are being intercepted.[9]

§19.5.2 Messages in Storage

Title III regulates the government's power to force a service provider to divulge customer messages "in electronic storage." It does not, however, deal with government compulsion of a subject to authorize disclosure of its records in a service provider's possession. Other laws (such as the Inspectors General Act) govern that topic just as they govern government demands for divulgence of records in a subject's home or office.

A government entity may under Title III force a service provider to disclose a stored message,[10] provided the government clears specified hurdles:

- If the message has been in storage in an electronic communication service (ECS) for 180 days or fewer, then the agency must possess a search warrant from a court.[11]
- If the message has been in storage in an ECS for more than 180 days, or if the message is in storage in a remote computing service (RCS), then the government must acquire (1) a search warrant, (2) a federal

[8] 18 U.S.C. §2518(3) (1988).

[9] 18 U.S.C. §§2511(2)(a)(ii), 2232(c) (1988).

[10] 18 U.S.C. §2703(a),(b) (1988). Under §2703(c), a government entity can, with an appropriate subpoena, warrant, or order, also compel a service provider to disclose transactional records about messages (which generally are billing and operational records).

[11] 18 U.S.C. §2703(a) (1988).

> or state administrative, grand jury, or trial subpoena, or (3) an adequate court order.[12]

A search warrant is generally more difficult to obtain than a subpoena or a court order. Thus, the hurdles are lower for (1) messages in storage over six months by an ECS provider or (2) any messages or data in storage in an RCS.[13]

The reason for the 180-day watershed seems to be this: Messages stored by an ECS for fewer than 180 days are intended to facilitate communication. Messages stored longer are intended for recordkeeping. Congress decided the former activity deserved privacy more than the latter.[14]

Congress elected, with little explanation, to apply the lower protection level to all data stored by RCSs. Regardless of how young they may be, all are treated the same as ECS messages stored for more than 180 days.[15]

Title III denies protection from the government to messages stored by an RCS that can use them for some purpose other than just providing the customer processing or storage.[16] An example would be where an RCS stores data for

[12] 18 U.S.C. §2703(b) (1988).

[13] Sections 2701-2703 of 18 U.S.C. apply to data stored by ECS and RCS providers (although §2701 applies only to the former). The definition of ECS in §§2510(16) and 2711(1) seems to cover service providers for e-mail, EDI, EFT, telex, and similar communication. Section 2711(2) defines RCS as "the provision to the public of computer storage or processing services by means of an electronic communications system," which seems to be the service provided by a so-called service bureau. *See* H.R. Rep. No. 647, 99th Cong. 2d Sess., at 23 (1986). It may, however, be difficult to discern which of these two categories some providers fit. A provider may support communication, but it may process data (such as by translating it from one format to another) as well.

[14] H.R. Rep. No. 647, 99th Cong., 2d Sess., at 68 (1986).

[15] This reflects a plain reading of Title III. Legislative reports may suggest that the 180-day distinction should also apply to messages stored by RCSs. *See* Podesta & Sher, above, at 42-43. As for electronic archives, *see* §19.5.4.

[16] 18 U.S.C. 2703(b)(2) (1988).

customers, but also may sell access to that data to others. Evidently, Congress considered such a service provider as having "concurrent authority" similar to the co-occupant in *Matlock.*[17]

Title III sets rules on notifying the customer that its stored messages are under examination.[18] If the government acts under a search warrant, notice is not required.[19] If it acts under a subpoena or court order, however, it generally must notify the subject.[20]

The government may postpone any required notice. If it must inform the subject, it can obtain an order to delay for up to 90 days.[21] The granting of delay requires a court (or sometimes an agency official) to find that without the delay, any of the following adverse results *may* ensue:

> (A) endangering the life or physical safety of an individual; (B) flight from prosecution; (C) destruction of or tampering with evidence; (D) intimidation of potential witnesses; or (E) otherwise seriously jeopardizing an investigation or unduly delaying a trial.[22]

Item (E) sets a very open-ended standard favoring the government.

Moreover, Title III enables the government to "gag" the relevant service provider with a court order. Where government notice is omissible or delayed, a court can command a service provider not to tell its customer about the search.[23]

[17]*See* §19.3.2.

[18]*See* §19.3.

[19]18 U.S.C. §§2703(a), 2703(b)(1)(A) (1988).

[20]18 U.S.C. §2703(b)(1)(B) (1988).

[21]U.S.C. §2705(a)(1) (1988). Under some limited circumstances, a court can extend the postponement of notice. 18 U.S.C. §2705(a)(4) (1988).

[22]18 U.S.C. §2705(a)(1),(2) (1988).

[23]18 U.S.C. §2705(b) (1988).

The court must first determine that any of the adverse results identified above *will* ensue.[24]

To summarize, Title III says this about government access to electronic messages stored by a service provider: The government can force the provider to open them, and can omit, delay, and forbid notice about this to the customer. Hence, the government can win secret access. All these powers are subject, however, to measured procedural checks and qualifications.[25]

§19.5.3 Assessment of Title III

Title III's treatment of computer messages in transit seems roughly equal to the legal treatment of other private messages in transit. Whether the government wishes to intercept a computer message, tap a telephone conversation,[26] or open

[24]A service provider may agree by contract with its customers not to divulge their messages. It is doubtful this contract could preclude the government from enforcing a warrant or subpoena under Title III, however. Such preclusion would defeat the congressional purpose of permitting controlled law enforcement access to messages. *Compare* Restatement (Second) of Contracts §178 (1981) (contract term is unenforceable if public policy clearly outweighs the interest in enforcement).

[25]Could Title III force a service provider to process and reconfigure data to aid an investigation? For example, a service provider might have chronological backup records of data from hundreds of customers. The government may desire a translation and analysis of scattered bits of information pertaining to only one such customer. Title III is unclear. It speaks of the disclosure of message "contents," not the processing of data. 18 U.S.C. §2703 (1988). Yet it also provides for cost reimbursement to the service provider for "searching for, assembling, reproducing, or otherwise providing . . . information." 18 U.S.C. §2706(a) (1988). *Consider* United States v. New York Tel. Co., 434 U.S. 159 (1977), in which a court compelled a telephone company to aid in the installation of a pen register for tracing calls. Title III did not then authorize such compulsion, but the All Writs Act, 28 U.S.C. §1651(a) (1988), which gives courts residual power to carry out their duties, did.

[26]18 U.S.C. §2518(3) (1988).

a first class postal letter,[27] it must usually acquire a search warrant (or equivalent order) first. When so armed, the government need not necessarily notify the target of the examination for some time, and any intermediary involved either can be prohibited from tipping off the subject or would be unlikely to do so.[28]

Title III's treatment of computer messages in third-party storage, however, should give corporate users pause. Title III embraces the notion, well-established in fourth amendment doctrine, that something in third-party hands is less worthy of confidentiality.[29] And Title III affords the prosecutor a prized weapon—the power to muzzle a third-party recordkeeper during an inspection. Although not unprecedented, rarely is this power as resolutely articulated as in Title III. Consider the extent to which this power does or does not exist in other areas:

1. Some federal courts hold that a witness (including one just producing documents) subpoenaed before a grand jury can be enjoined under the Federal Rules of Criminal Procedure from telling the investigation subject about the subpoena.[30] Other federal courts disagree. The controversy centers on the meaning of Rule 6(e)(2), which implies that witnesses may not be "gagged." The disagreement has peaked where

[27]The fourth amendment protects first class mail much the same as it protects private papers in the home. *See* United States v. Van Leeuwen, 397 U.S. 249 (1970).

[28]Title III bars an intermediary from alerting others to the existence of legitimate devices to intercept telephone or electronic messages. 18 U.S.C. §2511(2)(a)(ii) (1988). *See also* 18 U.S.C. §2232 (1988) (ban on warning others about a pending search warrant).

[29]*See* §19.3.2.

[30]*See, e.g.*, In Re Grand Jury Subpoena Duces Tecum, 797 F.2d 676 (8th Cir. 1986). Someone who warns the subject about an investigation under a pending judicial proceeding may also be liable for obstruction of justice under 18 U.S.C. §1503 (1988). *See also* United States v. Smith, 729 F. Supp. 1380 (D.D.C. 1990).

the U.S. Supreme Court's *Miller* decision on banking privacy[31] collides with contradictory state decisions.[32] In both *In Re Vescovo Special Grand Jury*[33] and *In Re East National Bank of Denver*[34] prosecutors acting under federal grand jury subpoenas for bank records warned banks not to alert their customers about subpoenas. But in each case the bank believed state law mandated that it notify its customer; and the court ruled that federal law would not penalize the bank for doing that.

2. Under Internal Revenue Code §7609, when the IRS issues a summons to any third-party recordkeeper within a specified class, the Service must notify the taxpayer under investigation so he can challenge the summons. The class includes certain financial institutions, attorneys, and accountants; however, it does not include simple keepers of computer records. Section 7609(g) permits a court, at IRS request and upon the showing of good cause, to suspend the taxpayer notice requirement. The Code does not explicitly say the recordkeeper may be barred from disclosing the summons' existence to the taxpayer, however.
3. The Right to Financial Privacy Act,[35] adopted in the wake of the *Miller* decision,[36] provides procedures the government must clear before inspecting the bank records of individuals and small partnerships (but not corporations).[37] It includes provisions for the delay of notice from the government or the bank

[31] *See* §19.3.2.
[32] *See* §19.4.
[33] 473 F. Supp. 1335 (C.D. Cal. 1979).
[34] 517 F. Supp. 1061 (D. Colo. 1981).
[35] 12 U.S.C. §§3401-3422 (1988).
[36] *See* §19.3.2.
[37] 12 U.S.C. §3401(4) (1988).

to the subjects.[38] These provisions served as models for parts of Title III.

So in the context of these other laws, it is clear that with Title III Congress outfitted the prosecutor well for the information age. The Act endorses reduced privacy for data stored by third parties, and it equips investigators with a potent means for surreptitiously combing through such data. It unambiguously authorizes the gagging of all electronic third parties that it covers.

Considering the government's power, a customer may wish to direct its service provider to purge data after a few days or weeks. Note that Title III empowers investigators acting under a court order, or a subpoena, to compel service providers secretly to make backup copies of data.[39] Unlike long-term records, however, these copies are unlikely to cover more than a few weeks or months of data. In addition, this tool aids the government only if it knows to use it before messages are purged.

Alternatively, a customer who does allow a third party to store records might insist on technical controls to prevent secret examination. The records might, for instance, be encrypted so that only the customer can permit them to be deciphered.[40]

§19.5.4 Caveat on Third-Party Archives

Title III is ambiguous concerning archives (as opposed to shorter-term records) of message contents kept by third parties. First, the type of message content record it covers is a

[38] 12 U.S.C. §§3406(c), 3409, 3413(i).
[39] 18 U.S.C. §2704 (1988).
[40] *See* §6.4.2.

communication in "electronic storage,"[41] which it defines as:[42]

> (A) any temporary, intermediate storage of a wire or electronic communication incidental to the electronic transmission thereof; and
>
> (B) any storage of such communication by an electronic communications service [ECS] for purposes of backup protection of such communication . . .

It is unclear whether this covers an archive kept so a transaction can be proved for legal and audit purposes. That might be considered "permanent" rather than "temporary, intermediary storage" or "storage . . . for . . . backup."[43] Yet it might be argued that Title III does cover such an archive since it explicitly covers a communication stored for more than 180 days.[44] It designates no specific time after which stored messages are not covered.

Second, not all third-party archivers of message contents necessarily fall within Title III's ambit. Title III pertains to stored messages only if they are stored by ECSs or RCSs. Yet an entity might store or archive message contents without providing communication or computing service.[45]

If the Act does not apply to a recordkeeper's inventory, then the customer's protection from government searches appears weak. It depends more on the fourth amendment,

[41] 18 U.S.C. §§2701, 2703 (1988).

[42] 18 U.S.C. §§2510(17), 2711(1) (1988).

[43] If Title III does distinguish between temporary and permanent records, it offers little guidance on when any particular message in storage graduates from the first category to the second.

[44] 18 U.S.C. §2703 (1988).

[45] Note also that, for RCSs the only stored messages Title III covers are those derived from "electronic transmission." 18 U.S.C. §§2702(a)(2)(A), 2703(b)(2)(A) (1988). Stored data derived from a tape-to-tape exchange arguably do not fit that description.

and as explained earlier, fourth amendment protection for objects under third-party control is doubtful.[46]

§19.6 CONFIDENTIALITY FROM PRIVATE PARTIES

Electronic business data can contain competitively sensitive information, including customer names, pricing and production data, and so forth. Technology affords service providers elaborate technical controls, including password schemes, to channel information to only the intended users and prevent divulgence to others.[1]

Yet a provider can be lax in safeguarding data. One unfortunate corporation used a service bureau when preparing contract bids, but it became suspicious when it lost a series of contracts to one competitor. Investigation revealed that the rival was stealing confidential data held by the bureau. First, the competitor had stolen the customer's service bureau passwords. (The customer had weak safeguards over passwords.) Second, the bureau had inadequate controls over backup tapes, and a dishonest bureau employee was giving the customer's tapes to the competitor.[2]

§19.6.1 Confidentiality under Title III

What confidentiality obligations do service providers and private interlopers owe to the electronic message user? The

[46]*See* §§19.3.2 & 6.4.2.

§19.6 [1]With effort, however, a snoop may uncover some secret information. The extent to which service provider employees can access information varies, although it can be controlled.

[2]Wilkinson, Auditing Clients Who Use Service Bureaus, J. Acct. & EDP 8, 10-11 (Spring 1986).

fourth amendment is inapplicable because it checks only government activities.[3] Title III, however, generally outlaws the following intentional acts: (1) the interception by an interloper of an electronic message in transit, (2) the disclosure or use of a wrongfully intercepted message,[4] (3) the access by an interloper of a private electronic message in storage,[5] and (4) the unauthorized disclosure by a service provider of the contents of a message in transit or storage.[6]

Four caveats are in order: First, Title III may not cover long-term archives.[7] Second, Title III proscribes a service provider's intentional wrongdoing, but not negligence. It does not require the provider to deter crooks with the use of security features. This is a service a customer must contract for.

Third, Title III's injunctions against disclosures by service providers apply only to "public" service providers. The Act does not define public. Presumably, it covers at least service providers who, for a fee, furnish services to independent customers. Clearly this would cover the typical VAN. But query whether a hybrid system, such as a service created as a joint venture by a closed group of corporate users, is "public."

Finally, Title III permits a service provider to disclose to other private parties records or other information pertaining to customers (excluding message contents).[8] Thus, if a customer wishes that its service provider not divulge transactional or billing records, or statistical analyses of messages exchanged with trading partners, it should obtain a contract to that effect.[9]

[3]Burdeau v. McDowell, 256 U.S. 465, 475 (1921).

[4]18 U.S.C. §2511(1) (1988).

[5]18 U.S.C. §2701 (1988).

[6]18 U.S.C. §§2511(3)(a), 2702 (1988).

[7]*See* §19.5.4.

[8]18 U.S.C. §2703(c)(1)(A) (1988).

[9]Pen registers and trap-and-trace devices aid service providers and law enforcement personnel in determining and recording the origin and

§19.6.2 Confidentiality under State Law

The common law affords a user additional protection.[10] Undoubtedly a customer may obligate its service provider by contract to refrain from disclosing messages intentionally and to exercise due care (or some other more specific standard) in shielding messages from interlopers.[11]

Moreover, common law may impose confidentiality and security obligations on the service provider implicitly. Cases suggest a telegraph company may be liable if it divulges a message without authority.[12] Banking law may also furnish an apt analogy. A service provider is like a bank in that it possesses much precious customer information; its customer naturally expects discretion regarding that information. The bank-customer contract carries an implied bank duty not to disclose confidential customer information to third parties. The seminal case is *Tournier v. National Provincial & Union Bank of England,*[13] in which a bank had told its customer's employer that the customer was doing business, through his own account, with a bookmaker. The customer sued the bank, and the court upheld an award to the customer on the implied contract duty theory.[14]

Trade secret law is perhaps the chief legal means by which a business may protect its right to exploit secrets. It

---

destination of telephone calls and electronic communications. Title III generally prohibits use of such tools except with special court order or in connection with the provision of communication service. 18 U.S.C §§3121-3125 (1988).

[10]The common law against eavesdropping might be stretched to cover electronic snooping too. *See generally* 25 Am. Jur. 2d Eavesdropping (1966).

[11]*Compare* Nagy v. Bell Tel. Co. of Penna., 292 Pa. Super. 24, 436 A.2d 701 (1981) (possible breach of customer contract for telephone company to divulge customer toll records to outsider).

[12]Moore v. N.Y. Cotton Exch., 270 U.S. 593, 605-606 (1926); Purdy v. Western Union Tel. Co., 97 S.C. 22, 80 S.E. 459 (1914).

[13]1 K.B. 461 (C.A. 1923).

[14]*See also* Peterson v. Idaho First Natl. Bank, 83 Idaho 578, 367 P.2d 284, 290 (1961).

enables the holder of a trade secret to recover damages (or other relief) from a competitor who illicitly acquires or uses the secret. Generally, a trade secret is any private commercial information, the secrecy of which the holder has taken reasonable efforts to guard.[15] Accordingly, prudent businesses take pains to mark their secrets as confidential, limit access to them, and enter confidentiality agreements with those who must learn them. The wise company applies those same principles to its sensitive electronic messages.

§19.7 LIEN ON DATA

When he anticipates not being paid for work on a customer's personal property, a worker's instinctive reaction is to hold the property hostage. An unpaid service provider, being no different, is likely to withhold data.

Until his just fees and expenses are paid, the artisan, mechanic, or other worker has under common law and some statutes a lien on personal property left in his hands for repair, modification, or other improvement. Thus, a seamstress who makes a dress from fabric given her may keep the dress until her employer compensates her service.[1] It has been held that even the transportation of property is sufficient improvement of it to justify a lien.[2]

A few cases have addressed service bureau liens on data. *American Consumer, Inc. v. Anchor Computers, Inc.*,[3] involved a dispute over computer tapes (containing mailing list data) between a service bureau and a creditor of the service bureau's customer. The customer's creditor sought to retrieve

[15]Uniform Trade Secrets Act §1(4) (1985).
§19.7 [1]8 Am. Jur. 2d Bailments §245 (1980).
[2]Farrington v. Meek, 30 Mo. 578 (1860).
[3]93 Misc. 2d 452, 402 N.Y.2d 734 (Sup. Ct. 1978).

the tapes from the bureau, but the bureau asserted its right to keep them. The service bureau apparently sought to satisfy a debt owed by the customer to the bureau. Siding with the service bureau, the court held the bureau possessed a statutory artisan's lien on the data and the tapes because it had enhanced the data's value.

In a dispute between customer and service provider, any lien inures to the provider's advantage. A customer can deny its provider this advantage by demanding its surrender in the service agreement entered at the relationship's outset. In *Smithsonian Institution v. Datatron Processing, Inc.*,[4] a service bureau feuding with its customer had detained computer data on the subscribers to the customer's magazine. But the court construed the service agreement to require release of the data, and issued an order to that effect.

[4] 3 Computer L. Serv. Rep. (Callaghan) 393 (E.D.N.Y. 1971).

Appendix

Suggestions for Using Fax Machines for Legal Purposes

Following are suggestions to consider when using conventional fax machines for delivering legal business documents such as bids and contracts. Businesses should consult their attorneys before transacting business via fax. Some special laws, such as government procurement regulations on sealed bids, may not yet recognize fax as a satisfactory medium. *See* Chapters 4-6 for an explanation of the procedures offered here.

A. SUGGESTIONS FOR SENDERS

1. Include in the text of the fax a clause substantially like this:

> The sender sends this document to the recipient by transmission from one fax machine to another. The sender adopts as her original signature the signature appearing above her

typewritten name as reproduced by the fax machine receiving this transmission. Each of (1) the paper fed into the sending fax machine and (2) the printout from the receiving machine (including any complete photocopy thereof) is a counterpart original of this document.

2. To protect against forgery by the recipient, sign and notarize the document before faxing it. Have the notary initial each page. At the end of the document, have the notary complete a statement substantially like the following verification. This verification is intended only to confirm that the signer did sign the document. It may not satisfy statutory requirements to notarize special documents, such as real estate deeds. (XXX represents information to be filled in.)

VERIFICATION OF SIGNING

State of XXX)
) ss.
County of XXX)

On this day, [name of signer] appeared before me, presented identification of [him or her]self, and stated that [he or she] signed the foregoing document. I have counted the XXX pages of such document, and for identification I have handwritten my initials, the date, and the time of day on each page. To record this verification, I have made a notation of it in my official records and [name of signer] has signed the notation.

Date and time of day: ______________________

____

[name of notary]
Notary Public in and for the State and
County identified above

My Commission Expires: ______________________

3. Be sure to have the correct telephone number and the recipient's permission to deliver messages of this type to that number.

4. If the message is confidential, ensure there will be adequate safeguards at the receiving end. The receiving machine should be in a secure room, be overseen by a trusted operator, or have an electronic mailbox that will store messages until a trusted user initiates printing.

5. For extremely sensitive messages (such as information on corporate mergers and acquisitions), consider the use of sending and receiving machines equipped with encryption features. Alternatively, consider breaking the messages into pieces and sending the pieces by independent routes.

6. Use a cover sheet to show the transmission's source and the telephone number to call in case of an error.

7. Number paragraphs and pages to protect against loss. Indicate the total number of pages. (For extra protection, number every line.)

8. Be sure to send the entire document. If, as is often the case with purchase orders, the document has information such as terms and conditions written on the back, transmit front and back. If the parties plan repetitive transactions, they might agree on terms and conditions in a "trading partner agreement."

9. Inspect the delivery confirmation report issued by the sending machine to confirm successful transmission.

10. Retain the report as circumstantial evidence of delivery, together with the original document.

11. Confirm successful receipt with a phone call or a request for a return acknowledgment, asking the recipient to scan the document for errors.

12. For extra assurance of successful transmission, request that the recipient sign and notarize the fax and fax it back.

13. If proof of receipt is important:

a. have the recipient sign, notarize, and fax the document back;

b. obtain a notarized fax acknowledgment from the recipient; or
c. send a counterpart original by registered mail or courier.

B. SUGGESTIONS FOR RECEIVERS

1. If the risk of fraud is great, as might be the case for orders directing the transfer of funds, devise a strong system for confirming authenticity. As with paper documents and telexes, the system's strength should depend on the risk involved and the speed with which fraud could be executed. These are some possible safeguards:

a. Return an acknowledgment by an independent route. If speed is important, as with funds transfers, a confirming phone call may be satisfactory, but the source of the confirmation telephone number should be something other than the text of the fax.
b. Demand confirmation messages from one or two independent sources.
c. Demand that senders attach secret passwords, test keys, or cryptographic authentication codes to messages.

2. If the risk of fraud is low, demand only that the fax be notarized in accordance with item number A.2 above. This provides security that is roughly equal to an autograph on conventional paper delivered through the mail.

3. Inspect incoming faxes for evidence of incomplete or illegible transmission. Request retransmission if necessary.

4. Have office routines for quickly routing incoming messages to addressees.

5. Use a plain-paper printer, or photocopy printouts made on thermal paper.

6. Order and staple sheets together.

Appendix

B

Suggestions for Using EDI and Similar Technologies for Legal Purposes

Some of the ways in which firms might use EDI for legal purposes are to (1) buy and sell goods or services, (2) guarantee payment, as with a letter of credit, (3) direct a third party, such as a warehouse, to release goods, or (4) represent information to be true, as in a regulatory filing. Following are suggestions for the implementation of EDI and similar technologies to effect such purposes. This summarizes many of the approaches discussed in this book. The points are worded as specific recommendations, but readers are encouraged to formulate their own creative responses. Many EDI transactions are relatively minor, routine documents (purchase orders and invoices) and therefore involve little risk. Therefore, users should, with the advice of counsel, exercise judgment as to the degree of effort expended on each issue.

References here are made to Parts, Chapters, and Sections in this book. Some references are also made to *EDI and*

American Law: A Practical Guide, by Benjamin Wright, published in 1989 by The Electronic Data Interchange Association in Alexandria, Virginia.

A. ISSUES FOR SENDERS

1. Ensure messages are properly authorized before issued. Examples of controls for doing this include the physical separation of computers from unauthorized users, and the use of profiles to check messages for erroneous content (such as a quantity of 1000 parts when 100 is the most ever needed). *See* Section 5.2.

2. Devise a method for proving, in the event of a later dispute, whether a message has come from the apparent sender. One method is to route all messages through a trusted recordkeeper before they go to the recipient. *See* Sections 5.4 and 6.4.

B. ISSUES FOR RECIPIENTS

1. Implement a system for checking message authenticity. The system's strength should depend on the degree of risk present. Among the tools available are:

a. passwords disclosed to any intermediary network, incorporated into messages, or both;
b. the checking of messages for unusual features, such as unlikely ship-to addresses;
c. the returning of acknowledgments;
d. serial numbers in messages; and

e. for extremely vulnerable transactions, cryptographic techniques.

Bear in mind that EDI partners often work very closely together. A successful message forger must know much about the special relationship between the sender and receiver—the types of data they exchange, the data formats they use, and the manner in which they act upon messages. Undetected forgery is not easy. *See* Sections 5.4 and 5.5.

2. Ensure that responses, such as purchase order acknowledgments, to incoming messages are properly authorized before being sent.

3. Implement a trusted recordkeeper for storing and proving messages. *See* Sections 5.4 and 6.4.

C. ISSUES FOR SENDERS AND RECIPIENTS

1. Ensure that the data communications system is technically reliable. Public standard EDI permits use of myriad error prevention, detection, and correction features, including functional acknowledgments, line or character counts built into messages, and serial numbers in messages. *See* Section 5.3.

2. Implement control features such as functional acknowledgments and serial numbers that are tracked so that abnormalities are flagged and investigated in a timely fashion.

3. Devise a system for tracking and reconciling related documents. For example, if a purchase order must be accepted by a purchase order acknowledgment, then some recognition should be made as to whether a sufficient acknowledgment has or has not been returned.

4. If confidentiality is very important, consider encrypt-

ing messages. Alternatively, it may be easier to break messages into small parts and send them by independent routes.

5. Sender and recipient should each maintain credible message records. From a legal perspective, the ideal place for making a record is the point at which messages enter and exit the firm. If properly secured and routinely maintained, a complete, unmodified log of this data, including message contents and all the surrounding envelopes and other data delivered by networks, would be very persuasive evidence of what the firm sent and received. Records of messages at some other stage in processing would be satisfactory, however, if the firm keeps a secure audit trail showing the link between the data sent/received and the data recorded.

6. Among the ways for each firm to secure a data log are these:

a. Designate a trusted recordkeeper to maintain and protect the log. It could be a special department within the firm or an independent contractor to the firm.
b. Take steps to prevent the fabrication of information fed into the recordkeeper.
c. Record the data on a medium that may be written to only once, such as microfilm and some types of optical storage. Alternatively, if records are stored on magnetic media, they can be guarded against alteration by keeping them under lock and key.
d. Periodically have independent auditors review and document the controls securing the log.

See Sections 5.4 and 6.4 and Part III. *See also* pages 12-15 of *EDI and American Law*.

7. Remember that records kept in the hands of a third party, such as a VAN, enjoy less confidentiality than records kept in-house. *See* Chapter 19.

8. Develop a written policy on data record creation, re-

tention, and destruction, and integrate it with the firm's general record retention/destruction program. Consider how long particular documents must be kept, taking into account the needs to prove documents in case of dispute, to keep records for regulatory purposes, and to store data for federal, state, and local tax purposes. Ensure records are easy to retrieve and expunge as necessary. This may require that records of different document types be segregated. Also, it is likely to require special planning to ensure that future researchers have the equipment necessary to retrieve records. *See* Chapter 6 and Part IV.

9. Consult internal and external auditors on system configuration and control to make audit easy. For purposes of generating audit and legal evidence, create complete systems manuals, and flowcharts to show how the systems are configured, how they process and record data, and what controls are imposed on them.

10. Develop appropriate audit trail procedures for tracing and controlling transactions after they have been communicated. For example, after a buyer receives a purchase order, an audit trail should show how that order is logged into the order fulfillment application software and later how the order is filled. Controls should be implemented to prevent error and abuse.

11. Consider the use of a trading partner agreement. It can clarify issues, including:

a. the point at which a message is legally effective;
b. each party's intent to be legally bound to messages;
c. satisfaction of statute of frauds and other writing and signing requirements;
d. the interpretation of EDI codes;
e. the sequences and timing in which messages must be exchanged to achieve certain results, such as a binding contract;
f. whether the agreement on how EDI works between

the parties implies any larger commitments, such as an obligation to conduct EDI competently or to use EDI to make any particular purchases.

See Chapters 14-16 and Appendix C.

12. Considerations that usually are even more important than those listed in item 11 are the trade terms and conditions applying to the transactions effected through EDI. These should be considered carefully. (An example of a trade term and condition is the warranty that applies to the goods sold through EDI.) Ideally, trade terms and conditions would be fully negotiated and agreed to in a master purchase agreement or a trading partner agreement. A form similar to Appendix D may aid negotiation. If agreement cannot be reached, however, consider sending a letter, such as the form Electronic Trading Letter set forth in Appendix C. *See* Chapter 17.

13. Issue internal guidelines for operators using EDI. These should explain how EDI may and may not be used, what the trading partner agreements say, and what controls and routines need to be observed. For example, the guidelines might explain to a user what sequence of transactions are necessary to form a contract via EDI (e.g., (1) request for quotation, (2) response to request, (3) purchase order).

14. Investigate, with any intermediary service provider that may be involved, the network security and control features and audit reports appropriate for the user's needs. Consider the extent to which special audit reports should be retained.

15. Establish an agreement with any service provider used, and, before signing any form agreement the service provider offers, review it carefully with counsel. Among the issues to be addressed from the customer's perspective are these:

a. the service provider's commitment to perform all the services advertised in its marketing;

b. the service provider's obligation to maintain data confidentiality;
c. the service provider's obligation to keep or destroy records;
d. ownership and control of data, especially in the event of a dispute between the customer and the service provider;
e. the service provider's obligation to exercise due care;
f. the service provider's liability for errors and disasters;
g. the service provider's obligation to issue advance notice to the customer concerning a reduction in service;
h. the right of the customer's auditors to examine the service provider's controls or to receive control reports from the service provider's auditors.

See Chapters 18 and 19. *See also* Chapter 3 of *EDI and American Law* for a detailed analysis of particular clauses in service provider agreements.

16. Concerning remote service providers to which the user's own service provider will link, consider the extent to which the user needs the protections described in item 15 above. Can the user obtain adequate assurances from its own service provider or from its trading partner that the remote service provider will perform satisfactorily?

Appendix

C

Sample Electronic Trading Letter

INTRODUCTORY NOTE

This letter would precede electronic contracting. The letter could itself be an electronic message if the letter is modified to so indicate. *See* Section 14.6.

The letter contemplates two supplements. Supplement A would set forth special terms relating to the communication of electronic messages. (For example, it would indicate which "Initial Messages" must be accepted by which "Acceptance Messages" in order to be effective.) Supplement B would set forth trade terms and conditions intended to apply to the transactions facilitated by the electronic messages. (XXX represents a blank to be filled.)

TEXT

(From Blue Co. to Green Co.)

Gentlemen and Ladies:

Blue Co. and Green Co. may exchange electronic messages (Messages). This letter (including the following Supplements A and B, which are parts hereof) fixes the interpretation, and states terms that shall be deemed a part, of all Messages from Blue Co. and all transactions facilitated thereby. Blue Co. offers to agree with Green Co. that the same interpretation and terms shall apply to Messages from Green Co.

1. If, subject to any stated conditions, a party or its agent adopts any code as the party's or agent's signature for Messages, the same shall be its legal signature.

2. No Message may be considered received or may create any obligation until it is (a) if sent to Blue Co., available at the electronic address identified in Supplement A (Blue's Address) or (b) if sent to Green Co., available at any electronic address reasonable under the circumstances.

3. The recipient of a Message (other than a functional acknowledgment) may not enforce it against the sender unless the recipient promptly transmits a functional acknowledgment to the sender's electronic address contemplated in paragraph 2 above. No Message identified on Supplement A as an Initial Message shall give rise to an obligation until the sender has received an Acceptance Message as contemplated in Supplement A.

4. Each Message's contents shall be: (a) interpreted under any standards and guidelines identified in Supplement A; (b) understood as an expression of the send-

er's legal intent; (c) deemed "written" if, in connection with its communication from one party to the other, it becomes fixed in a tangible medium of expression; and (d) deemed "signed" if the contents include a legal signature. If a Message's contents are deemed written and signed, neither party will contest the validity or enforceability of any obligation on the ground that such contents are not written or signed.

5. Each Message and each transaction facilitated thereby are subject to Supplement B's terms. Each Message shall be deemed to incorporate this letter by reference. ALL OF SUPPLEMENT B'S TERMS, PARTICULARLY THOSE IN BOLD OR CAPITALIZED TYPE, ARE CONSPICUOUS WHEN INCORPORATED INTO A MESSAGE. To confirm this paragraph 5, some or all Messages may contain the code XXX.

6. Action by the parties in accordance with this letter, including the exchange of Messages, will show a course of dealing and course of performance approving this letter.

7. Neither party shall be obligated to exchange, review, record, respond to, or maintain the confidentiality of Messages. Neither shall be liable for costs the other incurs to exchange Messages or acts or omissions of any communications service provider. Neither this letter nor cooperation to exchange Messages implies an obligation to enter into transactions.

8. If any provision of this letter is invalid or unenforceable, it shall be so to the minimum extent required and all other provisions shall remain valid and enforceable.

9. This letter shall be governed by and interpreted in accordance with the laws of the State of XXX and may be amended or terminated by written and signed notice from Blue Co.

10. The transmission of any Message by Green Co. to Blue's Address shall be Green Co.'s agreement to and

acceptance of this letter, including the offer in the beginning paragraph. Such agreement and acceptance shall be effective even if Green Co. does not sign and return a copy of this letter.

Please sign and return a copy of this letter.

Very truly yours,

BLUE CO.

By: ______________________

Name: ___________________

Title:____________________

AGREED AND ACCEPTED

GREEN CO.

By: ______________________

Name: ___________________

Title: ____________________

Appendix

D

Terms Agreement

INTRODUCTORY NOTE

This agreement is intended for attachment to an EDI trading partner agreement dealing with sales of goods. (XXX represents a term to be filled by the parties.)

The agreement was originally drafted by Ralph M. Savage, Esq., and is reprinted with permission.

See in Section 17.4.2.

TEXT

Notwithstanding any terms and conditions expressed by either party, the following four Articles shall prevail to exclusively govern warranties, delivery, liability, and attorney's fees under this EDI Trading Partner Agreement.

1. WARRANTIES—Seller warrants to Buyer that products and any services furnished hereunder will be free from defects in material, workmanship, and title and will be of the kind and quality described in the specifications. The foregoing shall apply only to failures to meet said warranties (excluding any defects in title) which appear within XXX months from the date of shipment. Buyer will promptly notify Seller of any defects and, if required, promptly make product available for correction.

If any product or service fails to meet the foregoing warranties, Seller shall thereupon correct any such failure either, at its option, (i) by repairing any defective or damaged part or parts of the products, or (ii) by making available, f.o.b. ☐ Seller's plant ☐ Buyer's facility, any necessary repaired or replacement parts ☐ installing ☐ not installing same. Where a failure cannot be corrected by Seller's reasonable efforts, the parties will negotiate an equitable adjustment in price.

The preceding paragraph sets forth the exclusive remedies for all claims based on defect in or failure of products or services, whether the failure or defect arises before or during the warranty period, and whether a claim, however instituted, is based on contract, indemnity, warranty, tort (including negligence and strict liability), or otherwise. Seller ☐ does ☐ does not warrant any products or services of others which Buyer has designated. THERE ☐ IS ☐ IS NOT ANY IMPLIED STATUTORY WARRANTY OF MERCHANTABILITY OR OF FITNESS FOR PARTICULAR PURPOSE APPLICABLE. The foregoing warranties are exclusive and in lieu of all other warranties whether express, implied, or statutory.

2. DELIVERY—Unless otherwise agreed in writing, delivery of products shall be f.o.b. ☐ point of shipment ☐ point of delivery, where risk of loss passes.

Shipping dates ☐ are ☐ are not approximate and are based upon prompt receipt of all necessary information.

Seller shall be liable for damages caused by delay in delivery only when due to its fault or negligence. In no event shall it be liable for delay due to causes beyond its reasonable control, including but not limited to acts of God, acts of Buyer, prerequisite work by others, and strikes. In the event of any such delay, the date of delivery shall be extended for a period equal to the time lost by reason of the delay. In the event of cancellation, Seller ☐ shall ☐ shall not be entitled to cancellation charges.

3. LIABILITY OF BUYER AND SELLER—Neither party's liability on claims of any kind, whether based on contract, indemnity, warranty, tort (including negligence and strict liability), or otherwise, for losses or damages arising out of, connected with, or resulting from (i) any contract formed under this EDI Trading Partner Agreement, (ii) the performance or breach thereof, (iii) any products or services covered or furnished thereunder, or (iv) any extension or expansion thereof (including remedial warranty efforts) shall exceed the greater of either (A) $XXX or (B) the price of the specific product or service which gives rise to the claim. Except as to warranty of title to any products furnished, the liability of each party shall terminate XXX months after shipment.

In any event, neither party shall be liable for specific, incidental, exemplary, or consequential damages including, but not limited to, loss of profit or revenue, cost of capital, cost of substitute products, facilities or services, downtime costs, or claims of either party's customers for such damages. This applies whether claims are based on contract, indemnity, warranty, tort (including negligence and strict liability), or otherwise.

4. ATTORNEY'S FEES—If litigation is necessary

to enforce the terms of this EDI Trading Partner Agreement, the prevailing party shall be entitled to reasonable attorney's fees, costs, and expenses in addition to any other relief to which the prevailing party may be entitled.

Glossary

Because this book melds knowledge from two distinctly different disciplines—electronic messaging and law—this glossary aims to help those readers unfamiliar with the terminology of one or the other discipline. The following are neither precise nor comprehensive definitions but rather conceptual descriptions. When using electronic messaging technology terms in a formal context, such as in a contract, attorneys should confirm their meaning with clients and then make their definition explicit for the context.

Terms are often used loosely in the electronic messaging field, and definitions are evolving rapidly along with the technology.

ABA Model: Model EDI Trading Partner Agreement and Commentary published by the American Bar Association. *See* Section 14.4.

ABA Report: The report issued with the ABA Model. *See* Section 14.4.

ABA Task Force: The author of the ABA Model. The members of the Task Force were Michael S. Baum, Philip U. Otero, Jeffrey B. Ritter, Thomas J. McCarthy, and Amelia H. Boss.

ANSI X12: American National Standards Institute, Accredited Standards Committee X12. The leading body for the setting of public EDI standards in North America. The EDI standards set by this body are often referred to as ANSI X12 or simply X12.

Answerback: A coded symbol uniquely identifying a particular telex terminal. The terminal sends the answerback, sometimes automatically and sometimes upon command, to another terminal to which it is connected. The answerbacks of particular users are generally known in the telex community. *See* Section 1.1.3.

Application Acknowledgment: A particular type of EDI acknowledgment message. It responds (with an acceptance, rejection, or the like) to the substance of the message it is acknowledging. *Compare* Functional Acknowledgment.

Audit Trail: The presence of information processing media (i.e., paper, tapes, or disks) and procedures that permit an auditor to trace a transaction through the various stages of processing, communication, and storage. A computer audit trail may include data logs, transaction control numbers, and controlled computer processing procedures, among other things.

Canadian Model: The Model Form of EDI Trading Partner Agreement and Commentary published by the Legal and Audit Issues Committee of the EDI Council of Canada. *See* Section 14.5.

Cause of Action (or right of action): A legal right of one party to sue another party and obtain relief. For example, if *A* breaches its contract with *B*, *B* has (under contract law) a cause of action against *A*. *B* can sue and recover relief from *A*, such as a judgment in the amount of the damages that the breach of contract caused *B*. *B* can then legally force *A* to pay that judgment.

CCITT (International Telegraph and Telephone Consultive Committee): International body that sets standards for fax and some e-mail facilities.

Common Law: The traditional law handed down by court decisions rather than constitutions or legislative statutes. The common law tradition originated in England and has been adopted in the United States, Canada, Australia, and other countries.

Contract: A mutually binding agreement. For example, *A* promises to buy 100 laptop computers from *B* for $1000 each, and *B* promises to sell them to *A* at that price.

Cryptography: Any mathematical method for scrambling (or encrypting) all or some extract from a message to render the message confidential or aid in showing the message's origin and integrity.

EDGAR: Electronic Data Gathering, Analysis, and Retrieval system, is the Securities and Exchange Commission's system for the electronic filing of corporate disclosure documents, such as annual reports.

EDIFACT: EDI for Administration, Commerce, and Trade. This is a public, international EDI standard set under the auspices of the United Nations.

EDP Auditor: An auditor specializing in the audit and control of computer systems.

Electronic Data Interchange (EDI): The computer-to-computer exchange of business data in a standard format. EDI is usually conceived of as communicated between two independent firms. *See* Section 1.1.4.

Electronic Data Processing (EDP): The processing, communicating, and storing of information with computers and related technology. Also called Automated Data Processing (ADP).

Electronic Funds Transfer (EFT): A transmittal of money value between banks via computer or other electronic message. In this book, EFT refers only to wholesale, not consumer, transfers. *See* Section 1.1.5.

Electronic Mail (e-mail): The computer-to-computer exchange of messages. *See* Section 1.1.2. E-mail messages are usually written in free-text, rather than in a structured format, as EDI is.

Electronic Messaging: A generic term encompassing all the major technologies discussed in this book for the exchange of messages electronically—fax, telex, e-mail, EDI, and videotex.

Electronic Trading Letter: A letter designed to establish legal terms in an EDI relationship. It may constitute a trading partner agreement if two trading partners agree to it. *See* Section 14.6 and Appendix C.

Fax (facsimile; sometimes called telecopy): The transmission of data in accordance with facsimile standards set by CCITT. In conventional fax, a sheet of paper is fed into one fax machine, which converts the sheet's image into a digital signal that the machine relays (via the telephone system) to a similar fax machine. The receiving machine reverses the conversion and prints the image on a new sheet of paper. *See* Section 1.1.1.

Financial EDI: EDI transmitting data, such as remittance information, related to payments.

Functional Acknowledgment: A type of message often used in EDI. When used, it is typically generated automatically by an EDI message recipient's system. It is returned to the original message sender to indicate the original message was received and that it appeared to conform to the syntactical requirements of the chosen EDI standard. It does not respond to the substance of the original message. *Compare* Application Acknowledgment.

Globex: A videotex-type system, developed by the Chicago Mercantile Exchange, the Chicago Board of Trade, and Reuters Holdings PLC, for automated trading of commodities futures and futures-options. *See* Section 2.6.

Just in Time (JIT): A business manufacturing and supply technique whereby the buyer seeks to acquire products only as and when needed. JIT seeks to keep inventory to a minimum. *See* Section 2.4.

Mailgram: A telegram delivered, on the final leg of its journey, as paper via the postal mail.

Machine-Readable or Sensible Data or Records: Data or records that a computer can read.

Network: Any computer facility providing a data communications, processing, or storage service to a user. A network may be a large, external system, such as a VAN, or a smaller system within a single office.

Proprietary Standard: Any EDI message standard that is privately developed by a single company or a small group of companies. *Compare* Public Standard.

Public Standard: Any EDI standard, such as ANSI X12 or EDIFACT, that is developed by a group of industry representatives.

Real-Time: Simultaneous interaction between two machines. Two telephones or two conventional fax machines, for example, interact in real-time.

Restatements of Law (such as the Second Restatement of Contracts): A series of authoritative statements of American common law. The Second Restatement of Contracts differs in some respects with U.C.C. Article Two. As a very rough rule of thumb to use when reading this book, the Second Restatement of Contracts covers all contracts (including contracts for general services and the sale of real estate) other than contracts for the sale of goods. (The latter are governed by U.C.C. Article Two.)

Service Bureau: A firm dedicated to providing data processing (or computer "time sharing") services to independent clients. Strictly speaking, a service bureau does not provide electronic messaging services to clients, but in industry the distinction easily blurs between service bureaus providing data processing services and networks providing data communications services.

Service Provider: Any firm operating a service bureau or a network.

Statute: A law adopted by a legislature. Statutes generally supersede any contrary common law. U.C.C. Article Two, for example, is a statute that displaces the common law of contracts as it applies to the sale of goods.

Store and Forward: An electronic messaging service whereby a network receives a message, temporarily holds it, and, at a convenient time, transmits it on to the next leg of its journey to the recipient.

Telegram: A communication effected through the offices and employees of a record carrier such as Western Union. In the conventional sense, a telegram begins when the sender requests the carrier to send a message. The carrier transmits the message to its office nearest the recipient, where it is printed. The carrier forwards the message to the recipient by telephoning the recipient, delivering the message by hand, or posting the message in the mail. A mailgram is a telegram delivered, on the final leg of its journey, via the postal mail. *See* Section 1.1.3.

Telex (teletype): Conventional telex is the communication, through a record carrier such as Western Union, between two teleprinter terminals. Each terminal looks and performs like an electric typewriter. Each prints a record of the communication. *See* Section 1.1.3.

Test Key: A type of cryptographic code attached to the text of a message to display the message's origin and the integrity of its contents. A test key is not as secure as other cryptographic methods, such as DES and RSA. *See* Section 1.3.

Tort: Generally, torts are a class of wrongs, other than breach of contract, for which the law provides the victim a remedy in damages. Contract obligations relate to the enforcement of bargained-for promises between consenting parties. Tort obligations, on the other hand, are imposed on parties by law; they generally arise independent of any contract. A general tort rule (negligence) is that one who acts must do so with reasonable care to avoid danger to persons and property. Put differently, one who operates a computer network must use reasonable care to protect network traffic. If she does not, she can be required to pay for any ensuing damages.

Trade Terms and Conditions (TTCs): Detailed legal terms intended to become part of any particular contract, such as a particular contract for the sale of laptop computers. An example of a TTC would be an understanding that the seller will, for up to 12 months after sale, replace all defective parts in computers at no extra charge. TTCs might be specified in a master purchase agreement. In paper trading, they are often written on the backsides of form documents such as purchase orders. *See* Chapter 17.

Trading Partner: A term of art in the EDI community meaning any company with which another company buys or sells goods or services or otherwise does business.

Trading Partner Agreement: The accepted term for an agreement between EDI trading partners. It sets forth the rules and terms for trading via EDI.

Trier of Fact: The person(s) in a trial who finally determines what the true facts of the case are. Traditionally, this is the jury. Sometimes it is the judge. The trier of fact weighs all the evidence admitted into the trial and makes its determination based on what it believes is credible and what is not.

Trusted Recordkeeper: Any entity that makes and holds electronic message records but that is insulated from the incentive and ability to fabricate those records. A trusted recordkeeper could be independent of any company sending and receiving messages, or it could be a secure department within such a company. *See* Sections 5.4 and 6.4.

Uniform Commercial Code (U.C.C.): A uniform statute, adopted in whole or in part by each state legislature in the United States, to govern specified fields of commerce. U.C.C. Article Two (adopted by all states but Louisiana) governs sales of goods. U.C.C. sections that begin with the number 2 (such as U.C.C. §2-201) are part of U.C.C. Article Two.

Uniform Rules of Conduct for Interchange of Trade Data by Teletransmission (UNCID): Voluntary rules for international EDI conduct (the "Ten Commandments" of international EDI). *See* Section 14.2.

Value-Added Network (VAN): A specialized network providing communications, store and forward, mailboxing and other services to facilitate electronic messaging between independent customers. Some in the EDI community may refer to a VAN as a "third-party network" or a "public network."

Videotex: A means of computer communication that makes information available to many remote users simultaneously. The simplest example is a computer bulletin board. *See* Section 1.1.6.

Table of Cases

References are to section and note numbers.

Table of Cases

Table of Cases

Table of Statutes and Related Sources

References are to section and note numbers.

State

Uniform Acts

Restatements of the Law

Rules and Guides

Index

References are to sections.